JIM DAVIDSON
NO FURTHER ACTION

JIM DAVIDSON
••••••••••••••••••••••••
NO FURTHER ACTION

THE DARKEST YEAR OF MY LIFE

JOHN BLAKE

Published by John Blake Publishing Ltd,
3 Bramber Court, 2 Bramber Road,
London W14 9PB, England

www.johnblakepublishing.co.uk

www.facebook.com/Johnblakepub ⬛
twitter.com/johnblakepub ⬛

This edition published in 2014

ISBN: 978 1 78418 005 8

British Library Cataloguing-in-Publication Data:

A catalogue record for this book is available from the British Library.

Design by www.envydesign.co.uk

Printed and bound in Great Britain by CPI Group (UK) Ltd

3 5 7 9 10 8 6 4 2

Papers used by John Blake Publishing are natural, recyclable products made
from wood grown in sustainable forests. The manufacturing processes conform
to the environmental regulations of the country of origin.

Every attempt has been made to contact the relevant copyright-holders,
but some were unobtainable. We would be grateful if the
appropriate people could contact us.

For my wife, Michelle – a remarkable woman.

ACKNOWLEDGEMENTS

There are many people I would like to thank:

Steve and Gillie Lamprell, for their friendship and help.

Laurie Mansfield, my manager and friend for the last forty years, for his advice.

Richard Desmond, for being a constant in an ever changing world.

Brian Shaw, for the hard work against all odds.

Chris Davis, for picking up the baton.

My children – Sarah, Cameron, Charlie, Fred, and Elsie – for having to face all the bad press and keep smiling.

Melve and Pam Cotton, for their understanding.

My brother Bill and his wife Billie, for being there anytime, day or night.

Goose, for being special.

Flo and Steve, for staying awake!

Charlton Athletic Football Club and the fans, for believing in me.

Sam Snelling, for never leaving me.

All the people who have made statements in my defence... even those I don't know!

My QC Trevor Burke, for being very clever.

And Henri Brandman, my lawyer, for his wisdom, friendship and advice, and for rolling up his sleeves – without all of which I'd have lost the will to fight.

'When the Himalayan peasant meets the he-bear in his pride,
He shouts to scare the monster, who will often turn aside.
But the she-bear thus accosted rends the peasant tooth and nail.
For the female of the species is more deadly than the male.'
    – 'The Female of the Species', Rudyard Kipling

'Let them be ashamed and confounded together that seek after my soul to destroy it: let them be driven backward and put to shame that wish me evil.'
    – *Psalm 40:14*, sent as a message by my friend Goose during a low period

CONTENTS

INTRODUCTION

JULY 2013

Most of you know me – or think that you do. I've lived my life in the spotlight and have had many ups and downs. My life has been a rollercoaster ride, that's for sure, but I was always steering the rollercoaster. This is different. For a while my life was completely derailed. What you are about to read are the recollections of my worst period.

On 2 January 2013 my world was turned upside down, suddenly and without warning. I was arrested as part of Operation Yewtree: the post-Savile operation set up by the Metropolitan Police to investigate paedophilia within show business. That in itself was *never* an accusation against me – but I was horrified.

No one will quite understand the pain that my wife, my family and I have endured, and as I write this introduction the nightmare is still happening. Some of this book is reflective and some of it was written seconds after the event. Passages of it were even written during the events!

Have you ever been dreaming and the dream becomes so scary that you wake yourself up to be free of it? Well, there's been no waking up from this. This is life with the future removed, and the only way for it to return to normality was for the police and the Crown Prosecution Service to start believing *me* rather than *them*.

There seemed to be a need for the police to convict and to be seen to convict. I felt that, in general, they would arrest anyone who was famous. I believe that the government was embarrassed by the Metropolitan Police's handling of the Jimmy Savile affair.

That was my worry: that no amount of counter evidence would work because the powers that be had already decided the outcome. Was there a secret agenda that we didn't know about? During the writing of this book I've always been aware that something else was lurking beneath the surface, something sinister and scary.

But the biggest fear was my inclination to sink, without warning, into an ocean of negative thoughts and to project a grisly outcome that I was powerless to prevent, despite my innocence. The desperate battle against self-pity has been a constant concern.

You'll become aware of this battle as you read on. The note-taking helped me concentrate on the facts. Without them, the demons would have taken over and I'd have fallen to bits. You'll notice on occasions that a dark sense of humour helped me to cope during many unfunny moments.

All of these words were written from the heart. I've tried to describe the wider implications of these accusations: the fear, the self-doubt and the total feeling of helplessness, of not being in control of my life. It also describes how my lawyer and I battled to get that life back, seemingly against all odds.

In fact, as I write this I don't yet know how this book will end! If it ends with someone else writing it then you'll know that justice and truth are not what the police have been looking for. That being the case...

I'll see you on the dark side of the moon!

For legal reasons, the names of complainants and certain locations have been changed throughout.

Chapter One

JULY 2011

I love Richard Desmond. I always have. He is one of those incredible people who are extremely likeable even when they're being rude to you. He's a very successful man but when you're his friend you're his friend for life... unless you piss him off!

Richard has a unique approach to business. He cuts through the surrounding bullshit and does what his instinct tells him to do, much to the annoyance of the people he pays to stop him doing it. He is brilliant, and a tad scary.

When we first met he owned a magazine publishing company and X-rated TV channels. He was great fun and had the knack of calling people 'arseholes' that I thought were arseholes as well.

He bought out *OK* magazine, which decimated *Hello*'s market, and then bought the *Daily Express* and *Daily Star* – which joined *Spank a Granny* in the Desmond publishing empire. All this money, fame and power didn't change my old friend one bit. He's *still* not one for sitting back or biting his tongue.

He works hard and plays hard, too. Richard is a great drummer. He had a kit in his office for years before the neighbours complained, and has raised hundreds of thousands of pounds for charities like the Teenage Cancer Trust – some of it with an all-star band including Roger Daltrey as lead singer, no less. They're very good; I watched them in Ronnie Scott's one night and it was a joy.

When he bought Channel 5, rumour had it that he sacked nearly everybody within the first week. That surprised no one. But I got a call to come and visit him in his penthouse office. I jumped at the chance, arriving at lunchtime. It has to be the best office in London, with a sensational view of the river Thames.

His butler served lunch. With his right-hand man at his side, Richard chatted about their plans for the channel. If I'd had a swear box I'd have been a millionaire! To say he was in a buoyant mood was an understatement.

'Do you know the reason I bought Channel 5? To get Jim Davidson back on the fucking telly!'

What could I say? 'Well, thanks.'

'What do you want to do?

'What do *you* want me to do?'

'Look, I've bought *Big Brother*. I want you to go in the house and sort all those arseholes out.'

Richard's man looked on impassively. This was not Richard showing off; he was making a genuine offer.

'I'll put you in there, pay you a fortune, jam it full of crumpet and find a gay bloke for you to upset!'

'I'll speak to Laurie.' Laurie Mansfield is my manager.

'Look, you know I like Laurie, but bollocks to him, what do *you* want to do?'

'Well...'

'And then we'll do a chat show. That'll make those other arseholes sit up, won't it?'

I knocked my glass over in shock.

It was a great meeting. I left with a smile on my face and a spring in my step.

I called Laurie, who instinctively knew what Richard really wanted. *Big Brother* was going to be his flagship and he wanted me to be controversial. But I'd had enough of that with *Hell's Kitchen*, in 2007.

The trouble with reality shows is they're not really 'real' at all. Only a tiny bit is live, which enables revenue to be earned from a phone vote. You can't vote on a programme that's been recorded last week.

Producers don't like live TV. Nasty celebs could say something horrid and the programme makers could get their arses sued. So the show is edited to show whatever storyline the producers want and to cut out the *actionable* bits.

During the filming of *Hell's Kitchen*, I fell out with former *Big Brother* winner Brian Dowling. Brian was very bright, full of life and extremely camp. It was also on my mind that he had no experience in show business whatsoever – apart from 'being popular for being popular', a celebrity just for being a celebrity.

It was edited to look as if I was bullying Brian over his homosexuality – you couldn't get further from the truth. I always try to treat everybody equally. That means everybody is up for grabs or a piss-take: gay people, straight people, black people, white people, stripy people. You're all in my sights; everybody is in my comedy crosshairs!

Later on, when we were sitting down having a drink, Brian came in and said, 'How much do you think Lee Ryan got when he stormed out of the kitchen?' He was another contestant on *Hell's Kitchen*, who then sold a story to the newspapers.

I said, 'How much?'

'I think he'd have got a hundred grand.'

I said, 'You're mental, that'd never happen!'

Brian also said he was offered over half a million pounds for his story by the *News of the World*. I called him a liar. The two girls leapt to his defence by saying, 'That's what *we get* nowadays.'

Then the crying started and Brian said through the sobs, 'You called me a shirtlifter!'

During the show I'd met that bloke from *Dancing on Ice*, the Australian with the new hair. He was sat in the restaurant bit with my old pal Bonnie Langford. She introduced me; he gave me a wet-fish handshake and a camp, disapproving, bad-smell-under-the-nose look.

I didn't know but I assumed he was gay. So I'd asked Brian earlier in jest why 'shirtlifters' have a certain look. I used the term because I assumed that, Brian and I being matey, he wouldn't take offence.

There are many slang piss-takes for homosexual men: 'poof', 'uphill gardener', 'little brown engine shunter'. I thought 'shirtlifter' was a light-hearted bit of fun. It was certainly not used as a way to insult him – if I'd wanted that I'd just have called him an 'untalented fucking arsehole'.

Complete misfire! But Brian had laughed when I said it, though he also said, '"Shirtlifter" is an awful word.'

It only had an effect later – when he was pissed. After a glass of wine or two, with his two henchwomen with him and the cameras rolling, he played the protected-species card.

I tried to explain that I wasn't homophobic. The actor Victor Spinetti, who was gay, once said to me: 'You know what "gay" stands for? Good As You!' And I totally agree.

Victor was in *Help!* with The Beatles and *A Hard Day's Night*; he was also in *Oh What A Lovely War!* and introduced me to the brilliant producer Joan Littlewood. His partner, Graham, died years ago; I used to have chats with him and Graham as he was lying in his sickbed. It was then I decided I'd vote for gay marriage, if ever the chance came. Because after Graham died there was terrible litigation over the money, and it just didn't seem like a level playing field.

Later, at Victor's funeral, I spoke about him and said goodbye. I got a tap on the shoulder from someone who said, 'Well done, Jim, Victor would have loved that.' It was Paul McCartney.

Brian's henchwomen didn't understand what I was trying to say though. They took it as an insult. I gave up then.

'How can you say that to him?' screeched that lanky footballer's bird, Abbey Clancy, and the other one whose name I can't remember. They used it as ammunition to stick up for their fashionable gay friend; it's like they wanted him to be their little Chihuahua. This pissed me off and prompted Dowling to wail even louder.

I said he was disgraceful to play the homophobic card. Of

course, the producers edited my side of the argument out to leave me saying, 'You're disgraceful.' Nice!

So reality TV isn't that real.

I don't use the term 'shirtlifter' now – not because I've been persuaded it's offensive but because people take offence, and there *is* a difference. The main thing was, as I said on a TV programme to make the director laugh, before they edited it out: 'It wasn't because he was gay that I didn't like him, it was simply because I didn't like him!' Do you have to like everyone *because* they're gay?

I think some people's perception of me is as a homophobe – they look at every little deviation from political correctness as a stick to hit me with. If I was to cure AIDS, feed the world and eradicate malaria, I'd still be that 'homophobic racist'. If it was a gay black guy I'd been talking about, could he hate me twice as much?

* * *

Laurie called Richard's man and, as it turned out, I couldn't do *Big Brother* anyway as I'd be in Australia at the time of recording.

The first *BB* show on Channel 5 included those two idiots from Ireland with the sticky-up barnets and the speaker's wife, Sally Bercow, who was having a break from the poison dwarf.

Paddy Doherty, the traveller and bare-knuckle fighter from *My Big Fat Gypsy Wedding*, should have knocked those two morons Jedward spark out; he won the show. I enjoyed it, but I was pleased I was busy. It was full on and, to be honest, I didn't think I'd have the stamina.

The second series included Julie Goodyear. I've employed her for panto and know this talented actress can be a bit diva-ish. She lived up to all the stories I'd heard. One day she called me and said, 'If my frock's not here in an hour I'm fucking off!' A girl after my own heart.

She was perfect for the house. Julie is one of those people who share the same fans – her, Barry Manilow, Josh Groben, John Barrowman and Joe Longthorne all appeal to gay people and middle-aged women. She got lots of votes for being herself. As for me, I don't know if I ever *am* myself. I'm not sure who *myself* is.

Martin Kemp and the eventual winner, Julian Clary, just sat about, did nothing and paid off their mortgages. Julian is another person with similar fans to Julie. I can't remember him in it much, but he didn't upset anybody. He was just himself: a charming gay man with no nastiness. He'd attract the majority of votes from viewers of the show, which peaks at ages 16–24. These are people who like *TOWIE* and Jordan and wear Ugg boots.

Julian was odds-on to win right from the start. No matter how nice a guy Martin is – and he is – he was onto a loser by being straight. Gay people seem to have the edge on this show. They're funny, different and outrageous. Just look at the gays on telly: Alan Carr, Dale Winton, Graham Norton, Stephen Fry, Craig from *Strictly* and the little Italian chap from the ice-skating with the speech impediment. Although I've never seen Stephen Fry play the gay card, he can be hilariously camp, as can David Walliams and his little baldy mate.

Rylan Clark is favourite to win *CBB* this year, as he's

funny and loveable. And who can forget Brian Dowling? I bloody can't...

You can't help but like some of these gay chaps unless you're a complete bigot – which, contrary to perception, I am not. To me, people are people – or, as Richard Desmond would say, 'An arsehole is a arsehole no matter how he shags.'

I emailed Richard and congratulated him on a great series. The returning email just read: *'Right you're in the next show call me.'*

Chapter Two

MARCH 2012

I called Laurie. 'He doesn't give in, does he?'
Laurie is not a lover of reality TV. It's alien to him. He was raised on great performers; seeing people whose only talent is reading the autocue is not up his street. He started life in the business as a record salesman and then moved on to be a producer, progressing to manage some great, great talents: Cleo Laine, Charlie Drake, Tommy Steele, Peters & Lee, Cannon & Ball, me! All great live performers. His company, International Artistes, has managed the cream of the variety world.

No longer with International, he still manages great talent, and produces some of the best musicals in the West End: *Buddy*, *Dreamboats and Petticoats* and loads more. He also manages Nigel Lythgoe, who is a mate, and Lord Lloyd Webber, who I think looks like those fish blokes who chased Troy Tempest in *Stingray*! So it's fair to say Laurie knows good telly when he sees it. He also knows what he doesn't like, and a load of C-list celebrities poncing about in the Big Brother house do *not* float his boat.

'Hi Jim, it's Laurie, I missed your call.'

'Richard Desmond has emailed me and asked me to do the next *Big Brother*.'

I was expecting the usual 'Don't do it', but instead I got an 'Oh'. The phone went quiet for a bit.

'Well, it wasn't right to do it the first time; maybe this is the right time. Richard has certainly given it a new lease of life... what's to lose? Let me give them a call.'

We called each other back later and agreed that, if I played my cards right and stuck to a game plan, I could get through *Celebrity Big Brother* without any collateral damage.

We went to see Richard in his office. This time he was joined by the head of Channel 5 and a charming lady who introduced herself as Ros from Endemol, the company that produces *Big Brother*. We had a great lunch, with Richard ignoring the fact that we had a lady with us.

'Don't be an arsehole, Laurie, you know you should do this. Jim, there's a generation of people out there who don't know who the fuck you are. Let me walk you around the building – you won't like it.'

He had a point. Richard was saying I was living in a shell – that I should get out and grab this new audience. It was encouragement rather than a slagging off.

The series would begin in the New Year. It was now the summer, so we had plenty of time to discuss it. We ate Richard's food and drank his wine and thoroughly enjoyed his company. It's impossible to dislike this charismatic man!

We walked to the taxi rank and decided we'd do it, if the money was right. That'd be Laurie's job. It'd be a good contest: the best agent in the business against the best businessman in the business.

A week later, Laurie called – the deal was done. *Big Brother* here I come, God help me. Get this wrong and I really *would* disappear.

Meanwhile, it was back to the grindstone for the stand-up shows. I needed to think of a way to break the news to the missus. Thank God we'd been given planning permission for an extension to our cottage.

'Mitch,' I called to my wife, Michelle, 'you know that I said we couldn't afford the extension? Well...'

Chapter Three

OCTOBER 2012

You know something is wrong when there are lurkers! Two guys were hanging about outside the house. They were standing by Lady Bridget's driveway. We call her that because her husband was Sir So-and-So – a colonel in the army. Lady Bridget often pops in to share a tipple or three. She's one of those wonderful people who remain young no matter what their age.

When they buggered off, Bridget came over and told us they'd gone down the road to get a signal on their mobiles. I smelled a rat... a great, big rat. A while later the rodents reappeared. I hummed a little tune I'd written for panto:

'I'm King Rat, I'm thinking that
My time has come to reign,
I'll take your loot and then I'll scoot
To a tax-free life in Spain.'

I took a deep breath, crossed my fingers and approached

them. I always look guilty. When I pass through customs, even though I haven't got anything hidden, I walk through the metal detector at the airport like a terrorist trying to look like a priest.

'Hello, Jim' said the braver, older man. He was a photographer, dripping with Nikons, and had one of those 'don't blame me' faces.

'I've seen you loads of times. Sorry I'm here for this.'

'Here for what?'

The reporter said he was from an agency. 'I'd like to hear your side of the story.'

'Weren't me,' I said with a grin. But curiosity got the better of me, as they well knew it would.

'What's the story?'

'We want to know about the allegations.'

I'd thought some bird might have grassed me up to the papers and they were after a kiss-and-tell story. I've often got up and read in the paper about women I'd 'been with' that I'd never met before in my life. I was so used to some reporter coming up to me and saying, 'There's some Page Three girl who's done a story about you.' I'd had so many in the past that were just upsetting and annoying, because no matter what your current wife says, in her mind she thinks, *'Hmm, there must be* something *going on.'*

But then I thought: *'Ah, they're here to find out who I think the next Jimmy Savile could be. Jimmy fucking Savile!'* This was after that investigative documentary on ITV. *'They want to know what I know. Phew!'*

A week before, I wrote an article on my blog about the Savile enquiry: 'The Jimmy Savile witch-hunt is going a bit

13

silly now. We all are starting to speculate and accuse... even in jest. So no, I don't know who's next. Well, if I was in the pub with the lads it would be a different story.

'Everyone has had the nod. Everyone is now an expert. Just pick someone you don't like and say it's them. So I'll be the first one to knock it on the head and belt up. How's about that then?'

We all knew Savile was odd. The only time I spoke to him was when he came on *The Generation Game* in the nineties. He seemed quite pleasant then, but all the other times I'd run away from him. You'd hear him coming along the corridor, speaking in that ridiculous voice – he never spoke in his own voice – and you'd think, '*Oh fuck, find an excuse and run off!*'

'Sorry Jimmy, I've got to go and play the organ for the parson!'

I went on to say: 'A bloke who's a loner, dresses and acts like a nonce and thinks he is the most important person in the world. Hmmm. I knew... and didn't do anything. Mind you, I had no proof. To me he was just another pervert.

'There are lots of them in showbiz. There seem to be more gay ones than straight, but that's because there are probably more gays in showbiz than most professions.'

Well, that upset all the gay bloggers and forum writers, with a pink website twisting my words to mean that there were more gay perverts than straight. Why do they have to do that? What I was saying is that if you're in a room where the occupants are eighty per cent gay, it stands to reason that any pervs there are more likely to be gay – *not* that gay people are inherently more likely to be perverted.

I also said that everyone in showbiz could be a target. (Little did I know!)

I had a picture taken and the little reporter, who looked about twelve and had acne, asked again about allegations in the papers.

'What allegations?' I asked, genuinely interested.

He seemed a bit lost, as if he had no information and was waiting for me to help.

'About you.'

'Me?'

'Yes.'

'What's the allegation? Have I been mentioned?'

'No.'

'So are you accusing me of anything?'

'No.'

'So what do you want?'

'Uh...'

'Listen son, you're barking up the wrong tree. The only time I've shagged a fifteen-year-old was when I was fourteen – I've always gone for older women.'

With that I went indoors and had an uncomfortable hour or so wracking my brains to figure out what the hell this kid was on about. Plus I'd stupidly admitted I shagged a 15-year-old. I'd given them a headline: 'Jim Davidson Sleeps With Girl Of 15!' The silly sods missed an opportunity.

The next morning there were more reporters outside the house and, more scarily, a TV cameraman. They'd already taken some film of me anyway, so when they said, 'Can you walk past the camera?' I told him, 'Okay, but what's it for?'

'I don't know, we have been sent to get some stuff.'

I did a silly walk like Laurel and Hardy, walking past the camera with a smile. Although I was worried, it didn't mean I couldn't clown around – I wanted to say, 'I'm not bothered about you lot, you've got this totally wrong.' I could imagine one of these TV cameras outside everybody's house.

Then, bizarrely, he asked for a still photo with his eight-year-old son. Surely he didn't bring the kid as a prop?

What was this about? I wasn't into kids, the thought of it revolts me, so it must have been some kind of kiss-and-tell.

I was to find out later that day. An email arrived on my computer from someone at the *Mirror*: 'We have a story about you and *The Stoker** attacking a girl in a Midlands hotel in 1988.'

I took no notice and thought to myself that this was a ploy to make me ring the paper and ask, 'What's all this about?'

I settled down for an uneasy night, wondering about what was going on. I racked my brains for an answer... but there was nothing!

The next morning saw a lane full of paparazzi and reporters.

What the fuck is going on?

I went out and spoke to a Polish photographer who handed me his mobile. A man came on from *The Sun*.

'Before you ask me anything, I have nothing to say.'

He said there had been an allegation in the *Mirror*. I told him I don't read the *Mirror* – and neither should he! I asked if the allegation was about me. He didn't know. I asked him who made the allegation and he didn't know that either. So I asked him what he wanted.

'Is this anything to do with you?'

I told him to bugger off and stop believing what he read in the papers.

When Michelle asked what was going on, I told her what the press had said.

'You should never have done that blog about Savile.'

'What's that got to do with it?'

'You *would* have to gob off.'

She had a point – otherwise it would have been out of sight, out of mind. But I consoled myself that whatever the story was, it would not be about underage sex. Though it might well have been someone trying to take advantage of the witch-hunt and cash in. What has someone like that got to lose?

The press lurked about for a couple of days as I shot off and did a show on HMS *Dauntless* with Bobby Davro, Claire Sweeney and, of all people, The Stoker. I asked him if he'd heard from anyone in the press.

'No,' he said, 'why?'

I didn't tell him about the silly email, as it'd be pointless to put him on edge over bullshit.

Bobby was so inspired that I just let him get on with it, sitting in the wings with a vodka shouting, 'Keep going!' How's that for man management? Claire got Captain Will dancing and showed me why she is a star. The Stoker was also on top form. What a show! It lasted two hours, the sailors had a ball and I had a belly full of vodka – it was marvellous!

When I arrived home I got another email from the *Mirror*, telling me Operation Yewtree was investigating me. How would *they* know? I called Laurie and my lawyer,

Henri Brandman, who both said, 'It's a fishing expedition by the *Mirror*.'

How would they *know?*

Henri researched the *Mirror* story online. It made no sense when he paraphrased it to me: A woman claimed that two men, one of them a famous person, took her to a gig at a sports hall in Wigan, then for an Indian meal. Afterwards, the minder raped her while the famous person watched and then performed a sex act on her.

I searched my brain cells. Had I ever been to Wigan? Where the fuck *is* Wigan? Would I have done a gig in a sports hall? Who was my minder in 1988?

This isn't me!

There was also a story from a dancer saying that, in 1984, a BBC star tried to rape her when she was on tour with him. It wasn't me. I never toured with dancers – not until 1993 and *Sinderella* anyway. There was a picture of this woman, now in her fifties. I didn't recognise her. What were these silly reporters on about? If it hadn't been so contrary to my nature, I might have gone, 'Oh fuck!' But because I hadn't done it I was simply annoyed with this woman. Why do they print this shit?

This is the way it works: the papers just print enough not to be nicked then they advise the person to go to the police. They can then go back to the press and say, 'I've been to the police,' and sign an affidavit that what they're telling them is the truth. But why bother with that when all you need is the headline 'BBC Star Raped Me'? At the time the press was hammering the BBC. They wanted to find out if it was a club for perverts and paedophiles. But I was at

Thames Television in the 1980s – I was nowhere near the fucking BBC!

* * *

I looked outside the next morning and the little man from Poland was still in his car. I walked down and asked him what he was doing.

'I'm waiting for the police.'

Shit! What does he know that I don't?

I drove up to town in the afternoon to meet with my son, Charlie. We had dinner and stayed at our club. I mentioned this stuff to Charlie, who'd just completed a degree in law.

'Don't worry about it, Dad,' he said, 'it's just people trying to get a few quid.'

So I don't worry and we proceed to put the world to rights, while drinking our Scotch. Charlie is the brains of the family. He has a really off-the-wall sense of the absurd and is a great orator. I love being in his company and so does everyone else.

The next morning, Michelle told me there were six cars parked up and waiting. I'd no idea why they were there. Surely it couldn't be this silly allegation from a woman about the eighties? She was in her mid-twenties at the time, which isn't what Yewtree is about. If the press thought it was me they'd have printed my name instead of waiting for me to confirm the story.

I decided to drive to my little office in Glasgow and do some work on the book of short stories I'm writing. While in Scotland I looked for the article in the *Mirror* online.

To me this was a fictional story, too. I read further that

she went to the police four years after the event and then again several years later. The police took no action because of lack of evidence. So why were the papers printing this stuff now? Was this the story the man from the *Mirror* emailed me about?

It looked flaky, to say the least. Surely Yewtree wasn't investigating this? So what was that tit from the *Mirror* on about?

This made me dig really deep and search my past for wrongdoing of a sexual nature. I found nothing, but it was worrying the hell out of me. Sometimes you think, '*Did I do that or did I make it up?*' When I look back on some supposed sexual exploit, did I actually do it or was it just something I made up for on stage? Some of my sexual stories are complete jokes. Then people come up to me saying, 'Yeah, I remember you doing that.' A story turns into a myth and it becomes confusing: '*Did I actually meet that person or did I not?*'

I carried on working on the book. Two days of the Chinese invading the Falklands later, I drove home.

Bridget had called to say, 'The coast is clear, they've all fucked orf!' Or words to that effect. The press had indeed 'fucked orf' and it had all gone away... or had it?

I only had four gigs in November, though I had a lot of other things booked so I was going to be quite busy. I also had to complete my book of short stories; these take me forever as I keep coming up with new storylines, only to replace them later.

* * *

I'd been doing pantomime in Glasgow for the last two years. I love the city, it's the hometown of my father and I feel at home there. The Glaswegians like my sense of humour, it seems, and I'm made to feel welcome whenever I visit.

I was once walking through the city centre one night when I was approached by a *Big Issue*-type of bloke who'd had a sip or two. His bleary eyes focused on me. A look of surprise came to his face and he said in almost untranslatable Glaswegian: 'Jum, oh Jum… you is brilly-ant, man, I love ya patter… giss a tenna.'

I told him I didn't have a tenner. His face changed.

'You're fucking shite!' He wandered off swearing.

For the first panto run it cost me £16,000 for hotel accommodation. This was too much. The following year I approached a letting agent to find a flat. He found me a beauty and I spent three happy months in Glasgow's West End, commuting into the city to do the panto twice daily.

Earlier in 2012, I'd been negotiating a third year at the Pavilion. It'd be another three months work, so the letting agent started looking. It got me thinking that I needed an office as well. My one in Hampshire is tiny and full of office stuff. Scotland would be an ideal place to work: I'd be out of the way with no distractions. I could also put myself about to get more work north of the border.

Innes, my letting agent, found me just the thing, an old house in the West End with offices in the basement. Old as it was, it had all the phone and email facilities I needed. The owners hadn't lived there for years and it was ideal.

Rehearsals would start in November and I'd take the offices from September. But one month later, Iain Gordon, owner of the Pavilion, decided to do *The Wizard of Never Woz* – a version of the 'Follow the Yellow Brick Road' musical. There was no real part for me. Iain and I tried various ways to fit me in, but in the end we decided I wouldn't be right for the show. It was a shame but the right decision. When Iain makes his mind up, it's made up.

Innes, the letting agent, said he'd speak to the owner of the offices to try to wriggle out of the lease. I told him not to worry. I'd still keep the place, as a deal is a deal and I could still do my writing and make my presence felt in Glasgow. It'd also be great to spend Christmas in Scotland.

My old tour manager Stevie Farr and my mate John Cannal and I went to tart the place up. My great friend Stevie is multi-talented and known as 'Fix-it Farr'. I've written much about his exploits in my book *Jim Davidson OBE: One Bankruptcy's Enough*. Steve can fix and repair anything while John, my old pal from Great Yarmouth, was his assistant.

A vanload of office furniture arrived. One week later, Steve's efforts ensured the offices were up and running. This is when I returned home to Stockbridge.

I'd now got into the habit of getting up early to see what the papers were saying. Operation Yewtree was in the news most days with stories of Savile and his deeds.

There were also stories that Yewtree was now concentrating on 'others' not related to Savile.

It seemed that anyone who was famous – or used to be – that had brushed past a woman who didn't like him would be up for grabs. This really was becoming a witch-hunt.

All the blokes in the pub were commenting on these allegations. They were united in their opinion that it was bonkers and money-grubbing women were coming out of the woodwork.

I told them I couldn't remember ever having sex with anyone against their will – after all, I didn't have to. That caused much piss-taking. Someone said, 'Yeah, I can see the resemblance to Brad Pitt.' It was fun but I could have done without it.

Next morning I was up at six. Our dog Benji was becoming unwell.

He was a Coton de Tuléar – a little, white, very proud dog who didn't *lick* much. Benji was lovely and charming. He was almost apologetic for being a dog – he didn't want to do a poo in the garden unless there was a curtain all round him. He just wasn't particularly 'animal', he had a bit of class about him. Benji almost put a napkin around his neck before he ate.

But now he was lethargic and miserable looking, and couldn't keep any food down. He would wake us up by being sick. Michelle was beside herself with worry about him.

I had other things on my mind as I'd seen a car parked just down from the house. I approached the driver. It was that little Polish photographer.

'What are you still doing here?'

'I am waiting for the police.' It obviously hadn't gone away. 'They might not come,' he added, trying to be kind.

I surmised he was an opportunist who'd hang around for days waiting for the money shot of the Old Bill knocking at the door. I was determined he wouldn't get that shot. The next two mornings at seven o'clock I went to my office and did some work.

I have nothing to hide, bollocks to 'em!

The trouble was that, in my mind, I could see the headline: 'Jim Davidson In Savile Raid'. It'd bring out the 'copycat killers', an open season for madwomen who see their chance. Anyone can accuse anyone, and thanks to the fuss this operation was causing it jumped straight to the front pages without the police or press checking the facts or details.

Why do people do this? 'Money!' other people tell me. Me, I think it's *schadenfreude* – pleasure from other people's misfortune.

I told myself I was safe because the allegation the papers told me about was full of so many holes it was like a keepnet. This was not me. I wouldn't have even recognised myself, had it not been for the *Mirror* asking me if it was me.

Michelle took Benji to the vets. They had a look and kept him in. We had a sleepless night of worry. The next day, they told us his tum was probably ulcerated and gave us some pills. Michelle knew better. Although she has a pessimistic streak and thrives on negatives, sometimes she can hit the nail on the head.

'What if it's cancer?'

I tried to reassure her, employing my poker face. 'It isn't.'

Benji was only seven. He'd never been really ill but was never a particularly well dog. He had a habit of chewing his foot and had tablets to stop him scratching himself silly. Benji also had to have special food and, like Michelle, was allergic to wheat.

On 14 December, the day after my birthday saw me working at the Lakeside Country Club, where they do the darts. Bob Potter owns it, he's an old friend and he's the reason I do it. It's a difficult gig, especially then as I had a terrible cold and a raspy voice. But Bob was in a happy mood and was looking forward to the darts, where he'd sell three million pints of lager a night!

After the show in the backstage bar I bumped into two old friends, agent John Ashby and wrestler Steve Veidor. The conversation got round to Savile. We'd all met him and in a way were as guilty of ignoring his activities as anyone. When he walked into a room where we were, we all ran away.

We never heard the specifics. We used to say, 'What is it with him? Is he gay or what?' 'No, he's into young girls,' or whatever. Everyone had their own idea; they just knew he was slightly pervy. He had 'perv' written all over him – anyone who looks like that, wears that tracksuit, talks like a moron dripping in gold, is either an albino black pimp or a fucking perv!

But we agreed that the witch-hunt was getting worse. 'Everyone is trying to guess who's been nicked but not named yet,' said Steve. I told them about the *Mirror*. They were disgusted but not surprised.

'Who's next?' asked John. 'Footballers? Rock stars? They won't have enough fucking police cars!'

Where will this end? *'Right, that's it, we got 'em all!'* says a spokes-moron from Operation Yewtree. *'There will be no more* Top of the Pops 2.*'*

I bade everyone goodnight. I wanted to get home back to Michelle, back to a bit of calm; back to my poor Benji. I was on edge from not knowing what was going on, from all the negatives, all the *what ifs*.

On 16 December I was back to Glasgow to play the

Pavilion. Benji was getting worse and Michelle was losing patience with our vet. I set off up the M6 with a heavy heart. Something else was nagging at me, as it was with Laurie. When I got to the Scottish office I called him.

I was concerned that the higher profile from *BB* would reignite the press's interest in me. The *Mirror* had already emailed and told me the police would be investigating me. Although Laurie and I thought it was bollocks, it was niggling away at both of us.

We chatted on the phone, with me worrying and Laurie trying to bring a common-sense approach to the issue.

'Let's look at the facts,' he said. 'The papers haven't named you. We both know it's *not* you. We both know that the story doesn't stack up.'

'You're right. I suppose that the police would have been here by now. Surely they thought the story was bullshit and the *Mirror* was lying, so they haven't bothered?'

We paused for breath, then Laurie came out with a Tarantino moment: 'Well, let's not start sucking each other's dicks quite yet.'

'Do you know what's worrying me, Laurie? I'm frightened the police are waiting for their moment – that they'll come to the *Big Brother* house.'

'They would never do that.'

'Well, they aren't shy when it comes to publicity. The dawn raids on old blokes' houses, what's that about? Maybe the papers and the police are in cahoots. Why else would they tell me that the police are about to investigate me?'

Panic was setting in. Something was afoot. I felt it deep in my guts. Laurie felt it, too.

He called *Big Brother*. They'd seen the silly allegations in the *Mirror* and were unimpressed.

'We want Jim in here, we'll look after him,' said Ros, the producer. 'These stories are just that – stories. Everybody knows that's not Jim.'

Laurie and I also thought that by pulling out we'd be seen as flaky, as if the accusation was getting to me... well, it fucking was. No matter whether there's any truth in it or not, the allegation does the damage.

Now I was fucked. I'd have to do *BB* knowing that, at any minute, the papers could start up again and the police would be forced to act. I'd be helpless and clueless, as in the *BB* house you're isolated from the outside world. I felt sick to my stomach.

I put all these negatives to one side, taking stock as I sat in the pub.

It isn't me and the story is bollocks – no problem.

'Large Scotch and water please.'

The Pavilion gig was, as always, full of life and people. Clandonia supported me for 15 minutes, those magnificent Scotsmen in their William Wallace-style gear. The show went well and I ended the night with just a thread of voice left

My cousins Bill and Jean came along with their partners and we went back to the rented house to get bad heads. I stayed for a couple of days before setting off for home, taking in a Charlton game on the way.

It's unusual to have Christmas off. This was the first time for a while. The plan was to have Michelle's family on the 24th, my kids on the 25th and then bugger off to Scotland on Boxing Day, to spend time with our good friends Brian and

Lisa Shaw, their two kids and my best pal, Steve Lamprell and his wife Gillie. We'd stay until New Year's Day, when I'd start my prep to do *Big Brother* on the 2nd.

The *BB* producers had asked all the inmates to report on New Year's Day to a hotel where we'd be kept in isolation till the show started on the 3rd. I got a pass till the 2nd but I had no idea who was going in. It's top secret. The papers, of course, claimed they *knew* who was going in, me included, but I'd spent weeks telling people I wasn't doing it.

The plan nearly went out of the window because of Benji. He was so poorly that we thought we'd have to cancel Christmas. On 23 December we'd taken him again to the vets. They did some blood tests and it was heart-breaking. We'd bought both our Coton de Tuléars in Dubai and flown them home with us. Benji was my favourite, the clever little bugger; Oscar was a 'special needs' dog, really grumpy and sulky... like me!

Then Michelle's lovely family came round and we had a great time. Even poor Benji tried to look happy. Michelle's sister Mandy and her husband Pete tried to cheer us up. Their two kids, Lauren and Ben, were great fun and our spirits were lifted for a while. Melve and Pam, Mitch's mum and dad, stayed the night with us.

Benji got worse in the night. Melve looked at me and gave me that *he's dying* look. I agreed. Michelle called a pet hospital and, at 10pm on Christmas Eve, we took our boy to see the specialists. We never saw him again.

We waved him goodbye and drove home. We both felt hollow, devastated. I tried to sound bright but it was hard. First it was the papers, then the *Big Brother* doubts, and now our lovely dog.

Michelle said we'd had nothing but bad luck since we came back from Dubai. She was right: Mitch's granddad died. My car blew up.

My play lost a fortune. It was the first play I'd written to be done live. I played the lead part but actually wrote it for Bradley Walsh. It was a story about a bigoted old white comic backstage with a talented young black comic, played by my mate Matt Blaze. Unfortunately, it just confused the public.

Then there was my 36-foot sports fishing boat in Shamrock Quay. I'd gone to the pub, and then I was chatting to people in the marina. As I walked back I thought, '*Fuck me! Someone's boat's on fire 'ere, this is exciting!*' As I got closer, I saw it was my fucking boat! You should have seen the firemen jump off as I told them I'd put 200 gallons of four star in it. It was an electrical fire. It's since been repaired and was part of my therapy during the arrest.

But back then there were demons in the air.

*The Stoker *is a friend I don't wish to identify, who used to work as a stoker for the Royal Navy.*

Chapter Four

DECEMBER 2012

Christmas Day came. We woke up and gave ourselves the presents we'd stored under the tree. We tried to be upbeat but it was difficult. We called the hospital and the vet said Benji wasn't eating. They had ultrasounded him and there was some stuff going on in his stomach. They hoped it might be an ulcer and would wait for tests. In the meantime, to help with his chronic anaemia, they were going to give him a blood transfusion.

Poor little sod.

Michelle, my poor girl, was suffering. We put on brave faces and awaited the incoming Davidsons.

The door knocker sounded and there they were. Thousands of 'em, all smiles and tinsel, just what the doctor ordered: Sarah, my eldest, with her bloke Wyndham, his two kids Tristen and Emily, and our granddaughter Tilly; next came Charlie and Fred; Elsie, looking as beautiful, as ever completed the set. My eldest son, Cameron, was doing his own thing somewhere and was not coming. But that wasn't going to spoil our day.

Let the fun begin!

We had drinks and dinner was served. All was well. The mood was lifted. The kids watched TV; we all played bowling on the Wii and we tried our best to forget Benji – as well as the papers and *Big Brother*!

My kids knew I was going on the show and all offered advice, especially about a gay chap called Rylan. Sarah said we'd get on great. I'd seen pictures of him, but I can't stand *The X Factor* so I hadn't a clue about what he does. I looked forward to meeting him though, and perhaps putting to rights some of this homophobia nonsense.

We all hit the sack about midnight. When I got up there were bodies everywhere. Charlie, Fred and Elsie left early, but the house was like a bomb had hit it.

We cleaned up and waited for a call from the vet hospital. It finally came at five thirty. Benji was doing okay and the blood transfusion was doing its job. We were pleased, even though there was a long way to go.

We also had to make a decision. We'd been kicking this about for days and now it was the cut-off time. Could we go to Scotland while Benji was with the vets? How could we cancel with our friends? Everyone was looking forward to it. But what state would we be in if we went up there knowing our boy was poorly?

Lisa and Brian's Uncle Bill had snuffed it, so they wouldn't be coming till the 30th. However, Steve and Gillie would be with us on the 28th. It was Gillie's birthday and I was going to cook.

What to do?

We called the vets. They told us to go to Scotland. Benji was in good hands and the results wouldn't be back till the 28th. We decided to go on the 27th.

On Boxing Day I went to see Charlton play. It did me good to take my mind off Benji and the newspapers. Fred and one of his mates went as well; he likes to be in with the singing mob at the covered end, so I met up with them after the game for a quick drink. My luck hadn't got any better as Ipswich beat us 2–1.

I drove home with a feeling that everything was going tits up. When I got home, Michelle was grim-faced.

'What's up? Is it Benji?'

'No,' she said with a look of concern. 'Your brother Bill has been rushed to hospital.'

Bill drinks a bit and things had started to go wrong. This time it was pains in his stomach and a swelling in the abdomen. He was as white as a sheet and his wife, Billie, called an ambulance when he couldn't drink a Guinness.

Bill is twelve years older than me. We get on great. He left home at fifteen and joined the Royal Navy, and then the police, before becoming a publican. '*Christ,*' you're probably thinking, '*no wonder he's ill.*'

Bill has a typical naval sense of humour, a desire to seek out the ridiculous and laugh his head off at it. He and I watching *Tom & Jerry* is a sight to see, two grown men rolling about on the floor, clutching our stomachs and screaming in hilarity. He also shares the humour that helps servicemen and police officers through the bad times, the cruel gallows humour of men in uniform.

I once said to him, 'Harry crashed his car badly. He has brain damage and two broken arms.'

'No wonder he crashed the fucking car,' retorted Bill.

I called his wife. She filled me in on Bill and I filled her in on Benji. Then Michelle and I had an early night. Things could only get better.

After a restless night we looked like two zombies. We bunged everything in the car, including the now confused Oscar, and headed off to God's country. I hoped God was watching and had His fingers crossed for us.

The drive took forever. We arrived at six and unpacked our stuff. Michelle called the vet. Benji had eaten something at last – good news. We told ourselves he'd be okay.

Some documents had arrived from *CBB*. I had to sign some forms quickly and send them back by email. That done, we settled down for the night and slept the sleep of the dead.

The next morning, halfway through my cooking breakfast, I heard Michelle crying. She was on the phone to the vet. As I walked in she hung up.

'He's got cancer.' She looked as if her world had ended. 'It's in his stomach and his liver.'

I did my best to console her. What I really wanted was to cry my eyes out.

Poor Benji, my dear boy!

I called the vet and went through what the options were. Michelle took Oscar for a walk to compose herself. While she was out, I called the vet and told her to give Benji 'the good news'. He died peacefully in his sleep.

I've got to stop typing now.

* * *

Okay, where was I?

We walked about the house in a daze and got ready to receive Steve and Gillie. They were driving up from Suffolk and would be knackered. But they'd cheer us up. They're wonderful people, someone to put a brave face on for.

I remember my dad saying, 'NO MORE ANIMALS IN THIS HOUSE!' Sambo had just died. He was eighteen, older than me, and I'd known him all my life.

I'd had two dogs run over when I was married to my previous wife, Tracy. Michelle left her dog, Harry, with her husband when they split up.

They break your heart. Why do we buy the bloody things? Because we love 'em... and more to the point, they love us

When the fourteen years which Nature permits
Are closing in asthma, or tumour, or fits,
And the vet's unspoken prescription runs
To lethal chambers or loaded guns,
Then you will find – it's your own affair –
But ... you've given your heart to a dog to tear.

–'The Power of the Dog', Rudyard Kipling

Chapter Five

Steve Lamprell is the eighth wonder of the world. Here's his story in half a page:

When he was a young man, his father and brothers decided business in England had hit rock bottom. As Steve puts it, Barclays had put them on their feet again – it took away their cars.

Drastic action was called for. The family sold what was left and bought an old fishing trawler, sailing off to Dubai to make their fortune. Sadly, their father passed away and Steve took over the running of the business with brothers Alan, Bob and Timmy. They were penniless. Times were difficult but, with hard work and perseverance and against all odds, they survived. Times were so bad that they would sleep in their car because they couldn't afford air conditioning in their house. However, things eventually things fell into place.

Today, Lamprell Energy is a thriving PLC. Steve and Gillie

still live in Dubai. They are busy people, spending very little time in the UK, and the fact that they came to see me and Mitch for New Year is a testament to the kind of friends they are. I know I could turn to them with any problem and they would help.

They arrived in Glasgow knackered after a seven-hour drive, but it was good to see them. We told them about Benji. They were sad for us but Steve said, 'Let time pass. You'll be okay. It was the only thing to do – you didn't want the dog to suffer.'

We had a drink and dinner for Gillie's birthday – prawn cocktail; steak and chips; good, old-fashioned comfort food – and a good natter, raising a toast to absent friends before an early night.

The next day, Brian and Lisa Shaw were coming with their two children, Tegan and Leila. Brian is my promoter. Lisa is Welsh, leggy and gorgeous; she and Michelle are great friends. We would all have dinner together and I was looking forward to it as much as Michelle. To be surrounded by friends and to cook for them is bliss.

Steve and Gillie would not stay with us that night as they were meeting Katherine Jenkins, the singer, after dinner. She was working in Edinburgh and would not be in Glasgow till midnight. As we had no room at the house, Steve and Gillie would move into a hotel down the road where Katherine would stay for the night.

The Shaws arrived early and we met for drinks at about six. I made paella. There was a lot of catching up to do and gallons of white wine to drink. All that Spanish food tends to make one thirsty!

Steve and Gillie left for their hotel at about ten; the rest of us hit the bottle while me and Brian chatted about the spring tour. He was aware of the press attention and, like most, thought nothing would come of it.

The year was planned: *Celebrity Big Brother* for January and a stand-up tour from February till June. Then summer season, a big tour with Bobby Davro and panto.

All was well as we swigged our Glendronach. Brian and I go way back. He was the bloke from 'oop norf' who came 'darn sarf' and put shows on. He had the unenviable task of looking after Freddie Star's live shows: Freddie was a genius, without doubt the best comic I've ever seen, but very unpredictable. Sometimes he'd not turn up or, worse still, do the soundcheck and then go home, saying he had vertigo or something equally silly. Brian's job was to harness this genius, and he did better than expected.

I didn't work for him very much at first, as International Artistes always used the promoter Barry Clayman, but Brian and I became great mates over the years. Eventually we started working together, firstly with my panto production business and then on the stand-up. The promoter's job is to facilitate live work; he'll book the theatres and sort out all the problems that go with working live. Brian loves cricket and is a devoted family man. If you saw his wife you'd see why.

The next morning saw us all pile into Brian's car and speed off to Loch Lomond. Cameron House is a splendid hotel situated at the loch. I'd put my kilt on for good effect.

Steve and Gillie had met up with Katherine Jenkins the night before and had arranged to have tea at the hotel. Katherine was pleased to see us. We'd been through a lot together: several trips to war zones and once nearly getting shot out of the sky in Iraq, but that's for another book!

Katherine looked gorgeous as always. She is one of those people you like instantly and never change your mind about. She is crap at phoning and texting, but she admits that.

Michelle and Katherine get on really well, and Lisa Shaw, being Welsh like Kath, fitted right into place. Steve and Gillie are like her godparents, though Steve gets pissed off when people ask Katherine if he's her dad. Hehe...

We all met for dinner in a fantastic restaurant in Glasgow called The Grillroom, which is part of James Mortimer's superb 29 Club. Dinner was, as Katherine would say, 'fab-lass', and Steve, as always, got the tab. Once the boys tried to find a way to beat Steve to the till. He asked for the bill, left his credit card and went to the loo. When he returned, my mates Les and Digby had cut the card up into little pieces. Steve went bonkers! They didn't do it again.

Katherine was jetting off the next day to France for a spot of skiing, before joining Steve and Gillie on their boat in Singapore. As for me, I was going to the dreaded house at Elstree TV studios. I still wasn't mentally prepared for this and wished I could have joined them. Still, at least I'd be earning some money and....

I ran through all the positives in my mind. Singapore won hands down.

Chapter Six

LATE DECEMBER 2012

New Year's Eve was going to be the hardest night. I couldn't drink too much, even though *Big Brother* had allowed me New Year's Day off. I was nervous. In two days I was off into the dreaded house and I still had the press on my mind. Would they spring into action when *BB* was aired? Was there any truth in the papers saying the police were investigating me? As I prepared dinner, I ran through the various scenarios in my head.

Thank God there had been no more press speculation about the silly woman in the *Mirror*. The police must have thought, as most people did, that it was just another attention-seeking money-grubber.

What if they come when I'm in the house? What will Michelle do? Would they dare come into the house? More to the point, would Endemol and Richard Desmond allow it?

They'd have no choice. The way the police investigation was going for a higher profile, it wouldn't surprise me.

No... it'll be fine.

I prepared the bollock-knees sauce and marinated the chops. Six o'clock soon came and I changed into my kilt. Everyone did his or her best to wear a bit of tartan. We had some drinks and the first course was served one hour late – fucking Aga! But that's the trouble with being in someone else's house. It was worth the wait though; the tandoori chops went down a treat.

'Right, we're not having main course yet as we're going to play a game,' insisted Michelle.

I protested. I didn't want to eat late. I didn't want to be up all night boozing either, as my last day outside the house would be spent walking round with a hangover, shaking and panicking.

Still, the game, Logo, went ahead. We'd played this on Christmas day at home. It was great fun but it was getting late: ten to ten. After the game was played, the girls set off to do the main course. It was served at ten past eleven, too late for me. I wouldn't eat any as I knew it'd give me acid all night. So I was immediately turned into the bad guy.

Things got worse. At twelve o'clock we rushed out into the street to find the famous Scottish Hogmanay was not happening – nowhere near us anyway. The street was deserted. My heart sank. Where were the fireworks?

I tried to get us to go to the nearest pub, but we had two children with us so that was a no-no. I returned to the house, had a row with Michelle and felt I'd invited people up for a Scottish celebration that wasn't happening.

We sang 'Auld Lang Syne' with me sulking. 'Happy fucking New Year,' said Michelle.

Steve and Gillie made the most of it and, in their usual style, tried to keep everyone happy. I, however, was feeling sorry for myself. It'd all gone wrong. By now we were all slightly boozy and, in the best can't-see-sense-when-pissed tradition, Davidson went to sleep on the couch.

Bollocks to everything!

I'd dug myself a hole that I couldn't get out of. What a way to end the year: moaning, sulking, without my dog, with only the prospect of making a tit of myself on *CBB* to look forward to. Things couldn't get any worse.

I woke up on the couch feeling like I wanted to be dead. I'd fucked up again. Everything was my fault. Why do I do this?

I climbed into bed with my beloved Michelle and prayed she'd forgive me. Maybe not understand me, but forgive me.

I tossed and turned, then went to the bathroom to be sick – one of those panicky dry retches. I was covered in sweat and sat up shaking. Michelle put her arms around me.

'Right' she said, 'you're not going into *Big Brother*.'

'I have to.'

'No you don't… try to sleep.'

She cuddled up to me and my main problem vanished. It's always *will Michelle forgive me again?* I always think it's entirely my fault afterwards but that it's all hers during the event. In reality it's a mixture of both. Mitch will say or do something to provoke an overreaction from me – 'bear-poking' I call it. She's fearless and won't give ground, and also has that woman's thing of never being wrong even after it's proven in black and white. She's what you might call feisty

I got up at six and scanned the papers online... nothing, great. I then wrote apologies to Brian and Lisa, and Steve and Gillie, and a soul-searching analysis of myself:

1 January 2013
The trouble with me...

I suppose it is about getting old and feeling unwanted professionally. People who love me want me, even though I go out of my way sometimes to be horrid to them. Michelle especially.

Michelle has a way, without knowing it, or perhaps well knowing it, to bring me down a peg or two, to piss on my chips, especially if our friends are about. I will react to the smallest remark she makes. Other people don't do it, just her. Or maybe I don't hear it, or maybe I do and take no notice. But then other people do not have the first place in my heart.

Michelle has a way of stating the obvious. She can see through my mask. She can see reality more than me. I seem to live in a world of performing and getting adulation and then waiting around for the next ovation. And when I'm not working I seek instant pleasure and spend my life seeking attention, from Michelle mainly.

I always do things for the outcome of the event, not for the event itself. Even fishing. I am more concerned about getting a picture of the whopper than actually catching it. Would I go fishing if I didn't have a camera and, worse still, had to keep my catches a secret?

With no adulation or reward I become worthless. Mr Booze will help... won't he?

I drink too much for my own good. I'm OK for the first

couple but then the last one brings out all the grumbles. It rips away the mask of confidence and ignites the fires of insecurity that lie within. It then turns me against the people whose remarks I have been ignoring and telling myself, 'They don't mean it.' For instance, Michelle will say something like, 'We can't go home yet.' Harmless in itself. But... if I want to go home I just don't react to that statement, I react to all the other things she has said to upset me. All the things I've been storing up. She doesn't understand that and counters with, 'Is this what this is about, because I said, "We can't go home yet?"' That makes me worse. She doesn't understand the straw-that-broke-the-camel's-back syndrome, and nor should she.

All our grief is through my drinking.

Is that true? I dare say that it certainly doesn't help. The arguments normally start at the end of the evening. Michelle has a knack of telling me off for saying things. 'Shhh' and 'stop it' are her favourite words. They are red rags to a bull. I just clam up and stop talking. Silly really, but I sulk. How can she control what I say and what I should and shouldn't say? Then later, when asked why I caused a scene or why I went into a mood, the argument will start with me once again, bringing up every gripe I have been storing up. I'm not right but she never learns... or does she? Does my reaction come as a shock to her, someone who claims to, and does, know me more than anyone else?

She is never at fault and is totally unaccountable.

'He drinks too much.'

Do I?

Sometimes I drink to feel better. Last night, after prepping dinner, I had a couple of whiskies. I was tired and neglected to heed the word HALT: hungry, angry, lonely, tired.

The second whisky woke me up and I became the life and soul of the party.

Heaven...

By the time we started to eat, I'd had quite a few Scotches and things had started to irritate me. In my boozy state I failed to realise that I was still tired. The whizz of the second Scotch had turned into a brain-numbing memory. So, in an attempt to regain that second Scotch feeling, I did what all drinkers do: I had another in an attempt to relive the rush of the one that makes you feel better. You know the rest of the story.

I drink when I have bad news or when I have negative thoughts. Then booze becomes a medicine, something to transport you away from the incoming doom. And usually the second one starts the ride to safety. The fifth and sixth ones start the return journey back through the storm and to a place worse than where you started from.

Negative thoughts are bad for me. If I can't drink them away, I feel like physically running away from them.

Negative thoughts are great for removing the mask of confidence. They tear down your barriers of self-deceit and denial.

Denial that it wasn't you that became impossible to work with. Denial that you use people for your own ends, denial that you really are finished on TV and hated, mainly because you hate everyone else! Denial that to be shunned and neglected in favour of people with less talent pisses you off beyond comprehension.

The mask provides the makeup.

I lie to others and myself.

'Why would I want to be on telly with those wankers? Why would I want to go on chat shows? They are all arseholes!' They might be, but they are the arseholes with the chat shows.

I really believe that the new guys are not funny. Millions of people find them totally unfunny.

They don't go telling them though!

Tomorrow I step onto the tailgate of a slim chance of correcting a few untruths. Well, a few perceptions would be a better description.

I am anxious about the show, as it is an unknown thing to me. When I went into Hell's Kitchen I really couldn't give a fuck about how people saw me, as long as I was seen to be able to put those fucking Z-listers in their place. I did, and look what happened. 'Who cares?' said the man in the mask. What else was I to say?

Now though, a different set of circumstances has arisen. Now I have a real chance of getting a foot back in people's hearts. People that I now know I need.

If I succeed then all is well and it will be a job well done. That is my intention and I will not, at this moment, commit to writing any of my negative thoughts. I am sure that they are hovering overhead, sponsored by the cunning and baffling alcohol.

I will try not to project how I'll feel as I step off the tailgate but will wait and see.

To be honest, I am frightened. Not of failing or saying the wrong thing – I've prepared for that – but of not being able to do it. Of being there and not having enough of the energy I know I need to do well. But the fear is projected fear. If I stop that then there is no fear.

I shouldn't have drunk last night, but I wanted to be UP and not repeatedly asked, 'What's up with you?' In the end my solution to it all went horribly wrong! My only saving grace was that the cooking was great... so I'm told.

I once again hurt the ones I love, especially my wife Michelle. Maybe if she paid a little more attention to me then I would be OK, but then I would be living in a false world. One where certain comedians crave an instant high and a 'well done, Jim' after every event. That's not practical, or fair, on her.

I'm doing this show for the right reasons. I will try and do well.

2013 has just begun and, after a shaky few opening minutes, promises to be a good year for me.

* * *

This was the state of mind I was in. The pressure was showing. Despite the brave face, this was not a good time for me. I can't deal with uncertainty; I don't know how to plan for the unplanned.

Steve and Gillie left for home at half past ten. He understood the pressure I was under, giving me a hug and wishing me luck before they made their way down south. I felt my safety net had gone.

The rest of us settled down and faced the day. Michelle repacked my suitcase, making sure I had my novelty nightshirt and hat.

By now I was feeling better about life. I felt I could cope. It would be okay; I'd stick to a game plan. Henri Brandman was on standby to deal with whatever the press could throw at us.

Michelle was exhausted by the time we got into bed. Our friends Brian and Lisa had been encouraging. They told me all about Rylan: he was a very camp man who'd been on one of Simon Cowell's talent shows, and although it didn't go very well he'd captured the hearts of the public. But would I cope with reality TV?

Six o'clock came soon and I was dragging my bag down the stairs. The cab was outside to take me to the airport. I felt okay and, what was more, I felt that Mitch would be okay, too.

Mitch and Brian said goodbye, wishing me luck as I set off for my much needed television reappearance. I hugged Michelle and wanted her to feel I'd never loved anyone as much as her. Maybe I should have told her... but she wouldn't have believed me.

I told her not to worry. I'd be okay.

Three hours later I was in a cell.

Chapter Seven

2 JANUARY 2013

The flight down from Glasgow was not as scary as I'd thought it'd be. My heart rate was normal and there was no panic. Instead I had a feeling of tranquility and well-being. I closed my eyes and looked to the future: two, maybe three weeks in the house and then a tour. Hopefully, the exposure on *CBB* would boost the ticket sales. It'd certainly introduce me to a new, younger audience.

I ate my little British Airways breakfast and dozed for a bit. The wheels coming down woke me up. We landed on time and the adventure would soon be starting.

CBB had sent a car for me. There would be a man at Terminal 5 with a little board. I wondered how Michelle was doing. I texted her while waiting for the bags: *Don't worry I can do this x.*

Freddie texted me, telling me all would be okay. I replied: *Wish me luck.*

As I was unloading my bags, the phone rang. It was Sam, my PA. She was whispering, which was odd.

'Jim, a policeman has called Laurie's office, they want to speak to you.'

The blood drained from my head.

'Tell them to call this number.'

I put the bags on the trolley and shook my head to check if I was still asleep on the plane. Three minutes later the phone rang.

'Mr Davidson?'

'Yes?'

'It's DC *Fuck-Your-Life-Up* here.'

'Hello.'

'I'm from Operation Yewtree,' he said proudly. 'I bet you've been expecting us?'

'No. What's up?'

'We need to speak to you today... where are you?'

'You're a good detective!' I said in an attempt to get a laugh. Nothing. 'I'm at Heathrow... listen, officer, I'm going into the *Big Brother* house today, can't this wait? It's not as if you don't know where I'll be.'

'We've spoken to the *Big Brother* people. My colleague wants to speak to you. Can I give him this number?'

'Sure.'

I waited an agonising five minutes, hoping that someone would call and say, 'Ha ha, gotcha!'

I called Henri, my lawyer.

'You are not going to believe this...'

He couldn't. Neither could I.

I'd spent a week in terror of doing *Big Brother*. But I'd got myself prepared and I was ready for it. Now, in an instant, I had to switch targets. Dump *Big Brother* and prepare to be arrested.

I paced up and down and got the brain in gear. I thought of my friend Goose; I always do when I'm frightened and at a loss for what to do next. What would he do? The wise Special Forces soldier's words came quickly and precisely to me:

Prepare... forget Big Brother, *forget everything else and prepare for this NOW!*

The same policeman called me back.

'Where are you?'

'You'll have to speak to my lawyer.'

I gave him Henri's number.

Now what do I do? Shall I get in the CBB *car or what?*

I called Mickey, one of the producers.

'Oh my God!' she said. 'What do they want?'

'Fuck knows...'

I thought it must be the *Mirror* allegation, seeing as they'd emailed about me and someone else allegedly attacking a woman. After all, they'd told me Op Yewtree was investigating me.

But then surely the police couldn't believe that story. According to the *Mirror*, the accuser has been to the police twice but they didn't do anything. And it was twenty-five years ago!

Can't be that... what can *it be?*

She handed me to Ros, the other producer, who asked me if I was okay and added, 'Don't worry, we will wait for you.' She was very understanding and kind, even though she must have been thinking, '*Shit, what do we do now?*' I was thinking exactly the same thing.

I knew that when I got to the station I'd be processed and put in a cell. I decided to get rid of my clothes to save time. I checked my bags into left luggage and waited. Henri called and explained the procedure.

'They will call and arrange a meeting.'

It was so good to hear his calming voice. I was to go with them to a local police station, where they would check if there was 'adequate space' to interrogate me. Adequate space?

Waterboarding?

'When they call me to confirm where you'll be, just give me an hour and I'll be there.'

'Thanks Henri.'

As I ended the call I felt terribly alone.

Shit, is this really happening?

I called Michelle, who had heard from Sam. She was calm and said not to worry. 'Kin 'ell, this was Superwoman!

I told her to call Laurie in Mexico and fuck his holiday up. I'd call as soon as I could. I told her I loved her and, although shit was happening, I'd deal with it.

'I know,' she said.

I'm funny like that, when shit is impending I fall to bits, but when it happens I go into let's-deal-with-it-calmly-and-logically mode.

Then I ran to the gents and threw up! Just kidding...

Funny though, isn't it? I'd been worried to death for weeks that something like this would happen, ever since that bastard in the car told me the police were coming. I imagined the scenario: arrested in full public glare; ridiculed; humiliated; with no chance to defend myself. The thought of it happening was terrifying.

Now that it *was* happening, the fear had left me and I was anxious to get it over with. I was also curious to see what the charges were... if any.

The phone rang. It was another copper.

'Hello. I'm DC Danny Root and I'm coming to get you. Where shall we meet?'

Northern Cyprus?

I tried to get him to do it after *CBB*. 'You're preventing me from work.'

He didn't care much for my argument, so he ignored it. We arranged to meet at departures. We kept our phones open and I guided him to me. He was with another DC, an obvious policewoman named Paula Derrick. He was bald, smart and youngish, looking like a cross between Jason Statham and Alf Garnett. We walked to a small unmarked car with another woman sitting in it. I wondered for a split second if this was the accuser, which was a bit silly

'The alleged offences are of an historical nature, dating back to 1988,' he began. 'Jim Davidson, I am arresting you on suspicion of a sexual offence committed against *Scouser* [my codename for complainant one]...'

Is this the bullshit story from the Mirror?

I relaxed. I'd never heard of this woman.

'... and [codename] *Wag*.'

This woman's real name was odd! I'd never heard of her either. I repeated her name in astonishment.

He laughed, raised an eyebrow and carried on reading me my rights.

After driving around for a bit because they were lost, we

arrived at Heathrow police station where I was processed by the sergeant. He was a young, friendly policeman who showed no emotion and made no comment, just went through the motions.

I emptied my pockets. They were concerned that I had a pink pill. It was, in fact, a beta-blocker, which I always shove in my pocket whenever I fly. They also freaked out at a piece of artificial sweetcorn in a pocket of the fishing jacket I was wearing. *Big Brother* had told me to wear something with a hood. They didn't want my face to be seen at the airport or in the car.

I told them the sweetcorn was a sweetie but they didn't laugh. I don't help myself... When I explained it and the pill, the station sergeant laughed. The Yewtree cop didn't, putting it in an evidence bag as if it was nitroglycerin!

I was fingerprinted, photographed and DNA swabbed, and signed for all sorts of shit. I was then put in a cell minus my tie, belt and shoes.

Have I murdered someone?

Things raced around in my mind.

Big Brother *will replace me; Richard Desmond will go fucking mad. No extension to the house. Shows cancelled. Wife in tears. Children ashamed.*

My thoughts ran wild. I thought of Goose again. What would he do? I stopped pacing and got my head down.

Thanks, Bro.

I tried to keep myself in neutral and nodded off. Then there was a knock at the door, a small hatch opened and a paper cup full of the worst tea in history was passed through by one of the custody policemen.

I took a few sips. It was important to keep hydrated, as I didn't want to be dry-lipped when they interrogated me.

The cell was modern and light blue. The bed-cum-bench was fixed to the wall. A loo was in the corner. I noticed there was no toilet paper – in case I hanged myself with it, I suppose.

Henri Brandman would be winging his way as quickly as he could. My mind started racing again.

What will they ask? Who is this other woman, Wag?

The first girl was basically the story in the *Mirror*, I was sure of that. I'd never heard of Scouser either, apart from the article in the paper. Henri and Laurie had read the *Mirror* and said, 'Don't worry, this story is silly.'

Not so silly now, eh boys?

The police told me The Stoker had been arrested, too. I felt sorry for him. No one should have this shit dropped on them from twenty-five years ago. I couldn't remember any of it for the life of me, so what could he remember, I wondered? Maybe he could shed some light on the matter.

Too late now. He'll be in a cell like this one somewhere, shitting himself.

How could I defend myself when I had no memory of the allegation? Back in November, I'd run through the worst-case scenarios until I was sick to my stomach. Now they'd come true, just when I felt it was safe to go back in the water.

'Let's not start sucking each other's dicks quite yet.'

How right Laurie was. It was a long time to have the sword of Damocles hanging over one's bonce. My saving grace was a deep sense of my innocence. Sitting in a cell designed to cancel out all normal thought, I took stock.

I can't remember. Why can't I remember? It isn't me – that's why. Why are they doing this? Who have I upset so much? The police have to do this; they're going through the motions... surely? But who the fuck are these women? How is Michelle coping? Why am I talking to myself?

I thought of my wife, swallowing the lump in my throat. I got a grip and thought of Stevie Lamprell.

What would he do?'One step at a time, Jim.'

I got myself together and had a little walk around. It was no good worrying about complainant number two until I heard what she was accusing me of

Why is this happening? How long have I been here?

I could still taste the tea as I searched for non-existent answers. I imagined Goose's words:

'Just be yourself, Bro. You've done nothing so you've nothing to hide.'

But I'm scared. Scared of the unknown. Scared of what's to come. Scared of the power of accusation. This shit will be hitting the news wires now. I'm already suffering from these accusations and nobody has heard my side of the story yet. I don't even know what my side of the story actually is. I don't know what they're accusing me of. How is this fair?

I tried to sleep again. My head span as it tried to make sense of it all. But there was no sense in this. The more I thought about it, the more concerned I became.

I was convinced the police were looking to arrest any celebrities, no matter how flimsy the evidence. I could tell by the look on the DC's face that he was pleased he'd captured *his* celebrity. This shit was political and I was being hung out to dry.

What seemed like three weeks later, the hatch opened and a key rattled in the lock.

Am I free to go?

Not quite. Henri had arrived and I was escorted to an interview room. Boy, was I pleased to see him! He looked flustered and put out.

'How are you, Jim?'

'I'm okay thanks, considering.'

He handed me a piece of paper. On it were the two allegations. I read with interest. The first was a more detailed version of the story in the *Mirror*, disclosing Scouser's statement:

'In 1988 I was a promotion girl at Catterick races where I met The Stoker at a function. He told me that his friend was the most famous man on TV. He arranged to pick me up and take me to see him in the Midlands. It was Jim Davidson.'

Where in the Midlands?

'We went to a hotel...'

Which one?

'...where I met Jim at the bar.'

What time?

'He made a comment about my wig.'

How did I know it was a wig? Okay, I'll shut up with the interruptions now.

'I was shown to a room that had two single beds. I said, "I'm not getting on the casting couch for you."

'Later I saw the show; it was in a sports hall. I think it was being filmed as I sat next to a cameraman.

'Jim then drove us in his gold Bentley to an Indian restaurant. I had four Bacardi and cokes.

'When we'd eaten Jim gave me the bill and said, "If you're not going to shag you can pay." He then laughed and paid the bill.

'I think they put something in my drink as I never felt this way before. They helped me to Jim's Bentley and drove back to the hotel.

'The Stoker took me upstairs and raped me.

'He then called Jim Davidson who turned up naked and put his penis in my mouth. I bit it.

'I woke up in the morning in bed with The Stoker.

'I went to the bar and saw Jim. I showed him the note he had written when I had asked for an autograph for my son. He wrote "To Stephen, your mum's a great fuck."

'I went home.

'I called Jim sometime later and he hung up on me.'

The second one was even sillier. It was codename Wag's allegation:

'In or around 1989 my friend and I went to see Jim Davidson at the London Palladium. It might have been another theatre in London.

'After the show my friend wanted an autograph. She was too shy to ask, so I went to the stage door on my own. I joined a queue of people and was shown by an Asian bouncer to a little room with a table and a chair.

'Jim said, "What a nice bunch of tits!" and grabbed my breasts. I dropped my handbag in shock and its contents spilled onto the floor. I bent down to pick them up and Mr Davidson dropped his trousers and pants and shoved his erect penis into my mouth.

'The Asian doorman came in and gave a high-five salute to

Jim. I bit his penis. He called me a bitch. I left and didn't even tell my friend, I just wanted to go home.'

Who would believe this? More to the point, how could they have a chance of proving it? I looked at Henri in disbelief.

'What do you think?'

'Laughable, if it wasn't so serious. I don't think we would ever have had allegation number two if we didn't have allegation number one.'

There was a pattern in the two allegations. One might not have raised an eyebrow, but *two* bitten cocks? He dragged out a file from his enormous case.

'Let's just check the newspaper's account of the same story.'

We looked at the press cutting. In the paper I wasn't mentioned by name, nor was The Stoker. The stories were similar but one was written in newspaper speak, the other in police speak. I looked at Henri, not quite knowing what to say.

'I don't remember any of this, neither of them.'

'Well, let's see what we do remember... allegation number one, Scouser, 1988?'

'Bloody hell, Henri, I've been trying to remember this since I read the newspaper story in October... do you know, if they hadn't emailed and said it was me I wouldn't have connected me with it at all.'

He gave a look that said *exactly*.

'Now in the paper...' he searched for the point he was about to make, 'she says she was traumatised and went to the police four years after the alleged event.'

He made a note on his pad.

'It also says they did nothing... she says she went to them again "several years later". Be interesting to see those police reports,' he said slowly as he was writing. 'When did she go to the papers?'

He wrote again on the pad.

'Did she receive remuneration for the story?'

I couldn't help much apart from pointing out the holes in her story.

'I've never had a gold Bentley. I didn't have Bentleys till the nineties, I think. Can't remember what I had then – a Range Rover probably. I would've had a driver though, Kevin Laming or maybe Rick Price. I'll ask them.'

'Are the police holding back stuff? I mean, it's a bit weird that they haven't mentioned the date or the place.'

'I'm sure we'll find out.'

We moved on to complainant number two, Wag. Her story wasn't mentioned in the papers; however, that didn't mean she hadn't approached them before going to the police. We would ask them.

Henri and I both thought this one was a bigger nonsense than the other. How could we work out what I was doing when this woman didn't know the year or the venue? Nor did her story ring true. Autographs and tables at a theatre? Never – not backstage anyway.

We decided we'd ask questions about this woman. Henri wrote out what I'd read to the police before they questioned me, and we spoke about the politics of this Operation Yewtree.

Henri is a brilliant lawyer. I've known him for years and he's done most of my divorces – so it's fair to say he knows me well. He's also my friend. I love being in his company. He is never down, always full of life and fun. Henri has something of the night about him, which is a great part of his immense charm. He's also the solicitor for West Ham, but despite that I like him enormously.

The door was opened. DC Root stuck his bald head in.

'Ready?'

He gave a rehearsed smile. We were escorted to a police interview room. It was exactly the same as you'd see on *The Sweeney*, save for a huge widescreen TV and a CD recorder our bloke had trouble working.

The policewoman joined him. Henri and I sat down opposite them, awaiting my fate. After DC Root struggled to get the CD started, *we* eventually got started.

He read out the caution again and asked me if I understood it, then rattled off who was in the room. He looked immensely satisfied with the situation.

Henri slide-tackled him.

'Before we deal with your questions, can my client – can we now refer to him as Jim? – make a short statement?'

There was a blank look on my interrogator's face.

'Uh... okay.'

I read out our ten points: 'We would like to know if the accusers have received or sought fees from the newspapers.

'We would like to see the interview records of Scouser, who claims to have reported her allegation to the police twice.

'We would like to see written evidence of the police's decision to do nothing.

'We would like to see Scouser's medical records as in her own words she was traumatised.'

And so it went on. We asked for information not covered in the allegation sheet.

'I strongly deny any involvement in these alleged offences,' I said at the end of it all.

Right – your go now.

At this point I hated the policeman. Did he know the hurt this would cause? I couldn't believe he took these allegations seriously. They could have been dismissed by a woodentop straight out of Hendon Police College. It seemed he was trying to ruin my life to save face for the Jimmy Savile squad, who'd sat back as Britain's biggest alleged paedophile offended with impunity.

In reality, and in fairness, he was probably acting on orders from some faceless, politically correct career copper looking for a gong. But did he have to look so fucking smug and self-satisfied about it all?

I was trembling inside and had to hold myself from exploding. I took a deep breath and put the anger in the hurt locker.

Let's just take it one step at a time.

My recollection of DC Root's interrogation technique is as follows:

'In 1988 you met a woman called Scouser...' (He used her real name, of course.)

'Did I?'

'I'm asking you if you have met a woman called Scouser.'

'I can't remember anyone of that name. 1988 was a long time ago.'

'Can I say a few things that might jog your memory?'

You got her pregnant, killed her and chopped her body up...

'1988 was the year that...' He rattled off three things that happened in 1988. He was precise and motivated.

'Sorry, I don't remember. I can't even be sure who I was with in 1988.'

'Do you know The Stoker?'

'Yes.'

'How do you know him?'

I explained that he used to do guest spots on my shows, supporting me on the odd tour and summer season.

'Would you say you are friends?'

'Yes, you could say that. As far as having friends in show business goes.'

'What do you mean by that?'

I explained that being a stand-up comedian is a lonely business, as you normally work alone apart from whoever's supporting you at the time. It's not as if you're a singer with a band or a dancer with a troupe. It's a solitary job.

I gave him a brief history of The Stoker: the navy, *Copy Cats* on TV, Capital Radio and then some disasters with a TV company co-founded by Richard Digance and Jethro.

The detective continued.

'What hotel would you have stayed at in Birmingham in 1988?'

'Uh... I don't know. Several.'

'She said you played a sports hall. Can you remember doing that?'

'No. I don't think I've ever played a sports hall in Birmingham. I don't think there's a sports hall there that holds gigs.'

'It was being filmed, does that help?

'No.'

I told him I'd read the allegations and couldn't remember any of it. He ignored me and carried on.

'She says you mentioned her wig, does that ring any bells?'

'Why would I know she was wearing a wig?'

He raised an eyebrow.

'Did you have a gold Bentley?'

'No.'

'A silver one then?'

'No.'

'Anything that could be mistaken for one?'

Yes, a red mini!

'No.'

'Do you remember taking this girl for an Indian meal?'

'Look, DC Root, you're wasting your time. Could you remember taking a girl for an Indian meal twenty-five years ago?'

'Call me Danny,' he said with his best smile. He was not a bit put out by my irritation. I started to get the feeling he was a clever man.

'Do you remember?'

'I've told you I don't remember any of it.'

He didn't seem to listen, or was maybe only doing what they taught him in detective school. Whatever he was doing, he was doing it well. He was letting me talk, knowing I was a talker.

'She said you may have put something in her drink.'

'Of course she did.'

'Did you?'

'Are you being serious? Do you actually believe this shit? *Do you?*'

I was getting quite annoyed. He looked embarrassed. Paula, the policewoman, said nothing.

'We have to take these allegations seriously,' he said calmly.

I laughed, wishing DC Root back on the beat. He reverted to his line of questioning

'She said you went back to the hotel. Do you remember that?'

'No.'

'She said that The Stoker took her upstairs and raped her.'

I knew this could never happen. The Stoker hasn't got a rape in him.

'Did he carry her? Tie her up? Put a gun against her head? What?'

I waited for Columbo's answer. He took his time.

'She said that The Stoker called you and you came into the room.'

'Really? What, instantly, or did he keep bashing away till I turned up?'

'Then you put your penis in her mouth.'

'Did I? How can you put your cock in a mouth that doesn't want a cock in it?'

The DC livened up and shared his wisdom with us.

'Oh, believe me, you can.'

'Have you seen *The Shawshank Redemption*?'

'What?'

'I don't want to belittle your theory, but in that film the lead actor says to a guy, "The jaw is the strongest joint in the body and could bite a cock clean off."'

'Well?'

'Well what?'

'Did you put your penis in her mouth?'

'Well, if a woman doesn't want a cock in her mouth she'll keep her mouth shut.'

'She said that The Stoker held her head and you forced your penis in her mouth. She says she bit it.'

''Course she did, what else is she going to say when asked, "If you didn't want it in there, why didn't you bite it then?"'

'She said that she saw you the next morning.'

'The next morning?'

'Yes, she says she saw you at the bar.'

'At the bar in the morning? With my dick in a bandage?'

He shrugged.

'She stayed the night then?'

'She says she showed you an autograph that you signed for her, saying, "To Stephen, your mum's a great fuck."'

'I can't remember that either.'

'She said she called you later.'

'How did she get my number?'

'From an agency maybe?'

I couldn't believe how this copper was trying to fit a square peg into a round hole. I told him it wasn't possible. How come the police didn't have my number but a so-called rape victim did? The only way this woman would have had my number was if I'd given it to her – obviously to hand straight to her lawyer. You couldn't make it up (though presumably someone had). It was seriously pissing me off.

'Look, this is all silly. She's been to the police twice.'

'Where did you hear that?'

He didn't know!

'This was in the papers.'

'Did they name you?'

'No.'

'Then how,' he smirked, sensing a breakthrough, 'did you know they were talking about you?'

'Because some arsehole from the *Mirror* knocked at my door and asked if it *was* me.'

This took the two investigating officers aback. I was convinced they didn't know the story from Scouser had been knocking around the papers for ages. The difference between the Savile thing and what happened to me in my younger life is that mine were kiss-and-tell stories. But these stories contained the extra ingredient needed: '*I didn't want to do any of this – he forced me.*'

'So do you remember forcing her to give you oral sex?'

'No.'

'Have you ever forced anyone to give you oral sex?'

'How do you do that without a gun?'

'Have you ever had sex with The Stoker?'

'Can you rephrase that please?'

He smiled.

'Have you and The Stoker had sex with a girl together?'

'I don't remember.'

'Have you had threesomes?'

'Yes, but normally with two girls. Two blokes is a bit off-putting.'

'Did you and The Stoker have a threesome with Scouser?'

'I don't recall.'

This statement galvanised the policewoman into life.

'You say you don't recall?'

'Yes.'

'Well, you have been saying, "I don't remember." Now, you don't recall.'

'It's the same'

'Why change it then?'

She thought she'd noticed a slip-up on my part.

'Well I got bored with saying, "I don't remember." I think "don't recall" is better English.'

'So you don't recall any of this?'

'No.'

'Then you could have done it?'

'Come on... what chance does that give me? Henri, how do I answer that?'

Henri, who had been quiet until this point, said, 'Jim, the question to answer is: "Have you ever had sex with someone against their will?"'

I said a definite, 'NO,' and then added with a smile, 'Against my better judgement sometimes.'

The policeman smiled and said, 'Right, let's have a break.'

'Good,' Henri said. 'Can someone get me a sandwich?'

I decided not to eat. My tum didn't feel great and, to be honest, a sandwich from a police canteen is not something I long for.

They talked about putting me back in the cell. Henri asked if we could wait in the interview room. They compromised and moved us both to a room that was smaller than my cell.

You might not believe this, but Henri and I talked about football for most of the time until we were taken back to the interview room. Then the process of inserting the CD, reading me my rights and making introductions started again. This time it was about complainant number two. Off went the master detective:

'It's alleged that in or around 1989...'

'Hang on a minute, when was this – 1989?'

'In or around 1989,' he said, without the slightest embarrassment. 'Can I remind you of three events of 1989?' He rattled off some facts. 'Can you remember 1989?'

Yes, I was having my cock sewn back on after the events of 1988.

'No, I can't say that much comes to mind... my son was born.'

'Did you play the Palladium in 1989?'

'I don't think so. I did the odd charity show there but not one on my own.'

'When was that?'

'Can't recall.'

'No others?'

'Not that I can remember.'

'Don't you keep records?'

'No.'

'She says she queued up at the stage door.'

'That's impossible.'

'Why?'

'You can't get to the stage door at the Palladium. There are gates and you need a pass.'

'She says she was escorted to a small room by the stage door.'

'There isn't one.'

'A doorman let her in, an Asian guy. Did you have an Asian minder?'

'Why would I have an Asian minder? Sorry, I didn't mean that to come out the way it did.'

'I understand. She says the room had one chair and a table.'

'Then it's not a dressing room – not at the Palladium.'

'She says you said she had "a great bunch of tits".'

'"Bunch"?'

'Bunch.'

'I wouldn't say that.'

'Why?'

'Did she have more than two?'

'Sorry?'

'A "bunch" indicates a numerous amount.'

'She says you then grabbed her breasts and she dropped her bag in shock.'

'Of course she did.'

'When she bent down to pick them up, you dropped your trousers and pants and thrust your erect penis into her mouth.'

'Here we go again. Erect, eh? That was quick…'

'She then bit it.'

'Christ! I must have a cock like a Toblerone!'

The policewoman raised an eyebrow. She asked if I had any abrasions on my penis. I told her no, but she asked if I'd object to being examined by a police doctor. I resisted the temptation to tell her, 'You can have a look now if you like.'

The questions went backwards and forwards. Root then told me something that was not on the allegation sheet.

'She said you had ginger pubes and freckles that stop halfway up your thighs.'

'Well, that's the first bit of truth I've heard all day.'

His eyes lit up, but I put him straight on that count.

'Come on, what colour pubes do ginger people have? As for freckles, you're not born with 'em. They're caused by the sun when you're young. Short trousers leave freckles halfway up your thighs.'

'Right,' he said. 'We want to search the following premises.'

My house; my office in Stockbridge; my accountant's office in Bond Street, where my production company is registered. What were they looking for? A twenty-five-year-old used condom down the sofa?

I asked to call my wife and sort some keys. I phoned Mitch. I tried to be as matter-of-fact and calm as possible. She was okay, she was coping, and she sorted the neighbours out with the keys.

I informed DC Danny that the Bond Street thing was silly, but they were welcome. Henri asked again if we could wait in the interrogation room while all this was happening. They said it was okay.

Two hours of small talk later they came back in, looking very happy with themselves.

'All done?' I asked.

The policewoman spoke first.

'Well, there was a small problem with the gun.'

'Ah... thought there might be.'

I have a loo downstairs that contains memorabilia from my times with the forces. In the corner is a Thompson sub-machine gun.

She smiled. 'Oh, don't worry. We've checked it out, it's been deactivated.'

'I know, I have a made-safe certificate somewhere. You've probably got it now.'

We went through the tape and intro thing again.

'Well, my colleagues have spoken to The Stoker.' Root waited for a response.

'Oh?'

'Yes. It was a threesome.'

'Was it? Is that what he said?'

'Well that's what the allegation looks like, doesn't it?' He was fishing. 'Why do you think The Stoker can remember a threesome and you can't?'

'To be honest, he's the support act. The top of the bill gets the threesomes.'

I wasn't joking. Over the years I've never seen a famous or rich bloke with an ugly woman. They like top-of-the-bills, who also get more threesomes. A support act getting one would be something to remember, I'd imagine.

The Stoker could have told them anything. I couldn't remember any of these allegations but that wasn't to say he couldn't. I'd no idea what he'd said to them. He could have said it was consensual. He might have said nothing at all. Wag didn't know where or when, so how were we to know?

It was all nonsense, but I had to assume The Stoker had told them something. He had three choices: I don't remember; it was consensual sex; I did rape her. Let's say the third one is a no-no, so one and two are up for grabs and it's his word against hers. I wondered what he'd said to them. I had to guess that it was consensual. I'd go with that.

I'd no recollection whatsoever, but had to assume The Stoker knew this girl and the sex *was* consensual. Why mention me though? If indeed he had. My mind was working overtime. Whatever I said I had to stick to the facts, but what did I know? Nothing! The woman's statement was silly – that was the only fact I knew.

Why would you risk putting your cock in the mouth of a woman who's struggling to resist it? All those teeth are a definite deterrent. God gave us two eyes, two ears, two arms and legs, two testicles, but ONE COCK!

The interview got wound up. I felt as if I'd done my best to answer their questions. These detectives were good, but why hadn't they checked the allegations out? It was puzzling and a little bit troubling. I asked Henri why they hadn't done their homework. He smiled and said nothing. That 'nothing' said a million words!

Chapter Eight

2 JANUARY 2013

I was released at 9.30pm. The bail was set after Henri said the first condition of my staying at home was impossible. I now had to let DC Root know where I was staying every night. The nice police detectives dropped Henri and I at Heathrow. We promised to stay in touch!

Henri had found out that the news was 'on the wire' and put out a statement to counter the obvious headlines. He made it clear the women were in their twenties and the allegations dated back to 1988. Twenty-five years ago! We wanted to let everyone know this was not anything to do with underage sex. People reading it would think, *'Why now?'*

As I retrieved my bags, Henri checked with his office to ascertain how the press got my name so quickly. I could almost hear the cogs going round in his head as he tried to get a full picture of events. I looked for a flight. There were none. A train? One left at eleven o'clock from London.

The police had taken my phone so I called Michelle from a call box, struggling with how the bloody thing worked. I was relieved to hear her. She'd called Flo, my old minder, and arranged for him to come and get me. Mitch said she'd hang up and tell Flo to leave Hereford. I was to find somewhere to wait and then call her so she could tell him the location of the RV.

I bade dear Henri farewell and sought out a cash machine. I felt alone again. A cab took me a mile to the Hilton and charged me thirty quid for the privilege. I called Michelle and gave her the number of the hotel.

I then went for the best pint of lager I've ever had. I hadn't eaten since the British Airways breakfast and the lager took away some pain. I felt truly alone and numb.

Two hours later, my old pals Flo and Steve turned up. I piled in the back of their car and we set off for Glasgow, 430 miles away. Flo has been with me on and off for fifteen years. He is as steady as a rock, hard as nails, trains personal bodyguards and keeps pigeons. I've known Steve since he was a young trooper in the SAS, and he's another hard bugger. He ended up in the training wing at Hereford and broke many a soldier's heart taking them through selection. Now he was taking me to Scotland.

We drove into the night, making small talk and saying what bollocks it all was. They felt angry; so did I, but I was too exhausted to moan. I was too tired to sleep too, so we nattered our way up the motorway like three girls.

Six and a half hours later we arrived at the hired house in Glasgow. It was now 6.30 in the morning. Michelle was waiting for me. I fell into her arms, feeling completely fucked up. Preparing for *Big Brother* and an arrest on the same day was a strange combination. I fell into bed. When I awoke four hours later, Flo and Steve were gone. I love those blokes; they never let me down.

> 'We are the Pilgrims, master; we shall go
> Always a little further; it may be
> Beyond that last blue mountain barred with snow
> Or across that angry or that glimmering sea.'
> –'The Golden Journey to Samarkand', James Elroy
> Flecker (as inscribed on the clock tower
> of the SAS barracks at Hereford)

* * *

The day seemed unreal. I felt strange, as if I'd been dreaming. I was all over the front pages and, of course, the headlines said, 'Savile Cops Nick Jim Davidson'. The only front page I was spared was the *Express*. Thanks, Richard.

I sat in the kitchen while Michelle cooked breakfast, and watched our house in Stockbridge being searched by the Yewtree cops on the news. It was bizarre! I thought of our lovely neighbours, who must have been well pissed off with all the paparazzi camped outside the house. But there was nothing I could do.

I would wait till later and call Laurie. He was still on vacation in Mexico and there was a six-hour time difference. I didn't know what to do till then. I wanted to run away, but from what?

How had it all come to this? I felt so sorry for myself. I

took a good long look in the bathroom mirror and told myself to get a grip.

Don't let these bastards get you down.

I was helpless, not in control of events, and the frustration was getting to me. Then my hangover from New Year's Eve started kicking in! It was all too much for me, but I needed to be positive and fight off the black dog that was coming my way.

What must poor Michelle be thinking?

I bet she cursed the day she first met me. But she made me a cuppa, gave me a kiss and told me she loved me.

The police had taken my Blackberry for 'interrogation'. God knows what they'd taken from our house and office. What had they carried out in those familiar plastic bags? They made it look so sinister, but it made for better TV.

Michelle showed me the texts and emails of support. There were messages from friends we'd not heard from for years. I imagined all the goodwill the police were picking up on the Blackberry. I checked my emails and there were scores of them, all stating their dismay and revulsion at what had happened.

Michelle had bought all the newspapers; for some reason she had to read them, while knowing it would upset her. The worst thing, of course, was the link to Savile. All except for Richard's papers had gone for spectacular Operation Yewtree stuff; only later in the story did they print Henri's statement that these were adult women in their twenties.

Brian and Lisa Shaw had delayed their trip back to England. When I told them the story they were horrified.

'The problem now, Brian – and this becomes *your*

problem, I'm afraid – is to reassure the theatres that the tour will still go ahead.'

Brian agreed that one or two might go wobbly. We all agreed on the unfairness of it all; I'd been accused, not charged. We talked about making a statement to say the show would go on. I'd talk to Laurie when the time difference allowed.

We kissed our friends goodbye and sat with a cup of tea, mourning our dog and our bad luck.

'What are we going to do?' Michelle asked.

'We're going to deal with this one step at a time.'

'You sound like Stevie Lamprell.' She smiled.

It was going to be tough. We'd just lost the *Big Brother* money and there was a chance that the spring tour could go tits up.

I called Stevie, who was in shock. He was furious that the police would do this just before *Big Brother* started.

'We should sue the bastards!'

He said he'd help in any way he could. He's a star, always there for me both spiritually and financially. When my play, *Stand Up and Be Counted*, started hemorrhaging money, he was there. When the Dubai comedy festival I produced went tits up, he was there. (I take it back – Steve, you're a fucking jinx!)

But seriously... I hoped to God I wouldn't need his help with this; that common sense and justice would prevail. Just having him there as a mate was help in itself.

Michelle and I spoke to Innes, the estate agent, asking to keep the accommodation on for a few more weeks. He was very understanding, one of many people who were going out of their way to help.

Laurie called as soon as he woke up. He was in a state of shock. We talked about the future.

'Right now, we should do nothing,' he said. I agreed.

'Brian will sort the tour out. I'm sorry about all this.'

'What for? You are the victim here, don't worry about that. I don't think from what I'm hearing that the public are going to like this, it's becoming a witch-hunt. Just have a rest. I'll be back in a few days.'

'Okay mate, thanks.'

We chatted and tried to find some humour in it. There was an old saying we used, attributed to Peters & Lee: 'It could be worse, it could be foggy.' You grab hold of anything at a time like this, don't you?

Laurie and I had been through some tough scrapes together. This was just another one, hopefully. Thank God I have him as my mate as well as my manager.

Michelle and I sat on the sofa together. I could see she was worried to death. I was too, but I had to show that things were okay. They may have been pretty fucking far from okay, but the train had started rolling and there was nothing we could do; we just had to wait for our stop.

We decided to carry on with life. I wouldn't hide away like some of the others who'd been dragged in. I'd rest for a couple of days and then life would continue as before. But how would people take to that? As I later found out, they would give me hope, support and make my heart soar.

By the early evening the phone was red hot. I must have had the same conversation fifty times. My saving grace was being able to say, 'I can't go into it too much.' My brother, my kids, all my friends, Michelle's friends, her mum and dad, all had called, concerned and outraged. It was good to talk and get the frustration out of my system. The funny thing is that the more I told the story, the more ridiculous the allegations seemed.

Michelle was treating me as if I was terminally ill. I'd had so many cups of tea my tongue had gone furry! She was wonderful, pushing her worries and anxiety to one side in an attempt to get the shock out of my eyes and look after me. Mitch is normally a negative person, but she became very positive during this period. Right then, I needed looking after. It was weird; one minute I was angry and the next frightened to death. It was probably all that tea!

I can understand Freddie Starr gobbing off to the papers about his innocence, as did Dave Lee Travis; it's the sheer frustration that makes you want to tell people. I heard that a certain unnamed star had become suicidal. If he felt like me, I can see why. It's the shock coupled with the anger that comes with the unfairness of the arrest, a sickly feeling that makes one feel helpless.

I paced the room searching for answers. None came because I had no recollection of the offences. All that went through my head were negatives about work, the scandal and the shame of being branded a sexual offender.

I switched my laptop on and checked the emails – forty, all positive and supportive – which momentarily lifted me out of the gloom. Twitter was buzzing with good wishes. I have my doubts about Twitter: anyone can be whoever he or she wishes; there are three Jim Davidsons (imagine someone wanting to be me!) so I wish they'd arrested one of the other buggers. But Twitter was full of support and Henri's statement was spot on. People knew I wasn't connected to underage sex, no matter how the press tried to make it look like it with their headlines.

I emailed Richard Desmond and said something like: *'Their timing is impeccable; sorry mate nothing I could do. Good luck with the series.'* I called the *BB* production team and wished them luck. They were sad I wasn't on the show and were shouting, 'We love you!' down the phone. It was really a shame.

Richard emailed me back: *'Call me, I have an idea.'* I was reluctant, as I knew what he wanted. I emailed instead: *'Can't call you, you'll talk me into something I can't do.'* He emailed back: *'Come into the house. You'll look as if you are running away if you don't. You will be on the front page of every paper and can get your point across.'*

What *was* my point? I called Henri. He basically told me there was no problem in doing the show with regards my bail conditions, but reminded me, quite rightly, that he was the lawyer and Laurie the manager, so Laurie had to make the decision. I started to come alive.

'Mitch, they want me to do the show. I *should* do it.'

'Oh Jim, do you think you're up for it?'

'Hmmmmm... I'll wait till Laurie calls and see what he thinks.'

Laurie called at five o'clock. He was appalled. He thought the timing of the police was deliberate.

'They wanted as much coverage as possible.'

'Why couldn't they wait till I'd done the show?' I agreed. 'Listen, Richard still wants me to go in.'

'What?!'

I heard a gagging sound.

'He wants me in the house.'

'Good God!'

'What do you think?'

There was a silence.

'Jim... I think it's best right now to do nothing.'

'Why?'

'Because he wants you to go in the house for *him*, not for you.'

'Might be more money in it.'

'I'm sure there would be, but one wrong move, one wrong word or an argument and you're fucked. I think you'll find the public is fed up with this witch-hunt. My phone has been on fire! There is a lot of goodwill for you out there, but why risk spoiling that for a TV show?'

'Hmmmm... the money perhaps? I might need it.'

'I really think I should talk to Endemol.'

'Talk to Richard, he's a pal after all.'

'I will, but let me speak to Henri and I'll get back to you. Do *not* speak to Richard.'

'Okay.'

I waited and waited. Laurie finally called back.

'Jim, right now there is a row going on between Endemol and Richard Desmond. Let them get the opening show underway and I'll call him tomorrow.'

'Okay.'

No sooner had he hung up than I got a call from Ros at *CBB*, asking about the terms of my bail. I told her there would be no problem.

'Could the police call you in for an interview at any time?'

81

'I guess so.'

She said Richard was going ballistic.

'Good luck, I'll hide.'

I hung up and emailed Richard. I couldn't just ignore him, he's a mate: '*Richard – you'll have to speak to Laurie about this. He's in Mexico with Nigel Lythgoe* [director of *American Idol* and a client]. *Talk to him. I have to go with what he and Henri say, good luck for tonight.*'

I then put Michelle on guard duty. She'd answer all the calls in between making more tea. Laurie called back. He'd had a talk with Endemol. It was decided we'd all chat after the opening show.

This little bit of excitement was just what I needed. Mitch sat and watched in bewilderment. One moment I was depressed, the next I was buzzing and packing to go again. She's right – she always says I'm mental.

We had dinner and settled down to watch *Celebrity Big Brother*. It was a weird feeling. As soon as it started I was glad I'd been arrested.

Well, not quite, but the programme does have that scary audience with banners, all chanting and talking over Brian Dowling – who is just crap at reading the autocue.

My obvious replacement seemed to be ex-footballer and old mate Razor Ruddock. The papers hadn't hinted at him coming on at all. I was pleased.

God, he's put on weight!

We're old pals. He's a great laugh. I hoped he won, earned a few bob and sent me a crate of booze as consolation for being banged up. (He didn't, in the event.)

Rylan Clark did indeed look a splendid specimen, as my

daughters had said. He's got a presence about him that says, 'Look at me and no one else.' Everyone was thinking that, because I'd argued with Brian Dowling in *Hell's Kitchen*, I was obviously going to argue with Rylan – they fell into that homophobic perception shit. But this guy was actually on television because of his talent. He and Frankie Dettorri were in the diary room, picking who'd go into a shitty basement room and who'd stay in the luxurious house.

'I bet that was what Richard wanted me to do, pal up with Rylan.'

Still, Frankie was doing a great job.

I looked at Twitter: there were still a load of tweets about me not going in and some saying I'd be a surprise guest which, if Richard Desmond got his way, I would be.

The next morning brought another email from Richard: '*Mick Jagger makes his own decisions not his lawyer and manager. Use your head,*' it ended. I didn't know what to do so, unusually for me, I did nothing.

Ros called later and explained that Richard and her bosses at Endemol were talking. Richard may own Channel 5 but Endemol make *Big Brother*. I wished her luck. She asked again about the row with Brian Dowling, for some reason; I went over the story of how I was edited to make me look homophobic when I'm not.

All day I phoned friends and old roadies to try and work out what happened in 1988. No one could remember much. All the years roll into one: summer season, tour, panto, spring tour, TV shows, summer season... and so on. It's impossible.

Laurie called at five. He'd spoken to all concerned and I wasn't doing it. Richard had calmed down. It was thought that, because we couldn't trust the police not to miss the opportunity of a lifetime, it would be best to bin it. So that was it then. No extension to our house. I now had a month off work and it was too cold for golf.

Stevie called: 'Right, come on, fly out to Dubai and then we'll go to Borneo and stay on the boat. Katherine Jenkins is coming.'

I told him I couldn't.

'I've got to try and get rid of these allegations.'

It'd take a lot of hard work and research. It'd also look as if I was in hiding if I left the country. He understood.

'Let me know if you need anything... anything at all.'

'Thanks, mate.'

My friend and Stevie's brother-in-law, Gordon, called me. He wanted to sue the world. Keith Emerson called, appalled: 'Fuck knows what will happen if they go after rock stars!' I got messages from generals, politicians, lords and ladies. A friend who worked for SOCA, the UK police's version of the FBI, called. He went on about the Met police and called them the worst 'bunch of tossers on earth... don't lie down and let them walk over you.'

I've never known such support; it made you re-evaluate the way you treated your friends. Life would have to be different now.

I still couldn't believe what had happened. I'd pace the room; I'd watch TV with unseeing eyes and turn the pages of a book without looking at any words. I'd go to bed early and be awake at five in the morning, checking the online papers and trying my best to locate 1988 and 1989 in my mind, all because of two girls talking about twenty-five years ago.

What else would come? What was to stop *anyone* making an accusation? What had they got to lose? How many of the Jimmy Savile accusers were real? Don't let us forget he's not guilty of any of these accusations because he's not been charged or had a trial. The report on Savile says that he abused 350 victims: where's the proof? This is surely against everything the British stand for: fair play, a fair trial and the chance to answer allegations. He can't, he's dead. If there was a few quid in it, I might say he grabbed my nuts one night – and what's to stop me? Whether I liked Savile or hated him, whether I knew something about him or nothing, he cannot be found guilty. That's the way the law works – like it or lump it.

Is there a report to say accusers 126 and 322 may be liars trying to get a few quid? Anyone nicked for fraud yet?

I called Chris Davis, an old friend and agent who manages many artistes and actors. He was pissed off with the witch-hunt as well. He told me a law firm had called him to ask if he had any female clients of a certain age. The lawyer said that if they'd worked with Savile and could say he touched them up, he could get them fifty grand each – less his commission, of course. Chris told him to fuck off. Lawyers were touting for business like on those awful 'Have you fallen over at work?' adverts.

Meanwhile, Michelle had decided life would go on. We'd stay in Scotland till all the press buggered off and we'd buy a new dog. It was not just for her: Oscar was missing his brother; a new puppy was just what he needed. She scanned the Internet and we found Bertie.

He was a twelve-week-old Lhasa Apso bred in Peterhead, 120 miles north of Glasgow.

Next morning after much to-ing and fro-ing and shall we or shall we not, I set off for the north. Michelle stayed in bed, nursing one of the depressions that turn up without warning. After five hours of talking with people from the north of Scotland, who sounded like they came from another planet, I came back with Bertie.

Michelle fell in love. Oscar hated his guts.

That night I went to Nick's Bar in Hyndland Road and met up with the lads. I was interested to hear what they'd say. All were pretty laidback; it was as if they couldn't even be bothered to give the nonsense headspace. All except my mate Guy, who took the piss: 'You won't get any sympathy here, boy!' I joined in and had my first laugh since I'd read the allegations.

On my return home, Michelle suggested I take myself off to another room and watch a box set. I sat down and watched the first three episodes of *Dexter*. A story about a serial killer wasn't really the type of thing to calm one's nerves – even if he was a 'good' serial killer – but boy, I enjoyed it. I was feeling like a mass murderer anyway and was treated like one, so I could relate to Dexter – he even had the same boat as me. Watch out!

The little dog slept in the bedroom with us. The crying and whimpering got on Michelle's nerves. I said sorry. As for Bertie, he never made a sound.

* * *

Up at six to check the papers. Richard Littlejohn had done a piece about the witch-hunt. He was very supportive in his piss-taking way:

Although Davidson has not been charged, it has already cost him his TV comeback as a contestant on Celebrity Big Brother. *Since his peak years at the BBC his career has gone downhill and the bookings dried up. Until this week the standing joke was that he couldn't get arrested...*

Why was it necessary to nick Davidson as he arrived at Heathrow Airport, as if he was some kind of international terrorism suspect?

Police also raided one of Davidson's homes in Hampshire and emerged carrying boxes of 'evidence'.

Were they seriously expecting to find evidence of a 25-year-old sexual assault tucked away in a sock drawer?

Over the past quarter of a century, five-times married Davidson has lived in more homes than most.

He once joked he wouldn't ever get married again, he'd simply find a woman he hated and buy her a house.

He spends part of his time in Dubai these days. Are the Nonce Squad also planning to fly to the Middle East to give that property a spin?

I got a call from Kevin, my old roadie, who told me he'd had a phone call from Jo Urch. She told him the papers were in touch with her. They would be, wouldn't they? In 1987, I went out with her for a while. She was lovely, and she worked behind a bar at Doodles nightclub in Torquay.

At the time I assumed she was eighteen. I found out later from the papers that she was sixteen but I didn't care: sixteen was fine; she was seventeen two weeks after I met her. What was she doing working in a bar at sixteen anyway?

I ended up in a fight with her ex-boyfriend and his doorman mates, but that evening I had Paul Hill and Jimmy D, two sergeants in B Squadron 22 SAS, with me. Paul's dead now – along with Nish, Al Slater and a few more Hereford hooligans who'd have laughed their heads off at these allegations. The police would have seen their pictures on my wall when they violated our house, searched everything, took away a load of bullshit and put blue and white crime-scene tape right round our driveway.

> 'When you're wounded and left on Afghanistan's plains
> And the women come out to cut up what remains
> Just roll to your rifle and blow out your brains
> And go to your God like a soldier.'
>
> –'The Young British Soldier', Rudyard Kipling

RIP, boys.

I told Kevin that the papers would be sniffing for anything they could get. We'd wait and see what Jo would say. I hoped she'd get a few quid.

Laurie thought the Sunday papers would be positive: 'Jim, you are the straw that broke the camel's back, people are sick of this and can see these Op Yewtree police for what they are. They are supposed to be arresting kiddie fiddlers, not people like you. Just watch, do nothing and you will see the whole country is on your side... the public are not mugs.'

I love Laurie Mansfield.

I woke at five on Sunday morning and slipped into the office to check the papers. I looked at *The Mail* first. Joanne had indeed spilled the beans. The headline made my arse go tight:

'Jim Davidson cheated on his wife with me – I was only 16: The dancer who had a year-long affair with arrested comedian defends "perfect gent" who seduced her.'

In the summer of 1987 in the vibrant seaside resort of Torquay, Joanne Urch was a confident 16-year-old trainee dancer when she first met comedian Jim Davidson.

At 34, Davidson was approaching the height of his fame and performing a seven-week season at the local Princess Theatre, while Joanne, who was working as a barmaid, was enjoying the summer break from her prestigious training school in London...

Davidson later told in his autobiography how he had been accused of having an affair with an underage girl and was forced to defend potentially harmful allegations that turned out to be completely false.

Now, Davidson faces further questions about his personal life and conduct...

'Jim really was the perfect gentleman – at all times,' Joanne insists. 'It wasn't rushed. I never, ever felt he was lecherous, or intimidating or forceful.'

In fact, it seemed as if it was precisely Joanne's youth that attracted Davidson. The comedian's fifth and current wife, Michelle Cotton, is also 17 years his junior.

But well done, Joanne. She stuck to the facts – well, nearly. I can't remember seriously asking her to marry me, as she said I did, not after having been through my third marriage!

She got 20,000 quid for it – because when I went down to see her in the summer, she picked me up from the station in a car and said, 'Thanks for buying this!' It does look as if the reporter was thinking, '*Oh shit! Come on, say something bad!*' because their narrative was '*he obviously likes young girls, his wife is younger than him*'.

It gave me hope. And there was more. Esther Rantzen came to my defence in Scotland's *Sunday Post*:

The latest arrest of comedian Jim Davidson is deeply confusing. Yewtree is about child abuse, isn't it?

After all, it was set up as a direct result of the Savile revelations. The NSPCC is supporting the Yewtree investigations because it is a charity dedicated to protecting children against abuse.

When Yewtree swoops – and celebrity after celebrity has been targeted by them – we assume they've uncovered yet more sexual abuse of children.

But it turns out that Jim Davidson has not been accused of abusing any children... But the danger is that he's now tainted, and will be forever.

And the taint is the false implication that he was somehow involved with the Savile crimes against children.

Laurie was right, there did seem to be a backlash against these arrests. I wondered what people really thought. I'd go back to London the next week and find out. A Charlton home game would be just the ticket.

I called my mate Mark Humphreys. He is a Charlton fan like myself, who has a great building firm, PHB construction, that does stuff at the Valley. (He was also lined up to do my bloody extension!) He's my mate, he makes me laugh, he makes people happy – unless you're a Palace fan! He and Charlton Athletic were just what I needed.

I do a joke about Mark in my act:

Mark found himself in a pub in Woolwich with two Crystal Palace fans. A row broke out and Mark reached up and punched one in the lip! They chased him out the pub, where Mark continued to yell abuse at these rather large Palace fans. They were gaining on him. Luckily, he saw the Woolwich ferry. It was six feet out! Mark realised that he had to jump or be killed. Superhuman strength took over as he leaped onto the ferry like Steve Austin. Relieved and breathless, he continued to taunt the monsters on the quayside.

'I'm Charlton till I die... wankers!'

An old lady tapped him on the shoulder: 'I'd shut up if I were you... we're coming in!'

I boarded the flight at Glasgow and was instantly transported back to 2 January, when I was worried to death about *Big Brother*. This time I was worried about the reception I might get at the Valley.

Mark and his business partner Steve picked me up at the airport. I told them the story. By the time we were on the M25 we were all laughing like loonies.

We were playing Blackpool. It was to be a tough game, but I needn't have worried about the Charlton crowd. I was patted on the back and there was a lot of 'it's all bollocks'. A Labour MP made his way across, put his hand on my shoulder and said, 'Jim, you are being hung out to dry.'

Charlton's owner, Tony Jiminez, came over and wished me

luck. He was disgusted at the events, as was the vice chairman, Richard Murray. All the directors and ex-directors made a point of showing support. They didn't have to do that and it meant a lot. I'd made the right decision in coming; I felt surrounded by love, in a place that I love more than anywhere on earth.

Mark always makes me laugh. He plays at being a bigot rather like I do on stage, but makes me look like the Archbishop of Canterbury by comparison. He's a person who will say the absolute opposite to what is politically correct just to get a reaction. Because he's so over the top, people know he's joking – I think he gets a buzz out of seeing a bad smell come under people's noses.

He kept telling me all would be okay. I hoped he was right and the police would see sense. It was a wonderful day and we beat Blackpool 2–1. I felt great as I flew back to Michelle and our new puppy.

Mitch watched *Big Brother*; I watched Dexter kill two baddies – bliss. I called an old mate, Clive Cooper, who lives in Blackpool and is a stand-up comic. He owns a hotel that he runs like a twenty-four-hour party with rooms. He's a happy chap and a dog expert, and was just what I needed right then. I wondered if he and his wife Jo wanted a couple of days in God's country.

They turned up after getting lost in Glasgow for an hour. They also brought their two dogs. This sent Oscar into grump overdrive but boy, did we have a laugh. It was great to have someone in the house, though we were conscious not to bore them to death with our problems. We probably did though!

Clive was a chef in the army and is a very good cook, so I wanted to do something special for them. I visited my Pakistani friend in the Asian supermarket and bought what looked like two racing chickens, the kind of thing you see hanging up in a butcher's in the James Bond films.

He then told me how to marinate them and we had a good old chat. He'd been in Scotland for five years and I was the only person he could completely understand during that time. We laughed our heads off.

The chickens were cooked tandoori style, served with salad and Bombay potatoes. Perfect. The dogs played and we had fun, even going to the pub with Michelle!

Clive and Jo left us in good spirits the next day. It was time to return to Hampshire. We made a decision to go home on Sunday.

On the following Saturday, I drove to Blackburn to see Charlton. I was back the same night. The weather was a bit grim. We packed our stuff and got an early night. We were to set of at 10.30 in an attempt to beat the snow.

I woke at my usual six. After checking the papers I looked at the weather forecast. I woke Michelle and told her we had to leave as soon as possible, as the Midlands would get snow at twelve. We rushed around like mad people, packed the car to bursting point, bundled in the two dogs and set off for the 450-mile trip home. Michelle was humpy and I was anxious. We were going back to face the music we couldn't dance to.

We arrived without incident, having just caught the snow as we hit Oxford. As we stood at the door of our cottage, we shared a look. We were going back into our beloved cottage that had been violated. What had the police been looking for? Or was it all part of the humiliation they seemed to revel in?

We entered with some trepidation. The cottage looked okay. We were home.

Bertie ran in and pissed on the carpet.

Chapter Nine

**' We are all honourable men here, we do not have to give
each other assurances as if we were lawyers.'**
- The Godfather, **Mario Puzo**

Meeting your QC is a moment when you realise that life
has become serious. This was not going away. I still
hoped it would, but the way my luck had been...

Anyway, if you want peace, prepare for war, as they say.
Laurie and I met at the Carlton Club in St. James's. I was
wondering what reception I'd get from this headquarters of
conservatism. I shouldn't have worried; people were queuing
up to shake my hand. They were all saying the same thing,
'Ridiculous.' It was things like this that kept me going. I got
a text from my friend Ridgie: '*The whole world is on your
side.*' It did seem to be the case.

Laurie and I sat and had lunch. We talked about what I
should or shouldn't do when I went on stage the next
month. We decided I wouldn't mention the case. I'd also
drop some of the more expressive sex routines, as the press
would be looking for another headline. I'd not mention

Savile either, unlike some of last year's gigs that played on the *Jim'll Fix It* theme.

Laurie was as concerned as I was that the complainants hadn't stated dates, or even venues, so it was impossible to pinpoint where I was at the time. We'd have to ask the QC if the police had disclosed everything to us. My QC was Trevor Burke. He's in the judicial premiership and reckoned to be the new George Carmen. Henri can really pick 'em – for a West Ham fan he has great judgement.

We arrived at Trevor's chambers and were shown to a meeting room. We were early; I was anxious. There were too many law books for my liking. It was becoming scary. But I liked Trevor immediately, like a fledgling bird that sees its mother with a beak full of worms.

He was in his late forties, I'd guess, and had a kind face. He wasn't dressed like a QC; in fact it was me who had on the chalk-stripe suit.

The first thing on the agenda was an anonymous email sent to Henri by some woman.

Oh shit, what now?

She wrote that she and her friend had met me and a pal in a bar. The lady in question was serving drinks. She told me what time she finished and I apparently said, 'I'll come back for you.' Much to her surprise, I did.

Apparently, we ended up at my hotel, where this girl decided she wouldn't sleep with me. She came to my room for a kiss and cuddle, but then said she couldn't do it because of the guilt she felt about her boyfriend in Australia.

I said, 'Okay, no probs,' and sat and talked to her. She says she stayed in the room and that I was a gentleman, calling her a cab in the morning.

How nice of her to come forward. Try as I might, I couldn't remember the girl. But whoever you are... thanks.

The QC said the unusual thing about this case was that normally, with high-profile accusations of a sexual nature, other complainants come forward. In this case the opposite was happening.

'People are coming forward in your defence.'

A glimmer of hope.

He undid a file and held up the accusations.

'This is really thin. It is flimsy to say the least.'

Thank God.

'However...'

Uh-oh!

'We must look at the way the police are behaving: the dawn raids, the TV cameras, the house searches...'

He opened the file.

'They are acting, it would seem, on any accusation made against celebrities. They are saying: "We messed up with Savile... is this what you want?" They couldn't stand, nor does the government want, another costly inquiry with women saying, "I went to the police and they didn't do anything."

'The fact that claimant number one has been to the police twice already would seem to show that the Op Yewtree police will take on anything, no matter how unwinnable it is. We must assume that it is likely they will press charges...'

Oh no...

'... and say, "We've done our bit, let a jury decide." But don't worry... they have no proof.'

Don't fucking worry?

'If this gets to court, we will tear it to pieces.'

'Yes,' I said in an effort to prise out some more good news.

'We must, though, try and get them to drop it now,' I said in desperation. 'If they press charges it'll seriously affect my work.'

Henri and the QC shared a look. Laurie exploded with some common sense.

'How can the police believe these people whose evidence is so obviously flawed? They can't even say where this was, or what date. "Around about 1989"? How can you defend that? Is that why they say it after all these years? Because it's unprovable?'

'Exactly... I agree with what you say.'

Henri could sense our frustration and wanted to keep the meeting emotion-free. He continued.

'We are dealing with a woman that for reasons best known to herself decided to go to the police – and don't forget we've only the story in the newspapers for that – *four years* after the event, if one is to believe the story in the *Mirror*. The police at the time said there was no evidence. There isn't any now! There are so many holes in her story that it would last two minutes in court. However, The Stoker might – and I say again, might – have given her story, and I use the term lightly, some weight.'

'I can't remember any of it. I don't know how The Stoker could either. I'm sure he was giving his account as well as he could. But why would he drop me in it – if indeed he has?

Then again, if he said it was consensual, why *not* mention me? What harm would it do? None.

'But I can't bloody remember,' I went on. 'It really is so frustrating. He might only be giving his version, without fear; to him it's the truth, even if his recollection is flawed. Or he might not remember it at all. It was twenty-five years ago.

'Don't forget though, Henri, this girl is saying it was in 1988. I didn't meet The Stoker till halfway through 1989. I called Richard Digance as I was sure he introduced us.'

Richard Digance used to be my support act, and still is occasionally, going on to have his own TV show. He's a funny folk singer – sort of like Mike Harding with laughs – who does parodies of songs.

I was on a roll now. 'Richard confirmed that it was at a charity cricket match that he'd arranged in Lyme Regis.'

'Can he confirm the date and does he have any proof?' asked Trevor.

'Yes, he has a souvenir brochure of the event: 25 June 1989.'

'Great,' Laurie said, his frustration slackening a little. 'Surely that shows her ability to remember events is somewhat flaky?'

'And before anyone says the passage of time is a two-way thing,' I said, 'according to her, she reported it to the police four years after the event. We only heard about it twenty-five years later.'

'*Alleged* event,' said a smiling Henri.

All that was going through my mind as we spoke was the fact that Yewtree would bring charges.

If I'm charged the damage will be done. The theatres will

cancel. The newspapers will start their merry dance. It will be a nightmare.

How long between being charged and going to court? Nine months! How will we live?

Is this what my life has come to? All the glory and the misery; all the times I'd been shot at in Bosnia; the trips to the Falklands, Afghanistan, Iraq; everything I'd done would count for nought. The money I'd raised – hundreds of thousands for dead policemen's families, firemen, soldiers – would be as nothing because of some women with axes to grind and a move by the Yewtree coppers' political masters.

I pushed the negative thoughts to one side and started on the facts.

'She doesn't say where this took place. She has the date wrong, and she can't remember the gig or the restaurant. She has the wrong car.'

Where had she been all day? Why stay the night with The Stoker and then go to the bar to meet me? Where did she get my telephone number? Did he take her home? Does she still have the signed autograph?

Trevor pitched in with more common sense: 'So apparently you signed a bit of paper saying, *"To Stephen, your mum's a great fuck."* Why would you do that if this woman was assaulted? It sounds to me that you were on friendly terms with her.'

'Yes, I agree. I sometimes write, *"Thanks for the blowjob,"* or something silly like that after assessing if the person will laugh and not be offended. You'd only do it to someone you felt comfortable with. It's like your audience: you act differently at a Royal Variety Show than at the

Circus Tavern. It's the difference between speaking to a music teacher and talking to a hooker: you adapt. Does that make sense?'

'Yes, complete sense.'

I like my QC!

'So let's work this out.' Trevor was piecing together the allegation. 'She goes to the hotel room with The Stoker all afternoon – and is raped. She then goes to see your show with him. You all go and have a nice Indian meal and drinks.

'The Stoker then rapes her again in the evening; he stops raping her and calls you. He then continues raping her and you join them. She bites your penis. And then what? Presumably you go to hospital, while The Stoker rapes her again. She stays the night, wakes up with The Stoker and sets off to find you at the bar, where you chat away. You sign an autograph saying she's a great fuck before she disappears. Then she calls you sometime later and complains.'

I like him a lot.

The more he said, the more ridiculous it all seemed. The fact that the police couldn't see this was criminal. Or maybe they could see it? A child could see that these allegations were silly.

The second allegation, by Wag, was discussed. Trevor tore it to pieces. I felt like there was a light at the end of the tunnel. Suddenly, going to trial seemed an attractive option. I'd have loved to see Trevor in full flow.

The meeting ended with all of us agreeing that criminal charges were the problem. We'd do our best to make sure they didn't happen.

Laurie and I left chambers two feet taller than when we

entered them. Laurie laughed when I blurted out the famous line from *The Producers*: 'That's our Hitler!'

Henri had chosen a winner.

Chapter Ten

It was time to do some hard work. We had to find evidence that could make the accusations seem unwinnable. There was a chance these women were bonkers but because of the bail terms it'd be difficult to find out. The police would take a bad view if I unleashed the dogs of war – my big, hairy-arsed spy friends from the 'dark side'.

I tried to piece together my life from 1987 onwards. I called my ex-wife Tracy – which was difficult as she never answers the phone and never, ever calls back! I've been in her house when the phone rings and she'll only answer if she fancies it.

Eventually, she spoke to me. She was very annoyed at the women's allegations and asked how she could help.

'When and where did we meet?'

She confirmed what I already knew. 'It was September 1987 at the Southampton Boat Show. At the Guinness stand, to be precise.'

'Was I with Dave Franks and Kevin Laming?'

'Yes, you were... I think.'

I knew I'd gone to Germany in October, because I couldn't sleep there for the thought of Tracy. When I got back she met me at the airport.

'I gave you a lift to your flat in Kensington.'

'Did you stay the night?'

'Can't remember.'

'Who was working for me then?'

'Rick Price.'

'Okay... I remember doing the Lakeside on my birthday?'

'Yes, and I called you at your flat the next day and told you I'd left my boyfriend.'

'Yes, and that cost me six million quid.'

'Eh?'

'Nothing. I got the train to Brum to meet you... why didn't I drive?'

'Don't know... didn't you say you lent your car to Paul Hill?'

'God knows, I know he drove it through a fence. I might have been banned from driving at that time.' I made a note on a bit of paper.

'We went to Paris for Christmas, I think.'

'Christ, we did!' It's amazing how much you forget. I also remembered playing a gig or two in Cardiff called *Jim's Blue Christmas*, but no one else could recall.

'Did you come to Cardiff with me?'

'Don't think so. This is murder, isn't it?'

'The way I've been treated you'd think so, yes.'

I told her the allegations. I thought that, as I was with her round about the same time, she'd say something horrid to me. She didn't.

'These cows ought to be locked up.'

She can surprise me at times. A while ago there'd been some stories about wife number three and I, on account of which I'd been called – and still am – a wife beater. Tracy had wanted the other wives to get together and disprove it but the papers didn't want to know. Enough said, eh?

I thanked Tracy and put a call in to Kev, 'The Badge', my old driver. All the people reading this who know him will be laughing now, as Kevin has a job remembering as far back as yesterday. His view on things was as follows:

'No! That's bollocks, Jim, that wasn't your game. We had birds falling all over us. Why would you want to assault one, for fuck's sake?'

'Well,' I said, 'I agree, but we've got to get something in writing to Henri.'

'Jim, I'm shit at typing, I'll have to dictate it to some fucker.'

Kev is one of life's characters. As you can see, his use of the English language is only marginally better than mine. He was my driver, but he was banned once for a year and I drove him!

I called Dave Franks, who does the cars. He was convinced we never had Bentleys till 1993; he'd check it out and put it in writing.

I tried to piece together 1988: I toured clubs for a bit in the spring, with Rick Price driving and Colin Reece and Smudge playing guitars. I may also have done a TV show but I'm not sure. Summer was definitely in Torquay, with

Hillary O'Neil as guest star. In August, Paul Hill and I picked up the new boat from Plymouth – a Princess 55 that I named *Afghan Plains* after the Rudyard Kipling poem.

Paul Hill went off on a secret op in September and never returned. We buried him at St Martin's in Hereford. I asked his sergeant major, *Gonzo*, what happened. 'Don't fucking ask,' he said, so I didn't.

Tracy was pregnant. I remember that much! I did Christmas panto at the Dominion, I think. I needed to make some more calls.

I called Richard Digance. He agreed to make a statement regarding meeting The Stoker. I'd try and find John Avery, general manager of the Palladium, who could disprove the stage-door fan thing. The idea was to find specifics, not just 'he wouldn't have done that' stuff. We already knew complainant one had the date at least six months out. We knew I didn't have a Bentley. We knew she couldn't remember the hotel or the gig. The rest of her story had great holes in it, so really there was no need to disprove it. It did that on its own.

As for complainant two, we knew she couldn't get in the stage door of the Palladium.

We knew she didn't have a date. We knew she'd been coached: her statement said, 'in or around 1989,' which, according to my son Charlie, is legal speak.

We also knew that both complainants said they bit my cock. I made a note to call Dr Fred Lim, clap doctor to the stars, and my GP during that period, Christine. Fred is a nice bloke and knows my dick better than Patrick Moore knew the solar system, so he'd know if I'd been to see him with my knob hanging off!

Chapter Eleven

I've just seen Stuart Hall on Sky News. He is eighty-three and has been charged with the rape of a girl in her twenties, forty years ago. How will they have a chance of convicting him? Does the alleged victim have cinefilm?

Talking to the press, Hall said, 'Like a lot of people I wonder why these allegations have taken forty years to come forward?'

We all wonder why – Hall's own guilt or innocence aside. I don't think there's a real answer to why these girls wait so long to report this stuff. Is it because their friends talk them into it, like a private gathering of *Loose Women* all looking to fight back?

My own two allegations probably started long ago as kiss-and-tell stories the newspapers turned down because of lack of proof. To get paid by the *News of the World* in those days you didn't need the nasty bit; it was a good enough little earner to say, 'Jim Davidson shagged me behind his wife's back.' Now, with me in semi-retirement and not newsworthy, so to speak, the story had to have an edge. What better than a bit of forced sex to jump on the Operation Yewtree bandwagon?

* * *

I had a funny moment the other day. I'd noticed a lump in my abdomen. It'd been there a while but was more noticeable when sitting up from a prone position. I told myself it was because there was nowhere else for the fat to go. Then, me being me, I told myself it was because my liver had swollen up and was pushing my stomach out; then I persuaded myself it was cancer.

I did some physical exercise and noticed that sit-ups made me look like the Alien was about to burst out. I emailed the doctor, telling him of the grisly symptoms, waiting all day for his reply.

'Come and see me Friday.'

Shit, I knew it!

Friday took a hundred years to arrive. Suddenly, it wasn't important that I'd been arrested. Charlton losing their last two games after being one-nil up seemed insignificant. Was I about to die? I could see the headline: 'Op Yewtree Cops Kill Jim Davidson'.

I have a terrible fear of going to the doctor's; it's the nightmare of being told you're ill. I don't mind going for sore throats and things like that, but I hate the yearly inspection.

When I lived in Dubai, I lost some blood when I was doing a whoopee do-do. I immediately thought my time was up; I had cancer. I called my doctor, Graham, who was also a mate and drinking partner – in fact, we'd been drinking until the small hours the night before. He told me to come in straight away.

Shit, this must be serious...

I arrived prepared for bad news. Firstly, he got something that looked like the glass tube you baste potatoes with and stuck it up my bum. He then pumped some air in and started to look up my bottom. Then the phone rang. He left me bent over with something up my arse that looked like a kaleidoscope and felt like a roll of lino, and left the room. It was then that I saw the Pakistani window cleaner looking in at me...

I hate being ill. The week crawled by at a snail's pace. I was worried to death.

I called my comedian pals Bobby Davro and Kev Orkian and told them to come to dinner. We wouldn't get pissed, as I didn't want a hangover while worrying about planning my funeral.

Bobby can be a bit down on himself sometimes, getting frustrated that his – and my own – talents are not used on TV more. So I listened, drank my whisky and filled in my own Schadenfreude Society application form. At three o'clock in the morning, I fell into bed legless. It'd been a great and funny night, just what I wanted – but oh, my poor head.

Two days later, I set off for London to get confirmation of my imminent death. I arrived early, walking around for an hour or two listening to the buzz of life, wondering whether I'd have six months left and if it'd be enough time to see off the accusations.

I ventured into the waiting room and bumped into Peter, my doctor.

'Come on Jim, let's get you sorted.'

Help!

Peter was concerned about the allegations and asked how I was coping. He also enquired whether I could sue for loss of earnings. When I told him the specific details he laughed.

'Come on then, up on the couch. Take your top off.'

I jumped on the couch, trying to look healthy.

'Right, bend your legs up... ahh, that's a small one.'

'What, a small cancer?'

'No, silly, that is a ventral hernia. Nothing to worry about. I've got one, want to see it?'

'No, I don't! What is it?'

Peter explained. 'You can have it operated on or just live with it. Up to you.'

He then did the dreaded feel-about. A frown appeared on his face when he got to the liver.

'I can actually feel white wine.'

I got dressed and received a lecture about fatty liver. I was told to cut down on booze and fatty foods.

'Okay, anything, doc. Now that I'm going to live, anything.'

I left the surgery a happy man and called Michelle. I told her I was going to live; she told me I'd left the milk out!

Chapter Twelve

FEBRUARY 2013

The time had come to go back on stage. What reaction would I get? I'd last performed in December at Glasgow. I get really 'ring rusty' after two weeks off; now it was two months and I had all the shit to deal with as well. I knew I couldn't talk about the allegations but I also knew that the fans would want to hear the gossip.

As the day got closer the more nervous I became. I'd stopped drinking since the doctor's bollocking. I figured a clear head would be the answer. It was. I was now convinced I should stay off the booze and prepare an act that didn't grab a headline. I sat staring at a blank sheet of paper for ages. What would I do? In the end I knew I'd have to decide the moment I walked onstage.

The first gig was on 12 February at the Churchill Theatre, Bromley. I hadn't played there before as I don't think the management likes me. However, this was for the

Charlton Athletic Community Trust so they took a chance on me.

The first gig is always a nightmare. But I'd be giving the box office takings to the trust, so if I buggered up I would do it for a good cause.

Brian Shaw's girls prepare a 'tour bible': in it is listed all the gigs, phone numbers and addresses. I punched the postcode for the theatre into the sat nav and set off. I was feeling good and sorted the act out in my head as I struggled around the M25. I wouldn't mention the allegations, but I would talk about the arrest.

I had decided to wear a suit on stage. I normally wear a casual shirt, blue chinos and boots, but this time I'd wear a pinstriped three-piece. The first thing I would say is, 'Does this look alright for court?'

Brian's office had buggered up by putting the front door of the theatre in their bible, which is up a pedestrian walkway. I drove up it to the theatre front door, stopped and called Steve Farr, my tour manager, on the mobile. No answer – nothing new there. I eventually went into the foyer to see Steve looking vague – nothing new there either! This time though something was wrong. He looked odd. I asked him where his phone was. He shrugged.

'Where's the stage door, Steve?'

He climbed in the car and said he'd show me, and then confessed he didn't know where he was. I called the theatre and we set off around Bromley's infamous one-way system. It took forty-five minutes. In that time I became convinced Steve was ill. He kept saying, 'Nah, there is nothing wrong, don't worry!' But he said he'd been having terrible headaches and the doctor had given him some painkillers. I assumed he'd taken too many. We arrived at the stage door and I told him to go and have a lie down.

I ran to the front foyer and spoke to Steve's girlfriend, Sue. She said he'd been acting odd all day and nearly killed them while driving the van. I told her that he needed to see a doctor; she nodded and had a slightly lost look on her face, saying, 'I'm really worried about him – he's acting worse than he normally does!'

The main priority now was for me to check what he'd done about the PA and the lighting. He'd set the stuff up but it was all wrong. The local theatre techies and I sorted it out.

The support act was John Moloney, a great comedian who has a brilliant routine about taking his stressed cat to the vets. I can relate to that, with all the problems I had with my poor Benji.

The interval was fifteen minutes. This is normally the time when panic sets in, but instead I felt calm. I felt this was a chance to put my point across, not about the allegations but the witch-hunt bullshit that was going on. How would they react?

John had gone down really well. The audience was buzzing; I could feel it from the wings. I was also aware I had to watch my words. The press were in and would be looking for titbits. What better for them than to have me being racist, or sexist, or any other kind of *ist*, even if I wasn't? We all know they have the stories in their minds already and to give them anything that fitted would leave them happy as pigs in shit.

My friends Mark and his girlfriend of the time were in, as

in fact were all my Charlton buddies. My comedian pal Matt Blaze came, too. That was good of him; he'd know how jumpy I'd be.

Peter Varney, a director of the trust, was in with his wife. He's a great guy and it was him who gave the show the go-ahead. He knows I'm a smutty sod and a bit controversial, but he understands that my audience loves it and would love to contribute to the trust's coffers. Charity shows don't just have opera singers; sometimes they have adult comics. Having said that, tonight I'd watch myself. Imagining what Peter would say afterwards would be my benchmark. He's one of those great people that you instinctively want to do well for and receive their praise.

All this stuff was going through my mind as I made the offstage announcement. It was what Pete always said if I made a near-the-knuckle joke in the away games boardroom: 'The views expressed tonight bear no resemblance to the views of Charlton Athletic Football Club, and the Charlton Athletic Charity Trust takes no responsibility for the content of this show.' It got a big laugh.

No booze; deep breath; house lights out; step into the limelight. I walked to the centre to huge applause.

'Would this suit look good in court?'

They loved that. I then proceeded to ask if I'd had sex with anyone in the theatre. And so it went.

One hour and twenty minutes later, I was round the front signing my funny cookbook, which takes the piss out of all these posy chefs and 'cooks it like it is'. It was a big hit and they flocked to buy it after the show.

It had been a success.

That's the first one out of the way.

I chatted with my pals. One said I was 'a little softer than usual'. That was good. I'd have to be careful not be seen to belittle the accusations, no matter how daft I thought they were.

Steve was nowhere to be seen after the gig. I urged Sue to get him to a doctor and left for home. He called me the next morning to tell me he felt better and was at his daughter's house in Hemel Hempstead. He also confessed to going the wrong way and ending up by the London Eye. Now he was setting off for the night's gig in Basildon.

At two o'clock, Sue called Brian Shaw in hysterics. Steve was walking about without knowing where or who he was. Brian called me. I sped off to Essex at warp factor ten. I was in such a rush I left the petrol station without paying. (Luckily, it was my local garage and they called.)

The crew at Basildon had called an ambulance. Steve was whisked away. When I arrived, the lads at the theatre had rigged my gear up. They were brilliant.

The mayor came to see me, as did the leader of the council. They were so supportive and, like everybody I was meeting, asked how they could help. The mayor even went to visit Steve in hospital; she is a star.

The show was a cracker, but I drove home with my friend Steve on my mind. I had two more gigs to do in Wales. Having no Steve meant I would be at the mercy of the in-house sound system. It also meant I'd have no DVDs or books on sale – yet more lost revenue. Steve's girlfriend sold the merchandise and didn't get paid – not by me anyway – so to hire a new roadie and new merchandise vendor would not be cost effective. I'd have to do without for the time being.

I settled back at home and awaited news of Steve. John Cannal, my pal, called to say Steve was being moved to Romford, where he was to be operated on.

Shit, this is serious.

I called the hospital the next day and pretended to be Steve's brother. They told me he was doing well. I jumped in the car and sped to deepest Essex. At the hospital I met Steve's daughter and we went in to see him together. He was on the loo, but he looked better despite the surgical scar and staples in his head. He also sounded better, though he was bitterly disappointed to be sick and off the tour. I told him not to worry and that his wages would still be paid. Steve felt reassured and resigned to the fact that he'd need a considerable time to get better. He said something to me that I'll never forget: it was totally incomprehensible, but I'll never forget it!

I said my goodbyes and left for home. There was one more gig, at Weston-super-Mare, and then it was up to Scotland to do some work on the books and have a rest.

My hernia was a bugger though. I had to get it done before it got worse. It didn't hurt but I was aware of it.

My brother Bill and his wife, Billie, would be joining us in Scotland. Bill was out of danger now but still having more tests on his dodgy insides. Us Davidsons were falling apart. We were also meeting up with our cousins, Bill Birrell and Jean Gibbon, in an attempt to forget our troubles and have fun.

Then Michelle noticed Bertie had a funny eye – 'cherry

eye', it's called – and we'd have to take the poor sod for an operation. She was sure we were cursed!

After a good night with the cousins, we woke with sore heads to a phone call from Bill's mate; their home in Dartford had been broken into.

We are *cursed!*

The evening started well though. Bill Birrell and his lady, Elivia, arrived and we opened the first bottle. So much for the not-drinking pledge. Cousin Bill is the son of my auntie Nann, whose real name was Agnes. She was in showbiz as a rather classy singer and actress in her day. Jean Gibbon is the daughter of Uncle Bill – to say that controversy surrounds her father is an understatement. Uncle Bill left home when Jean was two and came to live with my mum and dad. After I was born, Bill buggered off to Thailand and was never seen again. He fought in the last world war and stories of his adventures pose many a puzzle. We're still trying to piece together his history.

We all got on well. Brother Bill was the life and soul of the evening and we dined and drank till the small hours. It's nice to be in contact with our Scottish blood. My dear English wife has been made an honorary Scottish lassie.

The accusations, however, were never far from my mind. In the small hours I lay awake. Something was nagging at me. The first woman – she of the threesome – had said she contacted me by phone sometime later. I'd asked the policeman at my interrogation about this. He'd shrugged and said she must have called an agency. Why didn't he know how she got in touch? Was there something he wasn't telling me? How could she phone me without the number? I must have given it to her – that's the only way she would have got to me, if in fact she did.

This opened another can of worms. Why would I, an alleged attacker, give my victim my number? The fact that I couldn't remember didn't alter the fact that baddies don't give phone numbers to victims. The only reason I'd have given it to her was that I assumed she was up for a repeat performance – *if* there was a first one – or, more likely, to pull her for myself.

Would I have given her my number and said, 'If you fancy being assaulted give me a call,' or, 'Come and bite my cock off again'? Unlikely, don't you think? Maybe she hadn't spoken to the police about the phone number because it'd suggest that we were indeed friendly and nothing untoward took place. I only wished I could remember.

Chapter Thirteen

14 MARCH 2013

Chris Huhne and his wife, Vicky Pryce, have been banged up for eight months; we have a new Pope; an unnamed entertainer in his eighties is so depressed that the police fear that if they name him he'll kill himself; DLT has been rearrested as he returned to a police station to answer his bail.

I have to go on the 20 March. The police say that more people have come forward to implicate DLT. What's to stop them? There is no downside for them. You can't help thinking this is what the police want. But they must surely understand that there are nutters about and that one good allegation, with proper evidence, is the way forward. Twenty flaky ones with no corroborative evidence and no chance of conviction cannot replace this. There is no safety in numbers!

I wonder what else they've trawled up about me. They

must be trying everything: find a woman with a grudge; the bigger the celebrity from the past, the bigger the feather in their oversized caps. It seems there have been no sexual assaults for twenty-five years. Showbiz stars of today must be behaving themselves – of course they are!

Real paedos and pervs must be leaping with joy about this Operation Yewtree distraction. What a smokescreen it's providing for them.

I've never told anyone this apart from family, but I was molested once when I was a kid. Now before all you armchair trick-cyclists start leaping to conclusions, read the story first:

I was walking home from school in Charlton. It took about an hour and I'd vary the route to avoid boredom. One afternoon I was approached by what can only be described as a dirty-old-man-type. He was oldish, in a dirty jacket that matched his unkempt appearance. I was about thirteen, but I was a tough kid going on thirty! He didn't worry me.

He asked where a certain place was; I told him. He told me he was a knife sharpener, looking for a lad to help him. He wanted someone to knock at the doors and collect knives and scissors for him to sharpen. My eyes lit up as he said he'd pay £4 a day. All my suspicions left me as pound signs replaced common sense.

I arranged to meet him on Saturday, at the front of the shops on Shooters Hill Road. Saturday came and I waited at the bus stop, thinking it was all bullshit. Suddenly, there he was. We got on a bus and I asked him where we were going.

'New Eltham,' he replied.

I asked him where his sharpening wheel was. He produced

some sharpening stones from his pocket and said, 'I don't need a wheel.'

I thought, *'Funny!'*

We arrived in New Eltham and walked to a new housing estate. He then took me to the woods at the back and we sat under a tree.

'Right,' he said, 'go and knock at the doors.'

He told me the price and said to come back for him to sharpen whatever I got.

'We have to be somewhere out of the way.' He then repeated his rates: 'Four pounds if you're a good boy.' He put his hand on my crotch and repeated, 'If you're a good boy.'

Then, expertly and as quick as a flash, he unzipped my jeans and got my dick out. I thought, *'What the fuck is this bloke doing?'*

He seemed so determined, bordering on manic. So I let him. I wasn't too bothered and waited my moment. I let him have a quick fiddle and then told him that I wasn't ready for this *yet!*

I pushed him away but kept calm, putting Mr Wiggly away.

'Okay, look, go and get me some fags will you?' He produced a pound note and said, 'Twenty Players.'

I took the money, got on a bus and went home. When I got home, I told my pal Tommy Elliot. He laughed and told his dad. He *didn't* laugh. He went straight across the road and told my dad.

'Did you tell him were you lived?' asked Dad.

'I think so.'

'Well,' he said, 'if he comes round here he can have his pound back – then he'll get this!' He formed a fist.

And that was it. Life went on. I thought it was just one of those things. He was just a dirty old sod and I wasn't traumatised by it. But I can still smell him, to this day – like a manky old raincoat that smelled of iron filings. I was half-thinking of beating the fucker up and stealing his money, but he was holding a knife at the time so I thought better of it!

Okay, I was lucky and some kids are not so fortunate. They might run into some horrible nonce who's not as much of a pushover as that dirty old man. But the point is that I never let that pathetic bastard's behaviour cast a shadow over my life. I just had to put it down to experience – it didn't hurt me then and it doesn't hurt me now.

So do you think I should tell the police now? After all, he might be a celebrity forty years on.

Chapter Fourteen

A setback – a big one!

It's Tuesday morning. I've received an email from Henri. I'd asked him to inform the police I'd be staying in Great Yarmouth on Friday night. When he spoke to DC Root, my pal Danny, he was told they wanted to speak to me on other matters and would be re-bailing me.

What other matters?

We're not sure, but Henri thinks they have another complainant. Right now I've gone back down a snake. Funny, isn't it? One minute I'm full of hope, then the next....

I've a feeling that some other 'person or persons' has jumped on the bandwagon. The police will disclose to Henri what the 'other matters' are on Friday – three days and a thousand years away.

* * *

It's now Friday morning. I have to drive to Cromer today to do a gig on the pier. I've been awake since four o'clock. My mind is awash with what could be coming my way. I can't for the life of me think of anything apart from an old lover deciding to cash in.

It's now 9.30 and I've been pacing and panicking. I can't eat and I feel sick. The whisky bottle shouts at me from the shelf. I ignore it and try to concentrate. I can't. The reason is simple: I'm scared of what the 'other matters' are. If it's another set of allegations, then who, what? As I explained to Mitch, if I'd done something bad I'd know what it was and plan my defence. Not knowing what's to come is terrifying, because it will be fantasy. I try to recall every woman I've ever had, but no chance. The trouble is you don't remember the ones you've forgotten.

This is beginning to make me feel unwell. Not knowing what's going on is so unfair. Do the police do this on purpose? God knows what today will bring, but whatever it is we'll deal with it. We have to.

Michelle has taken this badly; she was expecting, as I was, for the cases to be dropped. Instead, here we are with this further black cloud heading our way.

* * *

I set off for Cromer at about twelve. By two o'clock I was still on the M25. It's always the same on Fridays; rush hour is all day long. At 4.30 the phone rang. It was Henri. I pulled over and answered. The next five minutes are a blur.

There were seven further allegations. My heart sank.

Henri, as calm as ever, rattled them off. I listened with a morbid curiosity.

Firstly, Wag has changed her mind about which theatre she believes the alleged assault happened in. It was not the Palladium; it was now a theatre in Slough – only sixty miles difference, that's all!

There's one allegation from a journalist in Chester, dating from 2010. I remember this woman.

From 2006, there's a hairdresser from Eastbourne crying rape! That was a real jaw-dropper.

I didn't pay much attention to the others: 1992, Stevenage; 1988, the Midlands; 1992, Babbacombe; and in 1978, the Green Man public house in Old Kent Road, London.

I told Henri I knew two of them: the journalist and the girl from Eastbourne. He said he'd email me the allegations as soon as I was back online.

I carried on with the journey like a zombie. How could they come up with this? I felt helpless. I told myself I'd been correct about sinister forces. How had these allegations come to light in such a short time after the first two? I was in shock. I felt really odd; I'd been sentenced to death but first I had to do a comedy show!

Steve Farr called; he was in Cromer and looking forward to seeing me. His head was better and he felt well. Some good news at last.

As I travelled the last few miles, my mind quickly ran over the two accusations I knew about. The alleged rape was easy to deal with – because I knew the girl and I knew all the circumstances, and I knew the truth. She was a nice girl I'd met while doing a show in Eastbourne – but why had she suddenly cried rape? Flo was with me at the time; I had to try to get in touch with him.

The other woman from Chester had interviewed me for a magazine. I couldn't think what I was supposed to have done to her. I remembered I didn't like her – she was far too full of herself.

Steve met me at the pier. He did indeed look well; ten times better than me, for sure. I'd have made Commander Data from *Star Trek* look suntanned.

I told Steve the story as we walked through the rain to the theatre. Steve joined me in the white-as-a-ghost look. John Cannal met us and couldn't believe my story.

'Where do they find these people?' he asked in despair

I called Laurie and went through what I could remember. He said that if I didn't feel up to it, I shouldn't do the show. I *didn't* feel up to it. I'd had very little sleep and my head was awash with questions.

I sat with John and moaned. It made me feel a little better. But I *had to* do the show. I couldn't let these people down. It was a full house and I needed the money. My bills were already mounting up!

To make matters worse, I had to do both halves of the show. Lloyd Hollett, my support act, had double-booked himself and was off entertaining people on a cruise ship. Nice.

I had a whisky and went onstage... Okay, I had two. It was a lovely little theatre and a fantastic audience carried me through. I was a bit slower than usual, as every time I stopped talking my mind reverted back to the accusations. But I did two hours with an interval, where I joined the audience in the bar.

Steve and John came for a nightcap at the hotel in Great Yarmouth, before I toddled off to bed and tried to sleep. The rape thing was a problem. I had a witness who'd confirm everything I said was true, although in reality it's very difficult to prove anything that goes on between two people behind closed doors. That's always the problem with sexual accusations – it's one person's word against another's.

But the real problem was that it was in 2006 and I was with Michelle. I'd have to tell her. I could only guess what was said in the statement. I told myself the truth would prevail and dropped off to sleep... for three hours.

It was 4am again. I was wide-awake. I needed to leave at 7.30, as Charlton were playing Millwall at the Valley at 12.30. But it was three hours before my alarm was due to go off. I decided to watch a new episode of *Sons of Anarchy* on the laptop and then head off for a slow drive to southeast London to see the mighty Reds.

I arrived in Charlton at eight o'clock. It was too early for anything so I headed to Blackheath for a walk. It was raining, I was tired and I felt so sorry for myself. I walked the roads I used to walk as a child; they comforted me and made me feel better. But I was so afraid. I felt like Operation Yewtree had decided to get me at whatever cost. They must have thought they'd hit pay dirt when the rape thing turned up. I don't know what made the girl do this. Surely she must know – or she should be told – that to make a false accusation is against the law?

All of these accusations sound coached. The statements were obviously taken down by a policewoman or policeman who wrote them in their style, rather than in the voice of the complainant. In my book, that is 'coached'. '*In or around*

1989...' What's that about? Be honest, could you remember what you did on a certain day in the eighties, apart from maybe dance to Duran Duran?

The Valley was a buzz of excitement, a local derby against arch-enemy Millwall. I, however, felt distant. I was tired and drawn, having only seven hours sleep in two days.

I called Michelle. She was concerned for me and lectured me on how positive I should be.

'Is there something you're not telling me?' she asked.

'No, 'course there isn't!'

'Yes there is. I can hear it in your voice.'

Her perception is like a witch's! I hadn't mentioned the rape allegation, as I was hopeful that when the police heard my version it'd all go away. But I still had no details and my mind was playing tricks.

Henri called my mobile and, although we didn't go through the accusations, he reassured me we'd work through them and deal with what would be thrown at us. I asked him not to reveal them to me until we met on Monday. Rightly or wrongly, I wanted a weekend that was relatively shit-free.

The Charlton faithful sang, we cheered and our team lost two-nil. For the first time ever I left the ground early. My world was closing down. What had I done to deserve this sense of doom? To say I was feeling sorry for myself is an understatement.

I drove to the Edward the Seventh Hospital, where my pal Steve Lamprell was treating himself to two new knees. Steve had played loads of sport all his life and consequently his knees were like a camel's – handy if you live in Dubai, as he does. He'd been putting off the op for ages, but now he'd had them done. He'd come round on Thursday and was in the critical care unit. Steve's ticker isn't the best so they were keeping a beady eye on him.

He asked me what was up. I told him and he couldn't believe it. In all the pain he must have been in, he still took time to reassure me and to say what everyone was saying: 'Just tell the truth and you'll be fine.'

His brother Timmy and his wife turned up, so I buggered off and drove home, arriving at the pub just in time to see England get stuffed by Wales. Henri texted me and asked if I wanted the details of the disclosures emailed. I told him no again and asked if I could come and see him on Monday.

Sunday saw me whizzing up the M3 to see Stevie again. When I got there he was back in the critical ward. As Gillie explained, Steve, always one for rushing, had taken a hot shower, got overheated and then sat in front of a cold air conditioning unit. He promptly fainted. They scraped him up and put him back in the bed with all the lights and buzzers. He was fine, he'd just done too much too soon after major surgery with a body full of drugs, working overtime to try to heal itself. That was a relief.

I kissed them goodbye three hours later, drove to the pub in Stockbridge and got pissed.

* * *

I'll never forget Mitch's face when I told her I'd been accused of rape. I told her the accusation and I told her what actually happened – and, more importantly, when it happened. It was not the best night of my life.

But do you know what she did? She cuddled me and said, 'Don't let these women do this to you!' She was brave. It wasn't just, '*He's my husband, he didn't do it!*' I'm sure if she'd thought I did it she'd have fucking told me!

She was more concerned that these women had said this about me, more angry with them than she was with me, and also exasperated with me for letting what they'd said really get to me. This woman is special.

She then stuck a bread knife in my ribs – well, she'd have had every right to. I *had to* tell her I'd had a mess about with another woman. That is a lot for a wife to take, but I have one hell of a wife!

I slept like a baby that night – slept for an hour, cried for an hour and shit myself! I actually slept the sleep of the dead, thank God.

But I woke with a hangover and a feeling of doom. It was the 'beer fear', as my mate calls it. It was time to see Henri and hear what these women had to say.

The drive to London took forever. I had lunch at the Carlton Club and then spent an hour with Steve in the hospital. Henri was doing something and couldn't see me till eight o'clock. I went back to the Carlton and tried not to drink.

He opened his door to me at 7.45. By nine o'clock I was feeling full of hope. All could be disputed. Some of the allegations were silly beyond belief.

We agreed that our disclosure to the police had prompted them to revisit Wag and inform her it could not have been the Palladium. She then 'remembered' it was the Slough Pavilion. That's cheating, isn't it? We had to make the police aware of our displeasure with this, because an attempt to be as truthful and helpful as possible has come back to hurt us.

We'd heard nothing new about the allegation of Scouser, so the new allegations were passed to me:

Codename *Sassoon*: she stated that we met in Eastbourne in 2006. She was leaving the place where she worked and bumped into me and a man she believes was called *Fleur*. She then went on to describe the person. She said I asked her to come to the show and arranged to meet her in the bar at our hotel. She and her friend met us at the bar and drank pink champagne. She said she then came to the theatre with us and was shown to the dressing room where there was a lot of vodka and orange laid out on a table. At one point I supposedly came out of the toilets with my pants down and said, 'Who wants to toss off Uncle Jimmy?' She said we went to dinner after and then back to the hotel, where she had drinks at the bar. She wanted to be sick and I suggested she do so in my room. She came to the room, went in the toilet and was sick 'for ages'. When she came out, she alleged that I raped her. She then got a taxi and went home, revolted that I was 'so old', and had a bath when she got home. She then said I called her a couple of times, trying to sweet-talk her by offering her a part in one of my shows.

Codename *Pushy*: she said she was walking in Chester in 2010 when I approached her. She told me she was a journalist and wanted to interview me. I asked her to come to the theatre and told her to wear stockings. She said she asked her friend to come as she didn't feel safe on her own. She also said that during the evening I grabbed her boob from behind and simulated sex movements. She also said I dropped my trousers in the dressing room, exposing my penis.

Codename *Flim-Flam*: she claimed to have been a silver service waitress at the Cresset Theatre, Stevenage, in 1992 or 1993! She said she usually worked in the upstairs bar at the theatre but was assigned to the dressing-room drinks. She reported that I arrived drunk in a chauffeur-driven Rolls Royce with a driver in uniform and a velvet suit on a hanger. I ordered a bottle of champagne and three pints of lager. She opened the champagne and poured me a glass. She then went to get the three pints of lager. When she returned she had to bend over to put the drinks down; I supposedly grabbed her buttock on the outside of her trousers and my fingers went into the crack of her bum. She said, 'What's your fucking game?' and I said, 'It's all part of the service!' She stormed back to the upstairs bar, where I later went after my 30–40-minute act. I bought a spirit, pursed my lips, made a 'sex noise' and called her 'ass frigid'. Her boss stopped her from swearing at me.

Codename *Duff*: in 1992 she was seven months pregnant. At a TV show where I appeared, she was in the green room with her husband and all the contestants when I asked to feel her baby bump. I felt her and then said, 'I like boobs best,' and cupped her breasts. She didn't tell anyone – until now.

Codename *Seaside*: in June 1992, she was with her daughter and her boyfriend. They came to the back of the theatre in Babbacombe to see me. I was with a dark-haired woman. They asked for a picture. I put my arm around the girl, placed my hand on her breast and made honking noises.

Codename *Wanderer*: she said that at Christmas 1988 I was playing a workingman's club in the Midlands. She had to go to the toilet; on her way back she walked in front of me. I grabbed her bum and lifted her skirt up to reveal her stockings. I told the audience to give her a round of applause.

Codename *Doggen*: she was at the bar in the Green Man in – get this – 1978. She said it was a Sunday. I saw her stocking suspenders protruding from her skirt and put my hand up her skirt to feel them.

So there we have it...

Henri and I went through each complaint carefully. They were all full of holes. We then had to decide if we told DC Danny where the holes were or waited for them all to be laughed out of court. We decided to hear first what he had to say about our previous disclosure and one of the complainants changing her story.

But rather than wait to be charged and go to trial, Henri and I preferred the 'short game', where we tell all and convince the police that the complainant's accusations are flawed. The 'long game' – where we get all of our evidence into court, make everyone look foolish and presumably walk away as heroes – costs a fortune. It's easier in a way to win, but the short game was a quicker and more cost-effective way of getting all this to vanish.

The trouble was that, as I was to find out at the police station, orders from the top said that, no matter how flaky the 'victims" version of events, they were to be taken as the truth. The investigating officers *could not* say to the complainants, 'I'm afraid that your evidence doesn't stack up,' no matter how daft it was.

That's unfair and a tad illegal, isn't it? It's fucking annoying – I can tell you that!

Chapter Fifteen

MARCH 2013

'SECONDS OUT... ROUND TWO... DING!'

I was to report to the police station at 11.30. The night before, I'd been to see Steve at the hospital. Michelle came with me. She'd got over the initial shock of her husband being a shit and was now in supportive mode. Steve looked much better.

It's funny who you bump into: Steve had to use the bathroom, so Michelle and I buggered off to the waiting room. Sitting inside was Nanette Newman and her two beautiful daughters, one of whom leapt up and shook my hand.

'Hello Jim, we worked together once – I'm Emma Forbes.'

We had indeed; she was a nice lady and didn't mention the obvious. We all had a good old natter and then went back to Steve's room. After I'd eaten all his grapes we took Gillie out to dinner.

I was a bit distant, thinking about my visit to the police

station in the morning. The girls realised this and reassured me things would be okay. I wasn't so sure. My head was full of conflicting facts and allegations.

I woke at five o'clock and paced about. I felt confident, wanting to start the ball rolling. The sooner I'd said my piece the sooner the wheels of justice would start turning.

Henri was at the police station waiting for me. We rang a bell and in we went. My pal DC Root arrived. Henri and I had been studying this policeman on the Internet. He'd been assigned to Operation Yewtree from a mob called Sapphire Cold Case, dealing with rape and serious sexual assaults. He's a big player.

We started a bit late as WDC Paula was going to be delayed. It turned out she was lost! The friendly station sergeant went through the procedure of re-arresting me while his oppo looked over at DC Root and me, giving me a knowing look. It reinforced my belief that ordinary coppers were embarrassed by this witch-hunt.

We went to the interview room and the process started. I sat opposite Danny and Henri was opposite the WDC. DC Root asked how I was, which was nice of him. I told him I was okay. He must have had some practice with the CD recorder, because we got going straight away on one of the original complainants: Wag.

'As you've been informed, Wag has changed the location of the assault.'

'Yes, I know. I want to say something about this.'

I told him of my displeasure that information I'd given at the first interview and from my legal team's representations had been passed to her. We'd produced a letter from John

Avery, general manager of the Palladium at the time, stating that her description of queuing up at the stage door to be let in was impossible.

'Is it a coincidence that Wag has changed her allegation? Or have you told her it couldn't be the London Palladium?'

'We haven't told her, she came to us.'

'So it's a coincidence, eh?'

'Yes, a coincidence.'

'Danny, please don't expect me to believe that! You – or one of your lot – have told her to change the location after we'd proven the first one was impossible. The Slough Pavilion is about as far removed from the London Palladium as Mother Teresa is from Chubby Brown!'

I told him I felt cheated. 'Especially by you, Danny. I thought you were seeking the truth, not forcing square pegs into round holes just to convict me.'

He flinched. 'I *am* looking for the truth,' he said with a strange look.

'And I'm helping you to find it. But you want to convict me and you're using the evidence that *we've* found to force a conviction. It's not fair. I could have used my right to remain silent and this allegation would've been thrown out of court.'

He said nothing.

Henri added, 'Not only that, it has brought considerable stress to John, an old gentleman of ninety-one, who was appalled to think these alleged offences took place on his watch. An old man has been worried half to death over an allegation which turns out to be completely false.'

Danny said he was sorry for that. I believed him and, for a moment, felt strangely sorry for him. I sort of liked this guy despite it all. He was a man I believed could ruin my life, but he could also make this nightmare go away.

Then I thought of the Stockholm syndrome, a psychological phenomenon in which hostages express sympathy toward their captors, sometimes to the point of defending them. But Danny was just doing his job. What else was he to do? In reality, he was doing what his bosses told him to.

I went on to tell him that, despite all that had happened, I'd assume he'd *not* inform the complainants but accept our information as facts to dispute their claims. Otherwise I'd shut up and we'd do it all in court. He confirmed that would be the case.

'Okay,' I said, 'Slough Pavilion: what do you know about that? Do you want me to tell you why it can't be that one either? What have you discovered about Slough?'

'It's shut down,' he said proudly.

'Yes, I know.'

'Did you ever play it?'

'Yes.'

'Would you have played it at this time?'

'What time is that? Wag doesn't know when she was there. She doesn't know what year it was. "In or around 1989," or some other time?' I said sarcastically.

'When have you played it?'

'Okay, I'll tell you why this is not on. I played it in the very early eighties and then got pissed and broke the dressing-room sink. I was banned and never played it again. Also, there's no stage door.'

They hadn't checked these things and it was again down to me to fill in the gaps.

I explained that the theatre had a shutter door at the back and everything was accessed via two sets of stairs.

'The theatre is on a raised level.'

Henri added, 'I hope on our next visit that the venue hadn't changed again... to Scunthorpe.'

I think we were being fair. My confidence soared. We'd made an important point and DC Root had denied passing information to Wag on tape.

We moved on to Scouser. Danny asked if I'd had any more thoughts on her allegation. I told him I'd tried to remember, but the only way something might come to light was if The Stoker told me about it. That was unlikely to happen. I asked if they'd dropped the case. Danny smiled.

Well, it was worth a try

We moved on to Sassoon. I told them straight away, 'I know this girl.' Danny asked if I'd seen the allegation. I told him I had and gave my side of the story. Paula, the quiet one, made notes. Danny tried to look into my soul. Here's the story as I told it to them:

I was appearing at the theatre in Eastbourne. The soundcheck was done and I had some time to kill. It's always good to have a little walk around the town. It lets people see you and jog their memory that I must be doing a show.

On this occasion I met a pretty girl who I thought was giving out flyers, I might be wrong on this. She was pleased to see me... gushing, in fact. She wanted to come and see the show. I told her I'd leave a couple of tickets at the box office. She said that she was worried that I'd forget and she'd get there and there would be no tickets. I reassured her that there would be. I even suggested that they get there and ask the merchandise seller for the tickets.

This girl and I finally compromised. Her and her friend would meet me and Flo at the bar of the hotel and they could come with us. She was happy with that.

The show starts at 7.30. The support act does forty minutes, there is a twenty-minute interval then I do one hour twenty minutes.

I met Flo, my security guy, at the bar that evening. It would have been at about seven. Two ladies arrived soon after and joined us at the bar.

Sassoon was wearing a pastel-coloured lightweight summer dress cut above the knee and nice girly shoes. She looked lovely. She looked as if she had made an effort. I do not recall what her friend was wearing. Everyone was looking at Sassoon. Her mate could have been wearing a beekeeper's hat and flippers and no one would have noticed.

We had drinks. Flo and I had soft drinks; I do not recall what the girls had.

Sassoon was full of life and chatted to everyone in reach. I got the impression she liked being the centre of attention.

After we'd had a drink we left for the theatre. I drove. I had a black Range Rover.

Danny checked his notes and chipped in. 'She says that she drank pink champagne.'

'I do not recall what she drank. We were at the bar for no more than two drinks.'

'She says that she went into your dressing room, where there was a row of vodka and oranges on a table.'

'There are only two glasses of vodka in the dressing room: a double and a single. It's a ritual we stick to, one to go on stage and one to have whilst on stage. Steve Farr, my tour manager, will confirm that if I have guests to the room, I'll order more drinks. On this occasion I didn't.'

'She says at one time you came out of the toilet with your penis out, saying, "Who wants to toss off Uncle Jimmy?"'

'I'd never do that.'

Wouldn't that give her a warning signal? But she still stayed, had dinner, had drinks and came to my room. This girl likes to shoot herself in the foot!

She says I showed her backstage – this is likely. I have in the past teased the support act by showing him females. It is an old showbiz tradition. I looked into the wings once and saw two topless dancers wrapped around [comedian] Dave Lee. It's fun.

On this occasion I don't remember being with her backstage, although I've no reason to doubt her. It'd seem that if she was backstage, she wouldn't have been drinking, as there are strict no-drink policies in theatres.

'After the show she states that you went to a restaurant, Avanida's. Do you remember that?'

'This is true. I know the owner well. I'll contact him to see if he can somehow remember. He may well even know the girl. It's a very popular restaurant.'

'That would be helpful.' He made a note.

I don't recall what we had to eat or drink. We then went

back to the bar at the hotel. I can't remember if they came
with us or joined us later.

Sassoon had made her intentions clear. She was holding my
arm and being slightly suggestive, 'heavy flirting' it might be
described as. Flo was with me at all times.

We had drinks at the bar. Sassoon was happy and bubbly.
I do not recall seeing her drunk. She had not changed her
demeanour since the early evening.

'She says she told you she wanted to be sick.'

'I don't remember her saying this.'

It does throw up the question – if you pardon the pun – of
why she would tell me.

'Why did she not, as all girls would do, tell her friend?'

Danny shrugged at my question. My mind was racing.

I find it impossible to believe a girl who prided herself on
being the life and soul of the party would suddenly tell the
man she was showing off to that she was going to be sick.
Why? She and her friend had visited the toilet in the hotel
while we were in the bar. Surely pride would restrain her? If
anyone, she'd surely have told her mate? What happened to
the friend? If her friend had already left, at what time did she
leave? Why did Sassoon not go with her? Why would she
leave her sick friend? Was she instructed to leave by Sassoon
as she was determined to stay with me? Was the friend only
there until Sassoon's mission was completed? If she left
Sassoon at the bar, it suggests they had no worries or
concerns. Hopefully, Flo can fill in some gaps.

'Sassoon says that you suggested she use your room to be sick in.'

'That has got to be the worst excuse to be in a man's room ever!'

'She then suggests that you took her to your room where she went straight into the bathroom to be sick...' – he checked his notes – '... for ages.'

The distance from the bar to my room had to be a hundred paces at least. We passed two toilets and had to go in a lift. She kept on at me to take her to the room. As lovely as she was, I started to smell a small rat. I had in my mind that perhaps this girl had an agenda. She was all over me, and I was perhaps outside the age group of her normal targets.

I thought perhaps this girl had a press story on her mind. I thought she might be trying to snare me into having sex with her to sell her story. This has happened to me many times before. I mentioned this to Flo when she and her friend had gone to the loo. He too was concerned.

I must admit I was intrigued. I told her I was going to bed. She grabbed my arm and said something like, 'Come on then.' I was not aware of her friend objecting. I was not aware of her friend at all. Maybe she'd gone by then, leaving her sick friend with two men they'd just met... how's that work?

Danny listened intently. Paula made notes.

We walked to the room, leaving Flo at the bar. She was giggly and suggestive, impatient even. She showed no signs of sickness. She was not unsteady on her feet. She did not appear to be drunk.

We went into my room. It was a standard hotel room with a double bed, an en suite bathroom and phone.

'She states that when she came out of the loo after being sick,' he checked his notes, 'you pounced on her.'

'Rubbish... come on, what would this girl smell like if she'd been sick "for ages"?'

Paula stopped making notes and asked me if I'd made love to her.

What did take place was consensual and private between two adults. It would be rude of me to explain fully here what went down, if you excuse the pun! I did, however, tell the police officers.

I explained my fear of headlines: '"He Made Love To Me All Night... He Was Built Like A Stallion!" Well, she ain't gonna say that about me!'

They smiled.

I got her a drink from the mini bar. I had one myself. I got the feeling that she didn't like the no-cuddling phase. I also think she wasn't best pleased when I suggested I call her a cab. She got dressed and I walked her back down to reception. We met Flo on the way. He was either on his way to bed or he might have seen us from his position at the bar.

We had a chat. Sassoon was now bubbly again after coming to accept there was no way I was going to let her stay the night. She gave either Flo or me her number, I don't remember, and she got in the cab. She was happy and smiley.

The WDC chipped in. 'Did you pay for the cab?'

'I think I did give her some money.'

The next day I called her or she called me, I can't be sure. I asked if she was okay. I was using the hands-free in the car. She sounded slightly guilty, with lots of 'Oh my God's' and things like that. I remember her saying, 'I hope I'm not pregnant.' What an odd thing to say! For a moment I thought I might be being recorded. I spared her blushes by not going into details but reassured her that there was no way she was pregnant. She was chatty and wanted a part in one of my shows. She wanted to be a singer.

She might have called me back or I might have called her again. I do remember that her asking about being pregnant was odd. She seemed embarrassed by her behaviour. I think she didn't want me to think badly of her. At no time did she accuse me of anything untoward.

DC Root read from her statement that she had in fact met me before. 'She says she was at the box office in Brighton where you approached her, pinched her bottom and said, "Nice girls like you could get me in trouble."'

I told him I didn't remember that and it was unlikely I'd be in the foyer prior to a show.

As I type this sometime later the thought strikes me: was this where the seeds of an idea were sown? Was it like a signal for her? 'Ooh, I can have him whenever I want, he likes me!'

'She says that later she saw you on a TV show where you talked about your girlfriend in Dubai and texted your mobile: "GIT!"'

'I never got that. But both Flo and I thought the whole thing a little odd, especially the phone conversations. I wouldn't have been surprised to see my name in the paper. But I *am* surprised at her plainly false allegation, and question why it's taken seven years for this to surface. Why did she not report this immediately or contact me and tell me her intention?'

I told Paula that someone should tell Sassoon to withdraw her statement. I added that I thought she was a lovely girl and I'd hate to see her get into trouble over this.

They looked at me and made a note. 'She said her dress was torn,' said Paula.

'I don't remember that. She would say that, though, wouldn't she?'

Paula asked a few more detailed questions and we moved on. Danny looked at his notes and asked about Pushy. I said I could remember this woman. I'd read her allegation.

'If you'd like to tells us, please go ahead.'

I asked if it was alright to rattle off and then he could ask questions later. Here is roughly what I said:

I was playing the Little Theatre in Chester. Steve Farr was having a break as my tour manager and my son Cameron had replaced him. Dave Lee was the supporting act.

I did the soundcheck and decided to walk around Chester to get a feel of the place. I bumped into a woman in her forties who asked if I was Jim Davidson. She told me she was a reporter and asked could she interview me for one of her magazines? I was about to embark on a new venture, a play called Stand Up and Be Counted. *I'd need all the publicity I could get. I said she could come to the theatre and do the interview there if she liked. I said I'd leave two tickets for her at the box office under my name and I'd see her in the bar while the first half of the show was underway. She seemed happy with this. As I left I said, 'Wear stockings.' I then did a camp walk and said, 'I'll be wearing mine.' She laughed at this. I was pleased; I needed the publicity and all the good press I could get.*

Danny made notes.

Showtime came and the audience went into the auditorium. I went into the bar area and found Pushy sitting with an empty glass. Hellos were said and I got her a drink, a white wine as I recall.

She talked about her magazines. We had thirty minutes to chat. I was aware that she was thirsty and by the time I had to run for the dressing room to evade the interval, she'd had a considerable amount of wine.

Dave Lee came to my dressing room and we had a debriefing about the audience. Pushy came through the pass door into the backstage corridor with her friend, an attractive, bubbly, blonde woman. My son called me out to meet them. Dave and I went and joined them in the corridor. Introductions were made. I had to get ready, so I walked to my dressing room door, dropped my trousers and said, 'This way, girls.' I waddled into the room like a penguin. They laughed and followed. Dave joined us. Everyone was laughing and in high spirits. It was a tiny dressing room.

At no time did I touch her boob as she claims, and there was no sexual innuendo. My son was there at all times and so was Dave Lee.

Danny listened. 'She said she had her son with her when you met her.'

'Did she? I don't remember.'

Danny produced some pictures. They were A4 blown-up photos taken backstage, about eight in all. They showed, among other things, me with Pushy. I sort of recognised her but recollected her friend more. I told Danny I didn't know why I remembered her and not Pushy. There were pictures of the two women with me; me and the blonde; both of them and Dave Lee. It was good to see Dave again. He'd died very suddenly a couple of years ago from cancer. His funeral was the biggest piss-up Canterbury had ever seen! I bet he was looking down and shaking his head in disbelief.

The photos showed these women laughing their heads off, but Danny didn't see them like that. 'If you look at this one...'

He showed me a picture of me and Pushy. She was laughing and I was pulling a funny face. My hand was hovering around her middle.

'Look,' he said pointing at a photo, 'it looks as if you are about to squeeze her breast.'

I laughed out loud. Henri grabbed the picture and said:

'For the benefit of the recording, the picture clearly shows that Jim's hand is nowhere near the breast area and the photo shows a woman laughing. All these photos show that these women were having the time of their lives.'

Once again, a sleepless night wracking the brain has come up with the goods. I now remember why I recognised the blonde friend and not Pushy. The blonde lady was charming and not pissed. She was chatty and flirty. I liked her. I think Pushy got the hump with this. That would explain why I didn't see them after the show. My money's on Pushy dragging her friend away to stop her getting the attention she thought she should get.

DC Root said, 'Right, let's have a break.' He and Henri went outside and I was left with DC Paula. She seemed a nice woman. We chatted and I asked her if they were busy. She told me they were as there were only six of them.

'I thought there were thirty of you?'

'No,' she said, 'we're *attached* to Yewtree.'

'It must be murder.'

She said it was, adding that orders from above told them they must treat the allegations as absolute truth.

'Even some of these silly ones? The pendulum has swung back too far – from doing nothing about Savile to this,' I added.

She rolled her eyes. In my mind she confirmed what the British public was thinking and it brought the MP's words back to me: '*Jim, you are being hung out to dry!*'

The break was over and we restarted.

'Okay,' said Danny, 'let's move on to Flim-Flam. Okay, Jim?'

'Yes mate, but I have to tell you there are some Palladium-type things here.'

'What do you mean?'

'I mean that this girl's statement is all over the place.'

I told him I couldn't remember this incident.

'Have you played The Crescent in Stevenage?'

'It's The Cresset, Danny, someone has got the name wrong. What year are we talking about here?'

'She says 1992 or 1993.'

'She doesn't know the year?'

He shrugged. 'Between 1992 and '93.'

'Okay Danny, if it's alright with you I'll tell you why this woman has got it all wrong. You haven't checked her statement have you?'

He said nothing.

'Well if you had, you'd have found some big holes.'

Henri, who prefers to stay quiet, added, 'And when he has, we don't expect the venue to change again... if we meet again,' he added with a smile.

Danny laughed. 'Point taken.'

I was staring to enjoy it in a weird way.

'It can't be the Cresset. There is no upstairs bar, not one that is used for a show anyway. Also, she said she was responsible for the backstage drinks. She wasn't, I have a rider attached to the contract stating what must be left in the dressing room. My roadies get the drinks, not waitresses. She says she's a silver service waitress but the venue is a sports hall-type place. There is no restaurant. They might have functions but not when there's a concert on.'

Danny chipped in. 'She says you showed up in a gold Rolls Royce... or Bentley.'

'Don't start with the Bentleys again.'

He smiled. 'She said you had a chauffeur... in a uniform.'

Henri chuckled and shook his head

'I don't have a uniformed chauffeur and I never have. What's more, I don't drink champagne and couldn't drink three pints of lager if you put a gun against my head. Nor did I go to the upstairs bar because there isn't one.'

'She said you were carrying a velvet suit.'

'Bonkers!'

Danny gave me a look that agreed with the sentiment. He asked if I'd touched this woman's bottom. I said no.

Henri asked if they'd confirmed the occupation of this woman. They said no. Henri had something up his sleeve.

This allegation is one of the many reasons the police should be a bit ashamed of themselves. Why had no copper whizzed up the A1 and checked out the location? I'm not an expert but that's what I'd do. Had they even checked the complainants out?

We moved on to the next one.

'This allegation is made by a seven-months-pregnant woman who was a guest on one of your TV shows. She says she was in a room where the contestants partied after the recording; that you said to her, "I like pregnant women," and that she looked good. You allegedly asked to feel her bump, cupped her breasts and then said, "I like boobs better."'

What bollocks!

I told him I couldn't remember this woman or a similar

situation, and that the green room we used as a post-show drinking venue was usually crammed full of people.

'She says that she was with her now ex-husband. She goes on to say that she never told anyone until now. Do you remember this woman?'

'No.' I told him there were many witnesses. Surely he should find some? Then the usual daft questions started.

'Would you have squeezed this woman's breasts?'

'No.'

I made a mental note to contact the contestant researcher for my TV shows. She'd been at the BBC for years. I was very fond of her, even though I did call her 'Dragon'. The nickname was more about her fierceness when controlling people, rather than her looks... honest!

We moved onto the next one, Wanderer.

'This woman said that she and twenty friends came to see you at a workingman's club in Walsall at Christmas 1988.'

I told him that at Christmas 1988 I was at the Dominion Theatre in London, doing panto. 'I don't think I ever played a workingman's club in Walsall. I was at the top of the tree in 1988, why would I do it?'

'You can't remember this woman?'

Have you not been fucking listening?

I told him no, I could not remember this woman. He made a note about the Dominion Theatre.

We spoke about the next one, Seaside.

'It was at Babbacombe in June 1992.'

'I don't think so.'

'Why don't you think so?'

'I play Torquay usually in the summer. It's a better theatre and you get the same crowd. Summer season starts in late July.'

'Do you remember these people at the stage door?'

'No.'

'Would you have put your hand on her breast and made honking noises?'

I stifled a smile. 'No.'

He moved on. No more questions on that then! The last one was the girl in the pub in 1978. 'She claims that you pushed her against the bar and put your hand up her skirt to feel her stockings, which were apparently on show.'

I told Danny about the pub and explained that it was always jammed. He asked if I could remember the incident.

'Danny, that's thirty-five years ago.'

He said, 'Okay, we're done,' switched the recorder off and gathered his notes.

'It makes a change for people to speak to us so freely, so thanks for that.'

I was getting to like this guy. During all this, Henri had listened and chipped in with all the necessary points I omitted. He was impressive.

I was bailed until May 10. I felt much better as I signed out at the sergeant's desk. The train was gaining pace, the station was in sight and justice would soon be done... please Gawd!

I felt confident all would be well, because we were dealing with facts. It was when I ignored the facts and thought about what else could be happening in the halls of power that I get scared. One minute I was convinced all would be well, the next I was certain it wouldn't. It was driving me crazy. I had to concentrate on the facts and leave the demons to Dan Brown.

I left the police station and drove to my friend's house in Shropshire, where I was to do two gigs. The first one, in Telford, was a bit of a problem as the local paper had announced the show would be cancelled. They eventually printed a retraction but the damage was done. I played to 300 people; of course, the newspapers turned that into 200. But the two shows went down a storm, with the audience leaping to their feet. After the shows, promoter Chris Davis and I got pissed. Why not?

The drive home through the snow on a Saturday morning was hell, but I was looking forward to seeing Michelle. She, like me, was happy one moment, then worried to death, then angry. We had a big mountain to climb but truth was on my side. I had to keep telling myself that.

On Sunday we went to the Ivy restaurant in London, for Laurie's seventieth birthday party. I was looking forward to it, despite having a cold. We joined Des O'Connor, Cilla, Max Boyce, Ronnie Corbett and fifty of Laurie's friends and family. I was the MC. Laurie is a great manager and has many friends, including nasty Nigel Lythgoe who flew in from LA and flew back the next morning.

We had video tributes from Neil Sedaka, Tommy Steele and Jimmy Tarbuck. I read some cards out, including two from Frank Bruno and Priscilla Presley. Then I read an imaginary card: 'Have a good night, Laurie, and well done, Jim, hope to see you soon... Chris Huhne.' It brought the house down.

The producer Bill Kenwright made a speech and ended by

thanking me, saying I was a star to come and speak for his friend after the week I'd had. Then I received a standing ovation – my third in a week!

Chapter Sixteen

'HURRY UP
AND WAIT...'

The problem with being innocent is that you can't think of ways to wriggle off the hook. You're stuck with it. The complainants can bend and distort the truth, as they already have. I, however, cannot. The truth is all I have. In a way it must be easier to be guilty, as you can try to plan a way out. All I have is the hope that the police and the CPS will see that it *is* the truth.

Henri called to tell me that, in light of the police's behaviour with regards our evidence, we're not going to be making any representations to them via our QC. This worried me for a bit, but then everything worries me. Life is out of my control. It's like you're driving but someone else is steering. You have to try not to think about it all the time. I've done all my thinking; I've run out of thoughts. I'll go with Henri every time, whatever he says goes. But it still doesn't stop me from waking up at the crack of dawn and feeling awful all day.

I decided I'd now talk to the two reporters pitched up outside. I called Laurie and said that, 'No comment' might not be the best response anymore. He agreed.

I walked down the road and their eyes lit up as if they'd won the lottery. They asked if I was okay, and why I'd stopped using Twitter.

'It gets on my nerves.'

'Do you think that this is a witch-hunt?' asked the one who looked twelve years old.

'I don't think that's for me to answer, seeing as I'm now a witch. I do, however, think that the public believe so. But then I think the police are obliged to take all these allegations as the truth, no matter how daft they think they are. The pendulum has swung too far back the other way, from doing nothing about Jimmy Savile to this.'

The young one scribbled like mad, as my old Polish pal, *The Police Are Coming*, snapped away.

'Is your wife supporting you?'

'No more than usual... look, you have to understand there's no need to support me about these allegations; I've not been charged. My wife and I are carrying on as normal – she supports me and I support Charlton.' I didn't say we both felt it was the worst time of our lives.

I called Brian Shaw and asked how the figures were. He told me they were great in some areas, not so good in others. There was no pattern. I told him I'd now do some press if it'd help, so he arranged the first – and last – interview

The call came from a young reporter guy on the *Gloucester Echo*. I hate doing interviews; the little sods can't help going for a scoop and it became obvious this lad was doing just that. He talked about racism, accused me of making fun of rape, of insulting the disabled, and sounded like a real New Age lefty boy. He was, and the ensuing article was awful. I called Brian and said, 'No more. These guys have an agenda before they speak to me.' Yes, I could have ignored his questions, but it's very difficult not to fight your corner when faced by kids with pens.

The two Steves were recovering well: Stevie Farr had gone to France and would be back at the end of April. Since he'd been away, I'd not been selling merchandise at the gigs, and boy, I needed the money! Stevie Lamprell was hobbling about on new knees, probably feeling as frustrated as I did. We could both see where we wanted to be but had no control over how we got there.

The boys in the pub had been helpful. It was a good chance to let off steam and they were eager to help me do it. My friend Graham, an ex-RAF fighter pilot, has a son who's a barrister; he thought the police had gone mad and were not following their own guidelines: 'To start off thinking that the complainant is 100 per cent truthful and the accused is guilty is not what is supposed to happen.' I had to agree.

Mindful of being accused of hiding, I went on Twitter again. It's funny: people who knew me knew these allegations were untrue; people who liked me but didn't know me thought the allegations were untrue; even people who hated me knew the allegations were untrue. I even thought the two police persons who interviewed me believed they were false.

So why is it happening?

* * *

Henri has now received a letter from DC Root. It stated that they (the police) were hoping that we (us) would make some representations to them (Yewtree) in respect of Flo's (minder) statement and one from Cameron (son), in regard to Pushy (cow).

Mindful of the Palladium/Pavilion discrepancy, Henri wasn't sure we should make any representations and would consult with Trevor, the QC. In the meantime, I'd call Flo and a few others to get some wool on our backs.

A letter arrived from Bert Hilton, Tracy's dad. We'd kept in touch and remained friendly after the divorce, and I'd written to him about Wanderer's allegation. Tracy was adamant that I hadn't played a workingman's club, but Bert confirmed we had in fact visited one to see the late Johnny Hammond: 'It was a great night. Johnny was very good and then you disappeared from the table and appeared onstage.'

Shit!

'You had the room in hysterics and then we went back home to our house.'

I called him. He could remember every detail and was convinced nothing untoward had happened.

I called Henri. He said we couldn't be sure this was the club Wanderer referred to, reminding me that she said it was Christmas 1988, when I was in London doing panto. Wanderer said she went to see *me* – not Johnny Hammond – and that after twenty minutes she'd gone to the loo. It seemed she was under the impression I was the star turn. Well, seeing that no one knew I was going to be there made nonsense of all that.

Henri went on to say that a statement from Tracy and her

parents might come in handy. Then Tracy called to offer support in any way she could. I asked her if I'd ever played a workingman's club in Walsall.

'No, not while I was with you... the only time we went to a workingman's club, we went to see Johnny Hammond. We were with my mum and dad.'

I asked her if she saw me fiddling with a woman.

'Don't be stupid. You only went on stage to show off to me and my mum and dad. Why would you mess with a woman with us watching? It's all crap.' She also told me she wanted to 'kill these fucking women', bless her.

I told her Henri would be in touch. That'd be fun. Henri handled our divorce!

Speaking of money, I was starting to get concerns about how much all this was going to cost. I hadn't budgeted for any of it: first *Celebrity Big Brother*, that's a six-figure sum gone; then panto, that was another six figures! There was also the on-going problem of theatres waiting to see what happened with regards to the charges; it'd give theatre managers who didn't like me that much an excuse.

The legal costs were not cheap, as you can imagine. This was the year I'd planned to do a lot of work in Scotland, so there were the offices to pay for plus the retainer for my accommodation agent.

I really would be happy if all this went away. I'm feeling the pressure.

Chapter Seventeen

Another piece of bad news came my way in the shape of a text from Goose: '*Fred Marafono has died.*'

He was a friend of mine for thirty years. Although I never saw him that much, he was one of those people that you fell in love with straight away and never changed your mind about. Fred was a huge bear of a man from Fiji. He was in the SAS and I first met him one New Year's Eve in the eighties.

In or around 1983...

I was dragged out on the beer by Minky and Snapper (don't ask). I was staying with JB, another giant from the regiment who was very, very tough. JB didn't drink, but the others made up for it.

We drank our way through three pubs and then went and knocked on Fred's door. He produced a bottle of whisky and it vanished in three glasses as JB, a fitness fanatic, watched in horror. I'd never seen people drink half-pints of whisky! Fred and Tak, his Fijian brother-in-arms, drank it like water. We ended up somewhere where I was challenged to a one-arm press up contest with Minky. Guess what? I lost and had to drink more as a punishment.

Through a hazy head the next day, we listened to Fred's great tales of derring-do. He told us he was part Catholic as his grandfather once ate a missionary. Fred was a sergeant major in B Squadron. During the Falklands war, he and his squadron were at Ascension Island waiting for the word 'go'. This would be the mission to end all missions, which they prepared for by having a piss-up on the beach.

As Snapper would say, 'If you can't do it on fags and beer it's not worth doing.'

Snapper wrote *Soldier 'I'*, the first of the SAS books, detailing his amazing life, the Iranian embassy siege and the battle of Mirbat, where eight SAS men took on 400 of the *adoo* (Arabic for 'the enemy') in scenes reminiscent of *Zulu* – although Snapper looks fuck-all like Michael Caine or Stanley Baker!

But what his phrase means is that if you really have to work hard at the job, your chances of failing are much greater. If someone really has to be at the top of their game then he's trying to do something he can't do, which is what the SAS try to weed out.

Fred Marafono invented the now traditional flaming Drambuies. At one stage, my late friend's Paul Hill's face was set on fire, and Nish threw a beer on him. They'll be doing the same up there now, I guess.

Fred and Charlie C partook in the ancient and gentlemanly

art of shark fishing. Expert tracker Fred had seen some fins circling in the bay. Fuelled by a desire to improvise, and a few Scotches, he devised a way of catching them: a meat hook tied to Para cord with a lump of meat on it. They found an old chair and rigged up a seatbelt to prevent one of Britain's finest from being dragged in. For backup, Charlie had a GPMG (a machine gun) and two pounds of PE (stuff that goes bang). Their planned special op was eventually cancelled, so half of the squadron parachuted into the sea off the Falkland Islands to continue their mischief.

Legend has it that Fred said to his wife one day, 'I'm just popping out,' before he went to Sierra Leone to fight for the government against the brutal terrorists destroying the country. These baddies were particularly bad: they hacked off the hands and arms of people they believed were on the government's side. Fred took to the country like a duck to water. He was a man of great conviction and hated what the rebels were inflicting on the innocent people of Sierra Leone.

While on leave, he came to see me and Mick Gould in Blackpool. Mick is the guy who 'taught the SAS how to fight' – he also choreographed the fights and gun battles in movies such as *Heat* and *Miami Vice*… and I love him! Fred watched the show where my band finished on a Pink Floyd song, complete with lasers. He was impressed. We had a drink at the bar and a beaming Fred hugged me till I nearly fainted.

'Great show, my brother! Did you invent those laser weapons?'

I asked him if he was getting paid in Sierra Leone.

'No,' he said, 'it is a poor country, the rebels are well armed. Our boys only have basic weapons and spears.'

'You're not being paid?'

'No Jim, but it's Africa... there are diamonds there some-where.'

Fred's book is actually called *From SAS to Blood Diamond Wars*. My very best army pal, Goose, and I had gone to find Fred in SL. It was our sacred mission, as we both missed him. He'd disappeared off the radar (supposedly to get a tin of peas!) and we were worried about our old friend.

A year before, the notorious, self-styled West Side Boys had captured some British soldiers. The SAS and the Paras were sent to get them back. Their first port of call was Fred, who advised on the area and on the rescue mission. The mission was a tricky one: an SAS team sat up to their necks in jungle shite for days, watching the target. The raid was split into two parts: the SAS attacked the compound where the captives were, with the Paras taking the nearby barracks. The rescue was a success despite several casualties and the sad death of Trooper Brad Tinnion, who got killed by friendly fire in the raid.

My old pal Jim A got a bit of grenade in his chest. As he was the medic, he told them all, 'I'm going to go into shock now, lads.' The sergeant major came along and said, 'Fuck me, Jim, you've gone whiter than me!' which was quite some-thing for someone who's mixed-race. But Jim has huge muscles and these saved his life. As he put it, as a Geordie, 'The shrapnel would have killed a normal bloke, bonnie lad.'

During all this, Fred was in a Russian attack helicopter, firing a machine gun like Rambo. He was in his sixties at the time! When I asked him about the baddies, he said, 'They ran like chickens, Jim.'

So Goose and I planned our trip. We were to fly to Belgium and then take the Sabina flight to Sierra Leone. I'd arranged for the British Forces Foundation to set up a concert for the British Army Training team, who were training the local officer corps. We took a pretty female singer with us – and her hat. She had a hatbox she treated like the Holy Grail. She didn't take her eyes off it, wouldn't let anyone touch it, but it was only a hat that a woman would wear at Ascot, in a round cream box.

We arrived at Freetown and had to fly by Russian Yip helicopter to some other place. All around this helicopter were crashed versions of the same model. Goose, with typical understatement, said, 'Wait till last to get on then we'll be near the door.'

After a short flight, we landed somewhere and were met by our escorting British officer who, I was reassured to see, wore his pistol on his hip. The show was in a casino cabaret room. I've never seen anything like it; it looked like something out of Cuba in the fifties.

We'd planned to do a soundcheck at six o'clock. Jo, the girl with the hat, started to sing. I don't know if it was because there were no monitors, or the fact that she really couldn't sing a note, but Goose went white and said, 'Wanna drink, boss?'

The house filled up. There were the Brit soldiers, of course, but also pirates, pimps, mercenaries, terrorists, tarts, poofs and people of every colour. Goose said it reminded him of the bar at the end of the universe in *Star Wars*. We went to the bar to chat to some lads and the 'night fighters' were all over us. The price of sex was the equivalent of 50p. It'd be like bungee jumping – the rubber breaks and you're dead!

The show was great, although I had to apologise for a bad sound system that made the singer sound out of tune. The poor girl was really let down, but she and her hat soldiered on. I was proud of her.

After the show we went to the bar – where the night fighters were all over Jo, the singer! No sign of Fred.

The next day I got a knock on the hotel-room door. I was told there was someone to see me in the foyer, so I threw some clothes on and set off to the lobby. There in all his Fijian glory stood Fred. He took my breath away; he was huge and had a presence that filled a room. You looked round and all the waiters and waitresses were stood there open-mouthed. They nearly bowed.

'Hello, brother,' he said.

The handshake and the hug were bone shattering. My eyes filled up. He looked well. I called Goose, and the two SAS men greeted each other as you'd expect. Their eyes shared the look of people who have shared adversity. I felt like an observer but I didn't care. I loved both of these men.

As we walked into the bar, the receptionist called me over. 'Do you know who that man is? He is a warrior!'

Fred whisked us off to his house, which was more like a walled compound. There were guards and staff everywhere. It was his headquarters.

A maid made us a noodle-soup lunch. While we were waiting, Fred told us of his exploits. We were spellbound. Even Goose, one of the hardest and most dedicated soldiers the Regiment has ever produced, was fascinated by our friend's times in this scary country. Such moments can never really be described in print, so I'll leave you with my best recollection of Fred:

I leant forward to help myself to some chilli relish.

'Careful, brother' said a caring Fred, 'that stuff is really hot.' He helped himself to a spoonful. His face looked sad as he said, 'I have to have it, for without it food has no taste.' Then he smiled in a way I'll never forget.

Fred Marafono MBE was a great warrior. I loved him like the brother he always referred to me as, and I wish he was here with me now.

Chapter Eighteen

APRIL 2013

Henri emailed and said that the QC had decided, in view of the quality of our evidence and mindful of the 'short game', that we *would* be making representations to the police after all. DC Root had indicated that it was what he was expecting.

Henri went on to explain that once again this was a double-edged weapon, as there was nothing to stop the police going back to the complainants and reporting our findings. But Trevor agreed with Henri that it was the best way forward to avert charges being brought, and I also agreed. Now it was time to see what the police and the CPS thought.

Another story was brewing in the Kent local press: it was reported that the manager of the Marlowe Theatre in Canterbury had banned me. This was not a new story; he'd decided long ago that my act was far too horrid and awful.

Online he'd said that I could be racist, and homophobic, and upset the disabled, but the simple truth was he didn't like me. So when the news programmes and papers called me, I told them to speak to him. It was nothing to do with me.

There are a few theatres that don't like me. Usually it's because of politics, but they don't admit it. They'll put on Frankie Boyle but not me! It's all silly and anyway, I've other things to worry about. Sod 'em.

* * *

4 April 2013

Two more people have been arrested. One eighty-two-year-old was detained in November and has now been arrested, and a sixty-five-year-old man from Somerset has also had his collar felt. There are rumours, of course, but I've no idea who they are.

I've cancelled my Twitter account. I'm fed up with nasty people sticking their noses in. It may be fun but there should be a way of preventing nutters joining in. That's why most celeb Twitterers have someone else tweet for them and never get into conversation.

To make up for that, I've opened the comments page on the website. Now the problem is spam mail and offers of Viagra... that's all I need!

I didn't sleep well again last night. I'm sure my body is complaining about all this stress. I've been up since seven and have to work tonight in Horsham. My days are being spent in limbo. I can plan nothing and I have to be careful about what I think about. There are three main worries:

money; career; outcome. All this heat and stress, just because the police have let anyone with a grudge have their say. It's so unfair but I must keep trying to not feel so bloody sorry for myself.

God knows how Michelle is coping. She is a tough lady but there are limits.

I am now having a slurp... *ahh*.

Flo has sent Henri a statement re: Sassoon; Cameron has sent a statement re: Pushy; Steve Farr is preparing a statement re: Flim-Flam and Sassoon; Tracy and her father are making statements re: Wanderer. As for the rest, I've no evidence to give. I'll find some, but first bed – if I can find it!

* * *

I'd put a call in to the nice man from the Marlowe Theatre, Canterbury. His name is Mark Everett. I was hoping for a call back but wasn't holding my breath.

Then the phone rang. It was him. I expected a massive row but he was charming. Still, I went on the attack:

'Mark, I don't mind you not wanting me in your theatre, that's up to you, but you've gone on record and said on the BBC website that I can be very racist and homophobic and upsetting to the disabled. Because of your quote I'm on the front page of a gay newspaper that says I'm banned because of my views on gay sexuality.'

'Oh no,' he said, sounding genuinely pissed off. 'Where was this?' I told him and he clicked it up as we spoke. When faced with his quote, he backtracked: 'Well, Jim, you *can* be racist.'

I laughed and said, 'Can be, or am?'

'I never said you *were.*'

'Mark, let's stop this blame assignment and move on.'

He agreed. We decided that when we found a vehicle that suited both of us we'd be delighted to work together. I actually like him.

He later called Brian Shaw for the first time in ages and had a positive chat. Brian had been inundated with messages of both complaint and support. He told Mark that in the thirty years he'd been in the business, he'd never seen someone polarise the nation as I had.

'No one sits on the fence with Jim Davidson.'

I'm glad Mark Everett called. I hate being misunderstood or treaded unfairly, so you can imagine what the false allegations were doing to me.

And for the first time all season, I was missing a Charlton home game. I had to go to Wolverhampton to play the Grand Theatre, and Saturday was the only date they had available. Michelle was coming with me; when the show was over we'd go to Scotland to catch up on some writing and admin. We left Stockbridge two minutes after Charlton scored the winner against Leeds. I was elated as we set off for my favourite English town, to be followed by my favourite Scottish one.

The gig in Wolverhampton was great. Michelle and the doggies stayed in the dressing room while I did the act. But the trip up afterwards was hell, and I only just made it without conking out.

I was starting to feel the effects of six months worth of stress. It's okay to put on a brave face and tell oneself all will be okay, but it's in my nature to be negative. I have to work really hard to be otherwise. The trouble is that, when I bottle up all the grief and ignore it, at a time of its own choosing it comes whizzing back.

Once again, alcohol proved to be the trigger. Don't get me wrong: I'm not sitting with a bottle and playing sad records like I used to, but drinking socially can be bad, too. I do believe that whiskies are like tits: one's not enough and three's too many. Should I be saying this?

On Monday night we went to Nick's Bar in Hyndland Road. It was five o'clock. We had a few and were home by seven for dinner, which I cooked. After a glass of wine I worked out how much I'd had to drink: five whiskies, one and a half pints of Stella. That's too much. I slept okay-ish but woke up feeling awful.

That following night I had a reception for the cast of *Sinderella McFannie*, the Scottish version of my legendary adult pantomime *Sinderella*. I felt rough and four whiskies didn't make me feel any better. So I drank spritzers – four of them. I felt okay but woke up feeling like shit!

What did I expect? Alcohol is starting to take away more than it's giving. I must take steps to break the cycle.

Of course, on the day you have a hangover something happens to make the day worse. Flo wanted to do his state-ment again as he'd remembered some more stuff, as had Stevie Farr. Their problem was trying to separate the gigs: we tried to make every gig the same in terms of dressing-room procedure, times, sound, lighting. It created a warm, rosy glow and a feeling of security, but something out of the ordinary threw us all. When Michelle or the kids came, everything changed and was a tad awkward.

We tried to duplicate everything we did to be consistent, so consequently it was easy to confuse one gig with another. Add to this the passage of seven years, with an average of seven gigs in the same venues, and you had a recipe for confusion. I went into panic mode, as I didn't want the lads to confuse the issue by transposing dates.

As I paced up and down waiting for Steve to find his diary, I became aware of my aches and pains. I looked in the mirror and a frightened old man stared back at me. I felt sick, tired, and I'm now getting sick and tired of feeling sick and tired.

Michelle said I should go to see Dr Peter when we got back. But what for? To have him confirm what I already know: I'm not exercising, I'm drinking too much, I've got a fucking hernia, high blood pressure and the stress I've had in the past six months would have killed the average man!

At five in the morning I did some research on the computer. I was amazed at the things people put on Twitter or Facebook – and, more importantly, the things they *didn't* put on there. One of my complainants had 400 friends, and each of them had 200, and I went through them all. There was not one mention by her, her friends, friends' friends or family of anything about her allegation whatsoever. I made a note of my findings and would soon be sending them off to Henri. Whether they would be of any use was up to him. But I felt a little better. Things were looking up.

Then I went into the front room and switched on the TV. Margaret Thatcher was dead.

Chapter Nineteen

9 APRIL 2013

GOODBYE MARGARET

I first met Margaret Thatcher because of my involvement in the Sharron Allen Leukaemia Trust. It was 1980. I presented her with a cheque from money raised by the charity. The SALT was run by an ex-MP called Humphrey Barclay, who was slightly 'different' to other people and without doubt the poshest person I'd ever met. It revolved around the brilliant Scottish cancer specialist Jim Sharpe, who took the name of a little girl recovering from treatment for the charity's name.

Humphrey took me to see Prime Minister's Questions in the house. It was just after the Falklands war. After watching Enoch Powell sleep through it, I was taken to meet Mrs Thatcher. She was pleased to see me, taking me to a room with table and chairs, and chatting about my upcoming trip to the Falklands.

'This is where we decided to sink the Belgrano,' she said.

She never told me why! She then added, 'I believe you are going to Beirut for me.'

I was going to entertain the troops. We had 150 guys – apart from the Regiment, which was never broadcast – from the 165th Lancers in Beirut as part of a peacekeeping force when the Israelis invaded in 1983.

The reason, I was later assured by other people, is that Michael Foot, who was Leader of the Opposition at the time, had jumped up in the House of Commons and said: 'Our troops are in deadly danger! Why are they in harm's way?'

Margaret Thatcher replied: 'They're not in harm's way, they're doing a fantastic job and have just had a wonderful show by Jim Davidson and his team!'

That's why they said to me: 'When you come back safe we'll announce it to the press,' rather than the other way around. So they weren't *that* sure: if I'd have got slotted, they wouldn't have made that statement.

I remember being up on the roof with one of the hooligans; I saw a pattern of red tracer rounds coming towards us, whizzing over our heads, and then heard machine gun fire. I said to him, 'Why are there no tracer bullets for that second lot of fire? Are these invisible bullets?'

'No,' he said. 'The machine gun fire you heard was the sound of those bullets that passed over your head 10 seconds ago.'

'How do you duck?'

'You don't.' Then he said, 'You never hear the one that kills you' – which was quite haunting and made me grab the whisky bottle for a swig.

I was later invited to Number 10 to give her the money that

Thames TV had donated to the NSPCC on her behalf. I found it flattering to be able to chat to a Prime Minister, and one event was to bring us closer.

I was invited to an exhibition of paintings an artist had donated as a fundraiser for the charity. The evening was put together with a chap called Anthony Hollandish, a big, tanned know-it-all who once told me Harold Wilson was removed by MI6 for being a Russian spy! He did, in fact, used to work for the intelligence services and just before the exhibition had released a revelatory book which pissed Maggie off no end. It would have been awkward for the PM to come face to face with the whistleblower.

So I was stood in a line of the great and good, David Frost and other upmarket celebrities, when Margaret walked in, straight past Hollandish and the painter, and grabbed me, whispering, 'Come with me.' She then got me to lead her down the line of guests and introduce them. You should have seen their faces!

When it came to the speeches, I thanked everybody for coming and introduced the PM. Her opening words left me speechless:

'I am here for one person... Jim Davidson.' She then went on to describe what a great bloke I was – and with that she was gone. I never spoke to Hollandish again, even when he spread a rumour that I was rude to a barman in the Savile Club.

When I formed the British Forces Foundation, Maggie was the first one I asked to help. Help she did, agreeing to become its patron with the caveat, 'Don't make me work too hard.' For our first fundraising ball at the Dorchester, she agreed to come but indicated she didn't want to speak. But I'd already printed menu cards listing her as a speaker. I went into a panic. The menu cards arrived at four o'clock, which left no time to alter them. Michael Wynn Parker, my friend and charity pal, had a brainwave: we Tipp-Exed Margaret's name out of her menu, but only hers!

Lord Archer sat next to Margaret and me on the top table. 'Shift over,' he said, 'I'll get her to talk.'

Simon Weston made the first speech. There was not a dry eye in the house. Simon, who was in the Welsh Guards, was badly burnt during the Falklands war. His life since, and his recovery, has been an inspiration to all of us I'm sure. But my other Welsh paratrooper friend, Denzil Connick, who lost a leg in the Falklands, limped over to Simon once and said, with a gallows humour only squaddies can understand: 'Hello Simon, we was only talking about you the other night. Was your fucking ears burning again?'

As Simon was speaking I saw Mrs Thatcher looking at her menu. A frown came across her face. She began picking the Tipp-Ex off.

Shit!

I looked on in horror. She glanced in my direction and gave a knowing smile. Then she spoke for forty minutes and received a standing ovation. It was a great moment in my life.

A rather funnier moment was when I had to sack the Iron Lady. The new fundraising man and now director of the BFF, Mark Cann, had arranged a polo match at Sandhurst. The Prince of Wales had got to hear of our charity and his equerry gave Mark the once over. Sometime later, Laurie produced a play about the Marx Brothers. He knew the Prince would love the show and he did, indeed, laugh his royal head off. His equerry dragged us aside and said, 'Now would be a good time to ask the Prince to become patron.'

We all went into a flap. If we asked the Prince to be patron, we'd have to ask Lady T to step down. We had an emergency meeting. In attendance were a general, a former First Sea Lord, an air vice marshal and the former second-in-command of the SAS. We fought and debated for hours but could find no solution. In the end, all these brave men told *me* to go and break the news to Lady Thatcher. I asked Sir Rex Hunt, the former governor and commander-in-chief of the Falkland Islands, if he wanted to tell her.

'Sod that,' he said with a look of horror. Dear Rex – what a man, a real hero, but not on that occasion! RIP, old friend.

I set off... straight to the pub near her house and had a large vodka. Then I was shown into her drawing room, where the great lady was waiting for me. I shook her hand and sat down, with my top lip stuck to my teeth and my heart pounding.

The first thing she said was, 'How's our charity doing?'

I nearly went into cardiac arrest. 'Uh,' I spluttered.

'Would you like a drink, Jim?'

'Yes please... a gin and tonic please.'

A Denis-sized drink arrived and I downed it as Margaret looked on in wonder. Deep breath...

'The Prince of Wales has expressed a wish to be patron of our charity'

'Splendid... we must have him... and I'll be president.'

We never thought of that, but *she* got it in an instant.

As time went on, I'd visit her at her house on several

occasions. After Denis died, a part of her died as well. Towards the end of our meetings over tea, I'd sit outside in the car afterwards and shed a tear or two.

I truly loved the woman... and I think she liked me.

Chapter Twenty

I've been studying how to be an amateur detective in Scotland. I've been burning the midnight oil and doing research with Henri.

Our research shows Sassoon has lived in Brighton since 2003. She already had two children, born in 2000 and 2001, and since then had another with a bloke who's not registered as father of the other two.

She recently registered with a modelling agency, which reinforces Henri's belief that she was using me to get publicity for her new career. Their website has a nice picture of her and she now has a showbiz version of her name. Her Twitter account shows her following mostly celebrities – hundreds of them!

So when her statement to Op Yewtree said she was going home from work – to where? Brighton? – how could she then get changed and be at the hotel in Eastbourne at seven? She must have been situated somewhere more locally. It's the same when she got a cab at the end of the evening: where did she go, Brighton? I suppose these questions will be asked if charges are brought against me.

* * *

The drive back from Scotland was brought forward as I have to go to Fred's funeral at Hereford Cathedral. Michelle has a chest infection. She's quite unwell and now has to sit in a car for seven hours. I've been a bit sick but I put this down to being stressed and never really allowing colds and flu to go away completely. I've also noticed the skin on my arms is a bit papery. I looked it up on the net: up with the vitamins, down with the whisky, more exercise, fruit and oily fish! Or maybe I'm just getting old...

Mitch's mum and dad are coming over to look after her as I go off to say farewell to Fred. They're quite marvellous and I don't know what we'd do without them.

By 6.30am I was off to Hereford. The weather was horrid and I reckoned it'd take me three and a half hours. I did it in two and a half. I passed the time with a visit to St Martin's Church, where the Regiment blokes are buried. Graveyards are sad places. They can't help reminding you of the death thing! Why do we talk to gravestones?

Hello Paul, been awhile. You'd never guess the shit I'm in...

Hello Vince, I wish I could've had that drink before you went to Iraq...

Hi Al, I saw you on that programme The Paras. *You looked good, mate. I see you were twenty-eight when you left us. Too young, mate, too young. Give my love to Nish...*

And so it went. I set out to find Laba Laba, the legendary Fijian killed in the battle of Mirbat. He was under a tree just away from the regimental plot. I said hello and left, feeling as low as I'd been in awhile. I shook my head to rid it of this self-indulgence. How could I feel sorry for myself while surrounded by these blokes? I shook myself out of it and set off for the cathedral.

The first thing you notice when you meet the SAS is that they're not all giants. Some are, but most are of normal stature with a look of confidence and determination. This never leaves them, even when they're all old boys like the ones in the cathedral.

I met with Goose. He'd flown in from Gibraltar to say goodbye to Fred and looked well. His hair was as long as ever and his Spanish cowboy boots gave him the look of a Gaucho. One by one, old mates shook my hand and wished me well. Sam Mallett, the colonel that runs the regimental association, asked, 'Are you coping with the onslaught?'

All the old and bold turned out, including Snapper and Mink. I told them I was the only one that hadn't aged and that they were now all old buggers.

The ceremony was sensational, complete with Fijian choir. General Arthur spoke, as did Fred's son Will and his fellow Fijian Jim Mac. When the service was over, I told Goose I couldn't go on the piss as the next day would make all my worries worse. He understood. I said my goodbyes and cut away. But it was a great day. I felt better for it.

On the way home I got a text from my friend at *The Sun*. I'd been barred from Margaret Thatcher's funeral. I went back down a snake and, at the time of typing this, I'm still there.

Why is this happening?

I called Mark Cann, director of the BFF. He'd had a call from Mrs T's old right-hand man, Mark, who told him I'd been invited by the family but someone from 'the State' said it'd be inappropriate. He didn't know who.

Michelle was dreadfully upset. She finds it so unfair and feels deeply sorry for me.

I drove to Cardiff to see Charlton play. And who should I bump into in the boardroom? Neil Kinnock.

'That's two of us not going then.'

He understood my anger, wandering off muttering something that sounded like 'fucking bureaucracy'.

Charlton played well. I sat with my friend Mark Humphreys, who always cheers me up.

'Fuck 'em.' He's right.

After a thrilling game, Cardiff got promoted and I went to the hotel bar. As I sat alone, drinking an undrinkable Spritzer, Mr Churchill's black dog came to visit me.

The next morning the dog was still there. I watched the funeral on TV. Terry Wogan's face appeared; Eamonn Holmes asked him why he was there. Quite right, Eamonn: what the fuck *was* he doing there?

Katherine Jenkins looked beautiful, but then she always does. She must have a frock for every occasion known to man! But I turned it off when Wogan came back on, feeling so sorry for myself again. This heaped more negative thoughts upon me. I felt rotten and desperately depressed. Michelle was in tears.

I opened Fred Marafono's book and read about his and Chief Norman's exploits in Sierra Leone. It was thrilling stuff. Chief Norman's now dead – he got arrested by the Sierra Leonean version of the human rights court at The Hague. But to me, and to Fred, he was on a par with Nelson Mandela: a Sierra Leonean who tried to cut through all the corruption and bullshit. All he had was the love of his people in his heart. That's why Fred loved him so much, I'm sure.

My mind, however, wandered at every opportunity. I couldn't concentrate.

This is the lowest I've been in my life and I'm in danger of losing it if I'm not careful. I've told the truth to the police but I can imagine DC Root and his PC mates using it to brief the 'victims', in an attempt to persuade the CPS there *is* a case to answer.

I'm now convinced that I'll be charged. But I shouldn't be. A ten-year-old could see through these allegations. The demons and the unknowns are smothering the facts and my will to win. Someone somewhere wants my head on a block.

Michelle called and told me that Simon Weston had mentioned me at Mrs Thatcher's funeral, broadcast on TV.

Good on yer, my old friend.

That evening I went to work at a little theatre in Cwmbran. I'd been there in September. It's only a small place, run by a trust; they have no money but the manager and his team love the place. So do I. The trouble is that when you look at the way things are done, you can't help thinking that these little places with no money don't have the same infrastructure for marketing as the big theatres. There's the quandary: big theatre, big cost; little theatre, low cost. It's a problem when you only really expect a smallish audience of less than 800. Is it better to have a half-full theatre of 1,200-capacity and pay 25 per cent, plus £1000 costs, and wait sixty days for your money? Or a little one for 15 per cent, with no costs, and get a cheque on the night? ATG and HQ theatres can add up to £3 on the cost of a ticket for a booking fee and restoration donation, which is scandalous. It's all about money, but John Bishop doesn't have that problem; I never used to have that problem.

*   *   *

It's now 17 April and we've still have not had the figures for the Charlton Trust charity gig in Bromley. See what I mean? But the little gig in Cwmbran was great.

Back to the lonely bar at the hotel again and then to bed with Fred Marafono's book. I wake up at 6.30, feeling no better than when I went to bed. It's going to be a long day and I'm getting scared. It's as if the whole state is against me. How can I win? Is the truth enough?

I can see why people who have been accused of this kind of thing hang themselves. The guilty ones don't; they *know* they're guilty. It's only poor fuckers like me, who have to accept a police force using everything in its power, including tipping off the complainants, to convict an innocent man. And for what? To prove a point? This is not seeking justice. What justice is there in a witch-hunt? This is persecution that's making both my family and I ill.

Has the woman in the pub whose skirt I was supposed to have lifted up ever endured this torture? Of course she hasn't.

I'm sorry I sound so angry. It's because of the funeral ban. This is a wake-up call, the first time that the reaction to these allegations has got personal. I fear I'll have to get used to this.

I wonder if the police will suggest counselling? When this is over I'll take steps – fucking long ones!

I got a call out of the blue from General Denaro. I've known him for thirty years; he became the commandant at Sandhurst and agreed to become a trustee of the BFF. He was livid that I'd not been invited to Maggie's funeral, promised he'd be there for me if I needed him and stated that he didn't believe I'd impose myself on women: 'Why would you have to?'

He trusted me. That call meant a lot.

This was followed by two texts, the first one from Smokey Cole, CEO of the Falklands Veterans Association: '*Hi Jim I really missed you today, it was appalling that you were not there and lots of people agree but that doesn't help you. Take care mate and I said the goodbyes for you. Smokey*'

Then there was Simon Weston: '*Mate, you were missed yesterday and we did think about you as you should have been here with us!! As you are one of us!! Take care pal Simon.*'

Another arrived later: '*Hi Jim, Said a little prayer for you yesterday to send your love* [to Maggie]. *Katherine Jenkins.*'

These had a double effect on me. They made me feel good that I had such great friends but reminded me of the position I was in. I lay on the pillow and wept silently. The black dog of depression snuggled up to me – the bastard!

The gig in Barry was a dump... move on! What a pleasure to come to Crewe and see a real theatre run by people who love it. Not many in though.

I'm sitting in the dressing room typing this. Jane Kennedy, one of my old dancers, has been in touch. It was lovely to hear from her again after all this time. She wants to help. I tell her of the allegations; she's angry. She's flying to Orlando tonight but promises to call when she gets back and, better still, will make a statement telling whoever reads it what's what!

I miss her. She was my favourite but we fell out over money. What a wasted ten years.

Emerson, Lake & Palmer assisted the drive home from Crewe. The sound was full on and the best three-piece in history kept me awake. They also kept my mind focused.

I arrived home and fell instantly asleep.

It was nice to be back after three days away. My PA, Sam, was staying over and we had a catch-up in the morning. But tax bills and demands and matters of extreme urgency mean nothing to me. I just have to concentrate on not going to prison for things I haven't done.

Rolf Harris is all over the papers. No sausages this morning, but how can I moan?

I set off for Charlton and call my musical director, Allan Rogers, to see if he'll do a statement for me. He's been with me since 1978; he's a philosopher, and he knows and understands me more than most. When I snuff it I want him to do the eulogy. His testimony won't help with specifics but it might give someone, somewhere, in this nightmare the idea that these allegations are daft.

We chat forever. Allan's life is one of great confusion. He has great talent, he's the most wonderful man, but his life is always a mess: he hasn't paid his VAT, or he's gone to the wrong gig, or he's lost his shoes. He's married to Joan, one of the country's great choreographers, who has the nickname of 'The Dolphin' (don't ask). They're the fairest, kindest people in the world; they have a daughter called Amy, who has cerebral palsy, and they've dedicated their lives to making her life comfortable. Amy is as bright as a button and has a really wicked sense of humour. She once spelled out on her alphabet board: *'Fuck off Jim.'*

Allan's son Sam – or Sam-Sam as we used to call him – was a sound engineer for me for a while. Sam, like his father, has a built-in digital delay. We had to call him twice, hence the name: 'Sam... Sam!' Sam is six foot four and married to a little person. I think the 'correct' term now is 'dwarf' but I hate it, it sounds so cruel. I know many 'little blokes', their lives are so different from the rest of us and kids stare at them. That makes them stronger in a way; they have thicker skins and a great sense of humour. But I digress.

Statements have now arrived from Allan, Jane Kennedy and Elaine from Torquay. My old pal Grant from the Windmill pub called, and said a high-ranking copper told him there's great pressure from Whitehall to take some scalps. It's outrageous!

It was St George's Day yesterday, so I set off for the Carlton Club for lunch. My son Fred came with me, as did my Charlton mate Mark. The guest speaker was Nick Soames; the larger-than-life MP gave a great speech beneath a portrait of his grandfather, Winston Churchill. The drink was taken and I'm typing this with a bad head. The day was full of good wishes and I signed Margaret's book of condolences:

Sorry I couldn't say goodbye.

I got up early this morning and flicked through the laptop. Freddie Starr has been arrested again. It seems he's been on bail forever and his nightmare is no closer to ending. I don't know what the allegations against Freddie are, and to be fair I don't want to know. I have my own problems, talking of which...

Michelle has been great but God, she has her moments. Like most women, I'm told, she's never wrong – even when the contradiction is in black and white in front of her – and nothing is ever her fault. Maybe these women who accuse me actually *believe* their stories too. It's mad...and a tad scary. I'm at the stage now that, if Miss World offered herself, I'd think twice! (Okay, maybe I lie...)

I have moments of negativity. I can't help projecting the worst. I fear that politics, not justice, is at work here. Every time I look at a newspaper, someone is in court for rape or something similar. I have to flick through these pages I've written and read the allegations again, and then I don't feel so bad. If our police are any good – and I believe my two are – then I shouldn't be charged, it's as simple as that. But if, as I suspect, they've been told to treat this flimsy evidence as the truth, the whole truth and nothing but the truth, or are being got at by superiors or someone who wants to prove a point, then I have a fight on my hands. Still, I'm innocent and that counts for something, doesn't it?

But I'm becoming lethargic. I can't be bothered to do things. Instead, I sit at the laptop all day, trying to find answers and a piece of information that'll convince the police this is all dangerously silly.

In a minute I'm going to run out of money. The bills pile up and I'm down £400,000 on income expectation, even before the legal bills. I just try not to think about it. When the time comes for panic, I'll panic, but until then life is on hold. No projects, no future and a feeling of doom.

I'm playing the little town of Lewes in Sussex tonight. I'll take the time to visit the 'Sassoon Hotel' in Brighton and see if I can find any evidence. At least it gives me some hope. Surely, if I can prove that this girl is mistaken, no amount of political pressure can reverse that fact? But should I have to do that? Shouldn't they have to prove that *I'm* lying?

* * *

The Sassoon Hotel was interesting. I filmed on my iPhone the distance from the bar to Room 169 (Brian checked his records for the room number). It's a hell of a long way. When I got to the room, two little ladies appeared behind me and let me take some pictures of the inside.

It just about has room for a bed and a dressing table. The loo is to the left as you walk in the door. It's far from the best room in the hotel. On my way out I had a strange feeling of *déjà vu*. Something was nagging at me.

It came to me at 6.30 the next morning: my plastic key didn't work. I'd said to her, 'Don't go away,' and raced back to reception for another one. When I returned she was gone. I found her sitting on the stairs, waiting patiently. Now I might have been confused, but I remember thinking: '*Of all the luck, the fucking key card has spoiled the moment!*'

She was waiting with a little smile and her shoes in her hand. But how do I prove that? Do I have to? Or does she have to *disprove* it?

Chapter Twenty-One

27 APRIL 2013

I'M IN DURHAM TO WATCH CHARLTON PLAY MIDDLESBROUGH.

Max Clifford has been charged with eleven counts of indecent assault. Michelle calls and gives me the news. She is panicking. I try to reassure her that I'm *not* Max Clifford.

But my mind was racing. Had we got enough evidence? Enough information? How much more was there to get? Had we done enough? There must come a point when you think, *'Right, there's enough here now to avoid charges by the CPS.'* Or maybe there was something we were missing?

Time will tell. In the meantime life goes on: meet Mark in reception at twelve; drive to Middlesbrough; keep fingers crossed.

Why is this happening? I feel dreamlike today.

Charlton have to win and Millwall and Bolton must lose if we're to make the play-offs. But what chance is there of that, with my luck?

Last night I had a drink or two with the Charlton manager, Chrissy Powell. He's a great bloke, I adore what he's done (or is still trying to do) at the Valley. We had a good natter and not once did he mention the elephant in the room, sat right there next to us. Eventually she got up and left!

He asked if I was okay and seemed concerned. He listened carefully. It made me feel better talking to him. I can see why he gets the best out of people. He has a way about him that makes you want to be a better person.

Please, gaffer, make all this go away!

Mark and I followed the coach to Middlesbrough and went into the director's lounge. We quickly buggered off when we discovered a better lounge, complete with proper food. After a nice lunch, a man announced that Graeme Souness would be speaking – then later he said that Graeme was busy. I told him I'd have a go if he liked. He did like, and five minutes later I had the place in stitches.

Mark said, 'You amaze me, you're worried to death and hungover yet you still get up and chat. How do you do it?'

I told him I had to do it. It's nice to remind myself of who I am. Today, at that lounge, I wanted to be liked, I wanted people to think, '*He's alright, him.*' That's me all over.

It used to be called a 'show-off', craving attention and love to boost one's self-esteem. Rape? It's not me. For me, rape doesn't fall into that pattern.

Charlton played brilliantly and at halftime we were two up! Typically, we then drew 2–2. Millwall lost and Bolton drew. Goodbye play-offs.

We took the scenic route to Glasgow and fell into the pub knackered. A quick pint and a pizza later, we collapsed into our beds. Mark left at 5.30 the next morning. I'll stay here for a couple of days to do some admin and find out where the next quid's coming from.

The *Mirror* has published another of those silhouette pictures; this time the suspect is a man in his seventies. I wonder who it is.

My mind is working overtime. I sit at the computer and search. I now know most of Sassoon's family. They seem to have a lot of different partners and kids. Sassoon has three by two and her sister four by two. Mum has a boyfriend and a stepchild from his previous.

I don't know why I do this. What am I expecting to find? A confession from her to say she was wrong? Well, you never know till you look.

* * *

It was Jimmy Tarbuck. What the hell is going on?

Some tit on the television, a so-called policeman, has announced that 'victims' must come forward and tell them if they've been abused. On the same day, Lord Patten, Chairman of the BBC Trust, referred to the Crown Prosecution Service's reasons to arrest. He might as well have put an advert online saying: '*If anyone else has got some complaints, don't hesitate. This is the season for arresting people without any fucking case.*' It was like putting a card in the shop window, it opened the flood-gates: open season against celebrities, fame and fortune for nutters and opportunists.

I have a feeling deep in my gut that this is not over. I feel that someone somewhere is creating a sorry story for money, fame and, best of all, the pleasure of fucking someone's life up.

Will someone stop this before something horrible happens?

Chapter Twenty-Two

Something horrible has happened. Henri emailed me: DC Root wants to move the bail date to July. He says that he's busy; I bet he is. He also wants to talk to me about two details that are, in his words, 'bubbling under'.

He mentioned the Falklands to Henri, and says it's about stuff that was in the *Mirror* in October. My alarm bell started ringing. The story didn't make sense back then, but now it does. She must have been an entertainer in the Falklands. Here's her story from the *Mirror*, eight months and a thousand years ago! My answers to this nonsense are in brackets:

Speaking about the alleged attack for the first time in the wake of the Jimmy Savile scandal, [codename] *Penguin, 48, said: 'He tried to rape me* [she later said I did rape her]...

Penguin who was on tour with the star at the time of the alleged attack [she doesn't mention the Falklands as the papers at the time were concentrating on the BBC] *claims the presenter would offer girls his gold watch to look after, and he believed if they accepted it they were consenting to sex...*

She says she alerted three people [who?] *about the alleged assault at the time but nothing was done.*

Penguin, from Liverpool, has now reported the alleged attack to the police. [When?] *Detectives are expected to approach the star for questioning in the next few days...*

Penguin claims the celeb's minder handed her a gold watch telling her: 'Look after this for him.' Then as the star walked off stage after finishing his routine she claims he growled at her: 'I'm going to f*** you tonight!'

Penguin says: 'I just giggled, laughed it off and didn't think much more of it. Then after the show finished we went for a drink. He just ignored me in the bar, didn't speak to me. [Did she have the watch? What was it?]

'I never stayed up too late because we were normally up early the next day to move on to the next venue.'

Penguin said her roommate didn't come back after disappearing with another man [who?].

She claims: 'I went to bed and I guess I was asleep for about an hour when I felt someone in bed with me [the military beds are tiny, there's just enough room for one]. *I didn't hear anyone knock or come into the room* [how did I get in?].

'I thought "this is strange," I thought it might be my roommate and said "is that you?" Then this arm came around me and he said, "No it's me!" [So the light was off?]

'I was up against the wall, crying [she was in bed, now she's against the wall], *'Get off, get out.'...*

'He tried to shut me up with his hand over my mouth. Then he hurt me.'

'I was hysterical, I screamed when he did that. He was starkers in my bed [where did I get undressed?]. *Then someone opened the door* [wouldn't a rapist lock the door behind him?], *they must have heard me. He just legged it out. He just disappeared.'* [Did I take my clothes or run off 'starkers'?]

Penguin said the star's minder later told her that accepting the gold watch was seen as an invitation. [Did she tell the minder she was assaulted?]

The following morning, Penguin told her roommate what had happened. [So she just went to sleep and didn't bother to wait for her friend – or better still, get dressed and report it?]

Penguin also told one of the tour officials [who?], *but after making the complaint she says she heard nothing else...*

She came forward after reading the vile allegations against Savile [get away!] *and says: 'I thought, "I'm not the only one." I thought, "If he's done it to me, then I know he will have done it to others."'*

Penguin, who now works as a counsellor in her home city, said: 'He needs to pay.' [But of course I do!]

A spokesman for Merseyside Police said: 'An allegation of an historic sexual assault has been received and enquiries are being made.' [Let's see what was said then!]

Penguin was not paid for this interview. [She must have sold the watch!]

This makes me so angry.

The headline was something like, 'BBC TV Star Tried To

Rape Me'. If you look it up online, she never mentions the fucking Falklands! It was the BBC – that's what they were hitting at the time. Maybe the press also said, 'Don't mention the Falklands, it'll be obvious that it's Jim Davidson' – they were worried about being sued as well.

However, the context made more sense: the only dancers I used on tour in the UK were from *Sinderella* and were all girls I knew. I'd have to go and see Henri to find out the disclosure. I bet with myself it'd be different from the newspaper story.

There was also another allegation they wanted to speak to me about. This time they didn't want to arrest me, just to talk to me... that was encouraging, but what was the allegation? Who else was jumping on the bandwagon and how good was their imagination?

Henri and DC Danny agreed to me seeing them on Tuesday. I wondered what the other allegation was. Richard Littlejohn called; he told me of a story *The Mail* wanted to run. I crossed my fingers and listened. He said the Met police had an allegation made to them about a girl in the Falklands, going on to say they were in a quandary because they'd no jurisdiction over the islands. According to Littlejohn, they called the Falkland Islands police who said, 'What do you want us to do about it?'

I told him the truth; I'd not been questioned by the police about the Falkland Islands. Richard was on side. He was fed up with the witch-hunt, we all were.

I promise myself to be positive, but first I had a gig on the Isle of Wight on Friday, 10 May. The gig was a strange one at the Medina theatre, which is actually on a college campus.

It'd been shut for a while and hadn't sold many tickets. The show would be less than half full, but so what? We'd all have a laugh... and we all did. I didn't do the normal stuff but just reminisced about my life in southeast London – happier times. They loved it and so did I.

Twenty minutes after coming off stage I was driving up the ramp of the ferry. I felt good. My message light bleeped. Henri: '*Call me when you can.*' I did. He told me to take a deep breath as he told me of the accusations. I felt the blood drain from my face.

Henri tried to calm me down, reminding me, 'Don't forget, they don't want to arrest you.' A waitress in a nightclub up north – 1977/1978/1979, 'She's not sure of the date.' – claimed she was sexually assaulted, as did a girl in the Falklands... we were right!

* * *

It's Sunday morning and I've had three hours sleep. For the second night running I've tossed and turned and sweated the long, scary night away. Michelle hasn't been much better. She called Laurie yesterday and asked him to come as she felt that the black dog was consuming me. She was right. Laurie and his wife Marilyn came at about five o'clock. It was good to see him – although it was like lying in bed ill, opening your eyes to see your kids all around the bed looking glum.

Laurie, however, was positive. We walked to The Three Cups for a drink. The pub was full of my mates and the whisky soon cheered me up. The story about the Falklands was front page of *The Mail*; there was a fair bit of piss-taking but all said how ridiculous this was becoming. According to *The Mail*: 'A spokesman said, "If Jim Davidson stands trial in the Falklands it will be the biggest thing since the war."' What a ridiculous thing to say! I bet that was the paper making up some shit. You can always tell when they say, 'A spokesman said.'

My son Freddie called and told me there was a chat show on LBC about it. Everybody thought that enough was enough. I still hadn't seen the disclosure, but I'd see Henri tomorrow and we'd deal with it.

We talked about the other accusation. Laurie laughed.

'What's so funny?'

'Well, this is a blatant attempt at getting in on the handouts, the police will see this for what it is.'

I hoped he was right.

* * *

I went to Glasgow today to get my laptop that I left in the office. I felt naked without it and had been using Michelle's A&D. As you can see, it dosmt haf a spell chickker...

The flight to Glasgow was a blur. My mind is turning me into a detective, one who can't get the answers he's looking for. I am becoming Clouseau!

Laptop grabbed and packed, I headed off to the pub to find the boys. I'd booked into the Hilton, as I couldn't get hold of the agent for an apartment and I'd probably go home in the morning. Guy and his mate Donny were in the pub, and had been for some time! I joined in as best I could. The pub was full of pretty women but I couldn't look at them. The accusers had put me off women for life.

I fell into bed at 11.30 and watched *Boardwalk Empire* on the laptop. I awoke at 4.30 and felt panic stricken. It was fear of the unknown; of knowing this shit could go on forever. What was to stop it?

The airport was busy. I tried to hide away and read the new Chris Ryan novel, *Osama*. I started reading where I'd left off. The chapter was about prison; I started to sweat and shake. I was having a panic attack, losing it big-time. I tried to focus. I went over the allegations again and again, trying to find a safe haven in the facts. All the accusations were deniable and stupid but my mind kept battling with itself. I was cracking up, shaking and sweating as I dialled Goose with trembling fingers.

Goose calmed me down by giving me a lecture on truth. He took control of the situation. He took control of me.

'You will win because you are a truthful man. You tell the truth; everything you do is the truth.'

'Yes Goose, but what about the demons?'

The 'demons' were the political undertone. Something evil was in the air.

'God will deal with the demons.'

I felt better and called Laurie. He reminded me that the allegations came from bandwagon jumpers. 'None of this is you, everybody knows that.'

Stevie Lamprell called. His voice calmed my nerves. Where would I be without these guys?

I boarded the plane and finished the book. The bad guy lost; the good guy won. I slept my first undisturbed sleep for three days. The wheels hitting the ground woke me twenty minutes later.

I got the bus to the car park and set off for Henri's office. One hour later I was reading the latest accusations. I was right: Penguin's police statement was very different from the newspaper article. She now said that I raped her.

We discussed the allegation by a waitress in a nightclub in the seventies. Once again, the police didn't want to arrest me. Something had changed. They'd started to have doubts about these allegations. It was about bloody time, but well done, Danny and Paula!

I told Henri about the Falklands in 1984. We were both puzzled by why this woman had made these allegations, but she had and so we had to deal with them. I told him I'd speak to Richard Digance and see what he could remember. There was also Terry the minder, Dave the soundman and the band.

The nightclub allegation was silly. 'I have spoken to Trevor,' Henri smiled, 'he hasn't lost any sleep about the accusation from the nightclub; this girl is a liar and has admitted it, she lied about her age and gave a false name to the club.'

Henri wanted me to check all the books I'd written. Were there any facts that helped the accusers put meat on their accusations? It was a good point. I'd have a look.

I arrived home to find a reporter on my doorstep. I spewed out the normal stuff and went in to my worried-to-death wife. 'It *will* be okay,' I told her.

Much to the annoyance of Michelle, I went to The Three Cups to see the boys. She has my sister in-law, Billie, staying and they get on like a house on fire. That gives me a pass for the boozer.

Dinner was wonderful. Michelle started to relax. I was in

bed for 9.30; it was a big day tomorrow and I wanted to be at my best.

I slept till 6.30, got up and did the usual routine: cup of tea, a bit of toast, check the papers for what's going down. There was a bit in *The Sun*: nice picture, but I must get my hair cut!

I got to the police station at Victoria early, parked my car and walked to where Henri said we should meet. I opened the door of the bar and the place was full of TV cameras. I'd walked straight into a recording of that dreadful 'reality' show about Chelsea. I legged it, met Henri and went to the pub for a glass of water.

DC Danny called; we'd be delayed, as Paula was probably lost again. We had another glass of water and talked about the problems ahead: not my guilt or innocence, but the fact that the British police didn't have any say on the Falklands thing. Henri promised to bring it up with Danny.

He called and we set off. I felt strange, as if I was looking forward to it, as if I was going to a police station to complain about what these people were saying about *me*.

Danny greeted us with a smile. We shook hands and made our way to an interview room where Paula joined us. She looked well but we made very little small talk. Danny and his colleague looked passive and unconcerned. I hoped they were but you never can tell.

Danny started the tape machine and we did the introductions. He explained they were interviewing me under caution but that I could leave at anytime.

'Right, let's start with Penguin.'

'Before we get going,' interjected Henri, 'are we to assume

that this investigation is being carried out on behalf of the Falkland Islands Police? It is unusual for a police force in England to question someone about an allegation made in what is basically a foreign country.'

'They have asked us to do the investigation.'

Henri came back with some legal speak I didn't understand, and I'm not sure DC Danny did either. We plodded on. I asked him if we were going to do our normal thing: me gobbing off on a monologue and him asking questions.

Are you sitting comfortably? Then I'll tell you the story just as I told it to DC Root:

My first visit to the Falklands was in June 1983, a year after the war ended. I returned one year later. I'd spoken to Thames TV about doing a Christmas show there. They were interested. I said I'd go down in June and do a sort of recce-cum-dress-run of the TV show. I got in touch with Combined Service Entertainment; Richard Digance came with me and a backing band of four musicians.

DC Root asked if I had the names of the band. I told him:

Frannie Heywood on drums, Pete Stroud on bass, Smudger on guitar and a keyboard player who I can't remember. There was also a sound engineer called Dave South and a tour manager called Terry.

'Ah,' said DC Danny, 'she mentions him.'

'His name is Terry Draper. He worked for me for a number of years; I'll find him and get a statement if you like.'

'Yes please.'

'I'll get statements from all of them except Smudger.'

'Why not Smudger?'

'Because he's dead.'

'Oh.'

'Anyway, CSE had arranged a dance group called Night Time Movers...'

'Did you know they were called Night Time Movers?'

'I'd forgotten what they were called until I saw the disclosure.'

'You hadn't met them before?'

'No, I met them at RAF Brize Norton. They were a typical CSE-type girl group.'

I explained that CSE relied on the fact they had a captive audience who were mainly men. They used girly acts who, quite frankly, would have had no career if it wasn't for soldiers. I explained that I did a routine onstage about certain acts including Night Time Movers... and a tap-dancing duck! Danny declined my offer of telling the tap-dancing duck story, so I got back to the dancers:

The name Night Time Movers says it all. They wore stockings and suspenders and flimsy nighties when they were onstage, and their choreography might as well have been by Stevie Wonder. These acts were really there to remind the blokes what they were missing. Funnily enough, the blokes didn't like them much.

I told him about the worst 'vent act' in the world. On the 1983 trip we had a woman ventriloquist who wore a short skirt and stockings. When she started dying on her arse, she'd whirl around and her skirt would go up to show the 'webbing'.

I didn't tell the police that, while she was onstage, we sexually assaulted her dummy! She was on with another doll, leaving the traditional ventriloquist's dummy backstage. We all got our cameras and did terrible things to the little wooden bastard.

I apologised for going on a bit. Danny smiled and asked about Port Stanley:

It was below freezing. We stayed in a thing called a 'coastel', a floating barge with Portakabins welded together. The girls didn't stay with us, they were shepherded away somewhere, I think. This was a military operation and they have strict rules.

I went on to tell him about the shows. They were done in Portakabins, kitchens and a gym on the coastel. We helicoptered everywhere where we could. There were lots of minefields and unexploded ordinance everywhere. Fast jets were constantly on patrol. The Falklands was still very much on a war footing. The new airport had not yet been built and the islands were still on edge.

Danny asked me about the allegation. Once again, after I'd said none of it happened he continued to ask about the details. I decided I wouldn't pick holes in her accusation; that was *his* job. I concentrated on what I could remember.

'She was a misfit. I got on really well with one of the girls who mixed well and fitted in with the difficult job we were doing.'

'She says that Terry gave her your watch.'

Henri butted in. 'Well, she says *that* in the newspaper interview and then changes her story in the police interview. Can I point out that there are a number of significant changes in what she told the papers and what she told the police?'

I grabbed a bit of paper that Henri had prepared and read through the differences. There were many. Danny nodded and took notes. The WPC asked a couple of questions that I answered as best I could. We then moved on to the other allegation. Listening to what Danny read to us, it was the statement of someone with nothing to lose. I told him this girl was a liar and that I'd get statements to disprove her allegation.

Henri asked if the other people mentioned in the allegation were being arrested. 'Or is it just celebrities... like my client?'

The policeman started coughing and spluttering, and said, 'Oh, I imagine.'

We discussed the story in detail. There were two guys that I knew – these women had said the three of us went back to the hotel with them and basically had an orgy. They said they were underage as well, which was bullshit. It was *all* bullshit but they were trying it on and the police were aware of that.

Henri said to me later that DC Root's answer should really have been: 'There's been no complaint about the other two.' It was only about me, not the club managers.

But they were happy. We were done. I thanked the two officers and said, 'I'll get the statements.'

'That would be helpful.'

'You know this isn't me, don't you?' I said to Danny. It was a statement not a question.

'I wish I could give you my private thoughts,' he replied.

We left the police station and got wet. There were no photographers until I got home and one poor sod was waiting in his car.

Smile and look as if life is fine.

I'm starting to have the feeling that it might be... but I'm not counting on it. I'm off to the doctors today about my skin. I've also been drinking and peeing a lot. It might be diabetes, or possibly a stress thing.

Fucking hell... what else?

* * *

It's not diabetes. Peter, the doc, thinks that I'm drinking too much water, rather remarkably. As soon as I open my eyes I knock back the best part of a large glass, then another in the kitchen and three cups of tea before breakfast.

'No wonder you're peeing a lot. Drinking too much water makes one thirsty!'

If you drink too much water you can get into all sorts of trouble. I'd better take that on board.

Large Scotch, please... neat!

Chapter Twenty-Three

A couple of summers ago I had a lovely surprise visit from Val, my girlfriend in 1976, who now lives on Dartmoor. We had a good old catch-up. She'd once lived with my old tour manager, Terry Draper, and told me Terry now lives abroad and has remarried. We had a good old laugh reminiscing, and I emailed her to see if she had a contact address for him.

Penguin mentioned him in her allegations; she said he gave her my watch to look after. I wondered what Terry would make of this.

I sat in the hotel room at Kings Lynn. I was to work that night at the Corn Exchange and I was feeling good. The newspapers had announced that a further six celebrities would soon be arrested, but I was starting to not believe a word. It's not right for papers to lie, but they *sooooo* do!

My phone rang. 'Hello Jim, you looking for me?' It was Terry. I hadn't spoken to him for years.

'Hello mate, are you okay?' We had a quick catch-up. He was in Switzerland. I asked if he'd seen the story about the Falklands.

'Yes I have and I've had bets with my mates... it's a dancer isn't it?'

'Go on.'

'I bet I know which one.'

'Who?'

'That little one in the middle.'

'What makes you think that?' *This* I was interested in.

'Because she was a gobby little bitch that wanted to cause trouble.'

Thank fuck!

We nattered for a bit. I told him about the watch thing. He laughed and said it was ridiculous. I suggested he look her story up on Google, and he agreed to make a statement.

The phone rang again; it was Frannie Heywood, my old drummer.

'Hello Jim, can I help?'

Frannie is a great drummer and one of life's characters. Everybody loves him. He's big, loud, from Yorkshire and likes a drink... or lots of them! The stories of Frannie are legendary. The only drummer who could out-drink him was Keith Moon. I've known him for thirty years. He never changes and seemingly hasn't got any older.

The 1984 trip saw Frannie at his best. On Ascension Island he'd crept off after the show and gone AWOL. He was spotted in the morning, face down. He'd met up with some old pals; in 1983, when I first went down, Frannie went on the piss with the firemen at Ascension Island. He could hold more liquid than one of their fire engines, so they asked him to their basha for a drink. Then, in 1984, he tried to make it back to our accommodation and nearly made it, apart from a volcanic crater in his way.

He lay in the crater all night, covered in scorpions and creepy-crawlies of every kind. In the morning he awoke and checked himself for broken bits: he'd hurt his leg badly but, to his amazement and everybody else's, he'd not broken anything, including the bottles of Scotch and vodka still clutched tightly to his chest.

Frannie was responsible for nearly sinking one of Her Majesty's warships. I think it was 1983 in the Falklands, but we were doing a show on either RFA *Fort Austin* or *Fort Grange*, huge logistic ships run by the Royal Fleet Auxiliary. These guys are civvies, so the idea for the show was that two warships would raft up with the RFA ship. The crews would cross deck, then return to the warships, slip and proceed; then another two warships would come alongside and show two would begin. These were my most enjoyable shows ever.

In between shows we were invited by two RFA sailors to their 'house'. They lived in a Wendy house in the bar and were raising money for charity. They'd been there all the time that they were in Falklands waters. We joined them for a drink; Frannie was already a bit pissed when they introduced him to the Navy's own beer. Fullers made CSB especially for the forces; it was beautiful but as strong as anything you could drink. I had a half and left.

We waited for the second ship, HMS *Falmouth*, to come alongside. She was late leaving the inner harbour and still had to navigate the narrow straits. Word got to me that

Frannie had had six pints and was feeling no pain. I asked the officer of the watch to call *Falmouth* and tell them to hurry up, as we wouldn't have a show in another two pints' time. The ship, fearing a cancellation, engaged warp drive, hit the side of our ship, buckled a gun and knocked a couple of lifeboats off. They crossed deck like a speeded-up Benny Hill chase and the show commenced.

Val McKenna, my girl guitarist, sang a wonderful song about missing one's loved ones. The sailors wept and so did I. These days were the happiest in my life.

As for Frannie, he was a legend. We soon found a nickname for him: I made up a joke that a soldier had asked what the drummer's name was. I told him, 'Frannie... Fanny with an "r".' Later, after a skin-full, the soldier said to Frannie, 'Want a drink, Crunt?'

In Port San Carlos, two hours before the show, Frannie was attempting to assemble his drum kit. A crowd of squaddies with nothing to do were sat waiting. They started to notice this pissed bloke trying to put the drums together, closing one eye to thread the cymbals onto their stands. When Fran had finished they cheered and applauded. Frannie, ever the showman, took a bow and promptly fell backwards into the kit, demolishing it. Cue hysterics!

He turned up in the mess. 'Frannie,' I said.

'Yes, Boss?'

'Go to bed.'

'Yes, Boss.'

Two hours later he was as right as rain, downing his cans of beer like there was no tomorrow.

It was good to hear his voice again. But his first words

about the allegations were, 'I can't remember a fucking thing... you know me!'

But he had a go and a two-page statement later came through to Henri. I also called my old friend Richard Astbury, who was appalled at the Falklands accusation. Richard had run CSE for a number of years, and would send a statement.

My friend Smokey Cole had been in touch with the Falklands and had heard nothing. Smokey was chief stoker on HMS *Intrepid* during the Falklands war, who famously had to throw a hand grenade out of a window when it was discovered rolling around in a tumble dryer. Smokey is now Chief Executive of the Falklands Veteran Association, which I helped to set up and which built a fabulous holiday home in the Falklands for veterans to stay rent-free and get rid of the odd demon.

'No one believes it, Jim,' he said of the islanders' attitude to the accusations against me.

Chapter Twenty-Four

23 MAY 2013

Jimmy Tarbuck is on the front page of *The Sun*; Rolf Harris has done a gig in Bristol; the newspaper reports of DLT and Gary Glitter have gone quiet; no news of The Stoker; I have to do a gig in Southsea; I'm having gigs cancelled and so far am £450,000 out of pocket; I've not been charged; I have two more statements to get in and then we go on the front foot, and keep hoping. If they don't charge me on 11 July, I'll be the happiest man alive. If they do... well, let's not go there.

Steve Farr has come back to work after his spell of R&R. He now has a dent in his head. It's difficult to tell whether it's affected him as he always acts so differently! But it's good to have him back, to have decent monitors onstage and to see a bit of merchandise again.

This morning sees the news full of the tragic and horrifying story of the soldier murdered in Woolwich. What a terrible thing to happen! According to people I know in Woolwich, armed police shot the two accused while their unarmed colleagues hid behind hedges and waited for the posse to come. I can't blame them, and I hope this action doesn't lead to a kneejerk reaction against Muslims. Most will be as horrified at this as anyone. During my time in Dubai I learned a lot about Islam. These murders are not part of this religion; the killers are nutters plain and simple – and born in Britain.

Also in the papers today: Rolf Harris being questioned and re-bailed until August; there is a sad report of a man hanging himself after accusations of being a paedophile; I keep hearing stories of people owning up and pleading guilty because they want the horrendous pressure to end. Fuck that for a lark! Not me – I'm going to fight the bastards.

Mark Humphreys calls me every day. He is a clever bloke and is convinced I won't be charged: 'They have to prove beyond a reasonable doubt.' I haven't gone into details about all the accusations with him, so let's look at them one at a time from a lawyer's point of view. I compiled this list because it was going over in my mind every day, and every day something else happened. So you make a shopping list: What have we got? Have we done enough?

1/Wag
A/The venue has changed from the Palladium to the Pavilion, Slough, after we proved it couldn't be the Palladium.
B/She doesn't know what year.
C/She has no witnesses.
D/She says she bit my penis. I have doctor's reports to say that's not the case.

E/Her story is childlike.

2/Scouser

A/She says it was 1988 – I didn't meet The Stoker until 1989.

B/She doesn't know the hotel.

C/She doesn't know the venue.

D/She told the papers before she told the police.

E/She's got the car wrong.

F/She claims she phoned me. How would she have got my number? Where would she call?

G/She stayed the night and claims to have spoken to me at the bar the next day.

H/She claims to have bitten my penis – the doctor's statement will disprove this.

3/Sassoon

A/She claims she was drunk but can remember details.

B/Where did her friend go?

C/Why did she 'go to his room to be sick' when it's 165 paces past a ladies' toilet?

D/No witness.

E/No DNA.

F/Why did she call me three times?

G/Why did she text '*Git*'?

H/I have Flo as a witness.

J/She has a desire to be famous.

4/Flim-Flam

A/She claims she worked at the upstairs bar – there isn't one at this venue.

B/I've never worn a velvet suit.

C/I've never had a chauffeur-driven Rolls.

D/Doesn't know what year.

5/Pushy

A/Pictures show no offence.

B/She never complained to the police at the time.

6/Duff

Witness statement from Dragon, my old contestant researcher.

7/Seaside

Witness statement from Tracy Belton (ex-wife).

8/Wanderer

A/Witness statement from Bert Hilton and Tracy.

9/Doggen

This is just silly so I've not bothered! How could anybody remember what happened in 1978? And is twanging a woman's suspender belt *really* that important?

I won't bother with the last two that I was questioned about, as I haven't been arrested for them – although we have eight witness statements re: these accusations that we've given to DC Danny. When I look at these it gives me hope... for a couple of days, and then I start to feel sorry for myself again and wish it was all a dream. It's like a constant toothache. Audiences haven't been good either and it'll get worse if I'm charged – though please God I won't be.

'*Is there no help for the widow's son?*'

Chapter Twenty-Five

28 MAY 2013

There have been no more arrests, despite newspapers claiming, 'More arrests are imminent'. We've made more disclosures to the police, collecting and sending a total of twenty statements. If nothing else, they must be happy that we're doing their jobs. We must now wait and gather more evidence.

Bertie is now playing with Oscar. The summer is coming. Michelle looks more beautiful than ever and life is good. However...

We're both frightened. We've had the worst six months of our lives. But we're together, and these women, for all their allegations, won't change that!

My pal Gordon emailed me, concerned that I shouldn't be telling the police everything as they'll use it against me. He believes we're wrong to provide statements from witnesses. I told him that, by doing so, we might prevent charges being brought, which is the most important thing at the moment.

But then a strange thing happened yesterday that makes you wonder if there really are demons in the air.

Richard Digance is coming to dinner. We're going to thrash out what we're going to do on tour. Having said that, we'll probably get pissed and talk bollocks.

I popped into the local fishing shop to get some stuff for Sunday's fishing trip. I said to the guys that work there, 'You buggers got me in trouble – a piece of sweetcorn was found in my fishing jacket at the police station.'

Then a smiling man behind me said, 'I haven't seen you for a while.'

I asked him where he'd last seen me. 'The Falklands... with the Night Time Movers.'

'Bloody hell!' I asked him how he remembered their name.

He said with a grin, 'It was those knickers and nighties.'

Well I never! I couldn't remember their name until I got the disclosure from the police.

I arrived home and there was a letter waiting for me. It was from Penguin's solicitor. She was claiming damages from me – demons or what?

Richard was on good form. I cooked a moussaka, washed down with a vineyard of wine and a barrel of Scotch.

I've a bad head today. I also have the 'beer fear'; the dreaded feeling that doom is around the corner. It wouldn't surprise me!

I don't know how much more I can take; each new thing is chipping away at me. I have one more gig to do on 6 June, then that's it till August.

If I'm charged, I'll deal with it and fight the bastards in court. Michelle is getting near the end of her tether as well, though she's been marvellous – so far!

I spoke to Henri regarding the Falklands thing. He says he'll speak to the police, because if we start corresponding with her lawyer we could be held in breach of something or other! I think she's shot herself in the foot. Firstly, she's claiming that the incident left her traumatised and unable to work. What nonsense is this? It was twenty-nine years ago. That's a lot of time out of work, even for a Liverpudlian!

The public will surely see what she's after, what this is *really* about. Henri points out that she has no witnesses – well she can't have, it didn't happen. But I have a few.

Richard has remembered a few more things. He told Michelle that Penguin announced to the audience, 'Oh no, I've started my period!' and ran off holding her Jack & Danny. He also pointed out that Penguin said I dropped my trousers in a marquee.

'But there weren't any marquees in the Falkland Islands, they would have been blown down the minute they were put up.'

Chapter Twenty-Six

JUNE 2013

My gigs have finished until August. They weren't busy, the worst attended I've ever done. The people who came loved the show, but there were only 300 of them... on a good night.

Brian Shaw says that business is bad everywhere. I agree with him, but some towns I've played in are almost closed. Margate seafront is now derelict. The town looks poor; there's no other way to put it. I don't think people want to spend twenty quid to see someone they saw last year.

I don't think the allegations had anything to do with it. They have, however, started to have an effect on future work. Some theatres are not having the show because of the 'current situation'. If I'm charged then none of them will have me. What will I do then?

Bill Roache of *Coronation Street* has an additional four charges of indecent assault. These allegations came one month after him being charged with the rape of a fifteen-year-old in the sixties. That was quick. Suddenly my ticket sales don't seem so bad!

We're now ready to present our new set of statements to the police about the latest two allegations. The QC has added that I've now received a civil claim from Penguin. This clearly shows her motive – she's after money, plain and simple.

As the days move closer to 11 July, my mind is becoming more cluttered as it works through the problems. The biggest one is money. I can win the court cases, I have no doubts about that, but where will the money come from?

If I'm not charged I'll try and get back on track. But what will happen if I am charged?

I can't believe my life has come to this. I'm the most frightened I've ever been. If I'm charged it'll be the worst miscarriage of justice in history... well, it will be to me.

I'm losing the will to go on. It's torture. It's like waiting for the results of a cancer test. I'm finding it difficult to keep positive.

Their evidence is non-existent and their allegations are flimsy, to say the least. But I have this dark cloud over me, and Winston's dog visits more frequently as the days go on.

Yesterday I went to see Bob Potter, the legendary owner of the Lakeside Country Club, 'the home of darts'. Bob has a fantastic lake which he allows me and Bobby Davro to fish on. I've had quite a few big carp out of it and, as I saw two great fish, for a moment all was forgotten. I didn't have any otherworldly thoughts – even the demons had gone away, replaced by monsters of the deep.

Nigel Farage was at the club, preparing to address a UKIP conference. He made his way over to me. I told him to bugger off; it wouldn't be good for the cameras to see him with me. His response?

'I couldn't care less, I just want to see if you are okay and coping with all this nonsense.'

What a great, no-bullshit bloke he is. He cheered me up, so I told myself to be positive. I went to the pub and laughed too loud with the boys at the bar. Michelle had gone to Wembley to see some girly singers and my younger son, Fred, was coming down to stay the night. I had to try and be positive, and not make him worried.

Fuck it, I will go fishing!

* * *

The first one was the biggest. As I scooped the landing net under it looked a good forty pounds. Could this be my biggest carp? Was my luck changing?

The fish had the biggest tail I've ever seen. I slipped it into the weighing sling and lifted. Thirty pounds dead...

Shit!

I shook the scales in an effort to get that needle to move toward the magical forty-pound mark. It stayed on thirty. It was a great fish nevertheless.

I'd arrived at the Lakeside and scanned the water for any signs. Some of them were still chasing; late spawning I expect. Everything is late this year! The weather, it seems, has also been affected by demons. We didn't have the mayfly hatch here on the river until a month after they should have done. Perhaps they were frightened to have sex in case they were arrested.

I tried again to winkle out the bigger fish that I saw before. *Whack!* Another fierce take. This fish fought harder than the thirty. It had to be bigger, though most carp fishermen would tell you different. They would be right: fifteen minutes later I slipped the net under a beautiful mirror carp of 23 lb 8 oz. Life was getting better.

The phone rang; it was a strange number I didn't recognise.

'Hello Jim... Mike Payne.'

Thank God!

Mike was the boss of Bailey's nightclubs. I was pleased to hear from him. He was a CID policeman before making his way up to running First Leisure, the company that owned the clubs. He was amazed as he listened to the woman's accusation.

'They said they were under eighteen and got paid in cash... could this happen, Mike?'

I waited for an answer. Mike wouldn't bullshit me. If what this girl was suggesting had legs, he'd tell me.

'Ridiculous. It couldn't happen, no one got paid in cash and everybody had to be eighteen.'

I breathed out. Mike would be happy to make a statement to that effect. He asked if the police were taking it any further.

'They haven't arrested me for it, Mike. I don't think they believe it.'

'Good, it's all rubbish... if this goes any further I'll come to court and be a witness.'

We chatted for a while before I said goodbye and returned

to the lake. The big'uns had buggered off. I caught two more fish and buggered off myself.

Three more people had offered to make statements, including my old friend John Cannal from Yarmouth. These could only help.

Chapter Twenty-Seven

14 JUNE 2013

Thirty-one years since the end of the Falklands war. This time last year I was in the Falklands attending a church service. Let's hope I'm not back there soon, attending court!

Henri has written to Penguin's lawyers, asking them to clarify what they're on about. He has also advised the police that her actions 'show her intentions' and they do, plain and simple.

Last night was a heart stopper for a while. Let me explain:

Henri called at seven o'clock. He was about to attend a performance of Helen Mirren's play *The Audience*, where she repeated the role of the Queen which she'd already played on screen. He spoke in hushed tones. His phone was cutting out. I heard: 'I'm its....ri....at ...eatre. I have re... ed one ...all from... olice.'

My arse went tight and I called him back.

'I have had a phone call from someone claiming to be a

high-ranking officer from Yewtree. Apparently, one of the officers is going into the *Big Brother* house.'

I butted in and told him I'd seen the story in *The Express*. He told me he'd missed it and initially thought the call might have been from a crank. But the policeman told him an email would be sent, and he texted me later: '*HAD EMAIL FROM POLICE WILL CALL AT 10.30.*'

It was a long wait.

Michelle and I were visiting her sister Mandy, to celebrate her daughter's birthday. Lauren was thirteen and we joined in the fun, mainly a bloody great Chinese takeaway. *Yummy*.

Henri called at 9.30. The email was, in fact, from the inspector in charge of Yewtree. It confirmed that a former Yewtree officer was entering the *Big Brother* house. We wondered about the implications of this event. A Yewtree policeman in the show they'd prevented me from doing? Who was the copper? Might it just be Danny Root? We speculated on it, as the policeman hadn't been named.

I woke this morning at six and scanned the online newspapers.

The policeman was a white man in his twenties. He was not *our* man. What a shame – life would have been fun for a minute! It also said he was gay, so I really hoped DC Root was his partner – Mr and Mrs Root, what a hoot!

But the *Big Brother* policeman was a Dan Neil. He was very gay, with one of those young Essex accents: '*What evaar...*' I didn't think for one minute he'd gob off about Yewtree, but something else bothered me.

Henri had written to *BB*, asking for tapes and transcripts to be delivered after Dan's eviction or the end of the show.

They wrote back and told him to fuck off, in legal terms. He'd also written to the inspector of Yewtree, but here's the thing: a policeman first contacted me by phone while I was at Heathrow. It was at about nine in the morning, on 2 January. Why pick that date and time? I told the policeman on the phone that I was going into *Big Brother*. He said, 'I know, I've spoken to them.'

However, while I was waiting to be collected from the airport by another police team, I called *Big Brother* to tell them what had happened. They were surprised. They hadn't heard – well, at least not the people I was speaking to. So who had this policeman spoken to? Did he have a higher pay grade contact in *Big Brother*? Could this copper on the phone be the very man who'd now gone into the *Big Brother* house? If not, was he at the next desk? Whoever had called me knew something that the papers and the public didn't.

All the *Big Brother* celebs went into the *BB* hotel on the first. Surely, if they'd wanted to arrest me prior to the *BB* show, they'd have made their move on the first? Why wait until the second, unless they knew in advance that I was going to be a day late?

Could it be that this policeman on the phone had already started a dialogue with *BB* and was privy to restricted information? Or did the conversation with *BB* lead to his applying to be a housemate?

Was Dan Neil that policeman? And if he'd started negotiations with *BB* at the time as a consequence of my arrest, wouldn't that be an abuse of public office?

Personally, I think it was plainly for publicity. They'd come across this openly gay policeman who'd taken part in Gay

Pride for the police and who wanted to be in the *Big Brother* house, and they thought, '*Wow, this is pretty damn good!*' As it turns out, the guy was very good in it.

Of course, everybody went mad, from the Chief Constable down. Everybody shat themselves, thinking, '*What's he going to say?*' If the police thought he'd compromise Op Yewtree or say something to help us, we didn't want to make too much of a thing of it – because we didn't want it known that this was our only fucking trick to play.

Henri had asked for the date that the negotiations between Dan Neil and *BB* started. I couldn't wait to hear their answer.

Chapter Twenty-Eight

20 JUNE 2013

My brother Bill, our wives and I were having a night in the Highlands; we hoped to visit the spot where we sprinkled our brother John's ashes. I say 'hoped to' because we weren't sure of the exact spot; someone might have built a council estate on him.

But we found it. It was on the battlefield at Culloden. John wanted to rest there because it was where the last battle between the Scots and the English was fought – not including Wembley. We all had our private thoughts but we made light of them, keeping the moment happy.

It was a long drive back to Glasgow, where we had too much to drink before an early night. We went to the pub for a couple and the defence against Sassoon's complaint came up. Bill is an ex-CID copper and shared his thoughts; he said they have no proof and he's right. What proof could there be?

I lay in bed imagining my defence. Here's how it goes: Sassoon was twenty-four and had two kids by then. She got pregnant at the age of sixteen and two months. She recently tweeted her sister and said, with regards to having children: 'Don't start as young as me.' I knew the name of her partner and her children; I had their DOBs. In 2008 she had another child by another chap, and is now engaged to be married to a further bloke. On her Facebook site she says she has packed to move and announces that the wedding has been booked. She shows a number of photos of her and her fiancé, and looks happy. Sassoon has both a younger and older sister. It would seem her life hasn't been blighted by her alleged ordeal. She hasn't written of it on Twitter or Facebook, nor have her friends or family – not even a *'what a time you've had!'* sort of thing.

At no time did I instigate sex with this woman. She took the lead; she didn't say, 'Stop!' or, 'No!' She wasn't sick, or pissed, and where was her friend when it was all occurring?

There, I feel better now I've got that off my chest. Sometimes pessimism can creep in. I have to keep reminding myself of the facts.

Sassoon mentions money for her wedding twice on her web pages. Is this the motive we're looking for?

* * *

I haven't watched *Big Brother* much. I've texted and emailed Richard Desmond but, unusually, have had no reply, which is odd.

Dan, the copper, is mincing about and there are a number

of reports of the police having to be paid overtime to watch the show, in case he reveals anything. Today, *The Star* announced that Dan had been blabbing about Savile. According to *The Star* – which, don't forget, is also owned by Richard – Dan has spoken to a housemate who's just been evicted. It's a headline designed to increase the viewing figures; Richard is a clever bloke and I can't help thinking that the copper on *BB* was his idea. The question is *when* did he have the idea?

This hanging about is hell. What are the police doing? They can't *all* be watching *Big Brother*, surely? Henri says we must assume there will be other accusations. The police and the CPS are virtually touting for business, so what is there to lose? Some women must think to themselves, '*I'll have a go, might be a few quid in it... never liked him anyway.*' But I'd hate for anyone else to have to go through the same thing: not charged but financially 'up against it' all the same, because the police have taken these flimsy allegations seriously without verifying the facts.

Let's have a look Wag's evidence, for example: well, there fucking isn't any!

There... I'm feeling much better now! I'm off to the pub. Bollocks to the world!

Chapter Twenty-Nine

The strain is starting to show. Brother Bill and his wife Billie are staying with us in Scotland as I write these words, but Michelle and I are not seeing eye to eye – on anything. It always seems to happen when she has an audience – but of course, this is my imagination. She'll say: 'This is not me, look at yourself!'

Michelle takes any contrary statements the wrong way and says loudly, 'You've got it in for me today,' or she'll puff out her cheeks and sigh, as if to say, 'Here we go again, look at what I have to put up with!' Billie is her audience of choice, her soulmate, someone who can relate to her suffering – someone who is married to a Davidson, perish the thought!

I've always known how Michelle is never wrong and can never be held accountable. Now, because of the stress, it's getting worse. I try to hide out of the way and she does the same. Shopping trips take longer and bedtimes are different.

I go to bed first, then she comes up when I'm asleep and reads. I get up early, she gets up later. She doesn't eat breakfast and never offers to cook me any without begrudging it. Sometimes, it resembles two people with nothing in common sharing a house: her with her *Coronation Street*, me with *Dexter*.

With all that said, Michelle will be another person next week. She might even like me, until the next negative thought. She's the first one to attack anyone who's bad to me, but is blinkered to her own behaviour. I'm also liable to fly off the handle at the slightest thing. I've started to react badly to people who are getting facts wrong, or jumping to conclusions.

If someone says to me, 'You wore that red shirt yesterday,' and I know I didn't wear it, I'll make a big deal of it for no reason. I'm turning into a Vulcan – the only thing that matters to me is absolute truth and logic. If someone says, 'It rained all day yesterday,' I'll say, 'No it didn't – it stopped at four o'clock for ten minutes,' because facts have become so important to me and I'm just so sick of people getting them wrong, even tiny little things.

I'll hide away and concentrate on the allegations, waiting to see what awaits me. I'm really low at the moment, that's why I'm moaning at Michelle's behaviour. I should really be looking at my own. Mind you, when there's no one here to play to and it's the right week, there's no finer woman alive! I love her.

* * *

It was time to look at some more evidence, in the hope it'd cheer me up. I summed things up in my panicking mind:

How can you have a blowjob if someone doesn't want to give you one? Unless you have a weapon to threaten them with, of course, as the jaw is one of the strongest joints in the body. And the $64,000 question is who'd risk having their cock bitten off? Not me!

I want beautiful ladies to want me. I don't want them as trophies or for bragging rights, I want them to see me as *their* bragging rights! It's a form of boosting my self-esteem. I've wanted lots of ladies over the years, but I'd give up on them if I found they didn't want me. I pursued them, yes, or at least the ones I wanted to keep – but they had to want me or there was no point. I left my wives when I thought they didn't want me anymore.

I love sex, I love women, but I *know* if they don't want it and there's no point in forcing it. It's like forcing someone to accept an autograph: if they didn't want one I'd be devastated, so I'd never do it. Does that make sense?

I've had many sexual encounters in the dressing room and I don't remember them all. But I've never had sex with anyone against their will and I *never* will.

* * *

We had some friends coming tonight and I was dreading it. The party went well despite my fears. Comedians and actors Dean Park, James McInerney, Nicola Park and pals mingled with some old panto cast members, including Deone Robertson, aka Miss European. Cousin Bill and Elivia, the wonderful Scottish singer Clarke Stuart (who appeared in my Scottish *Sinderella* romp) and his lovely missus all had a good ol' time. It was kind of a working dinner, with me catching up with what's going on. I have a part in a play that I want Dean to look at that'll suit him down to the ground – a drunken clown who hates kids.

(It's one of these plays that I write thinking, 'This'll be brilliant,' before I go off it and write another one in the hope I'll write something good one day. I'm turning into Ernie Wise...)

My mobile doesn't work very well in the Scottish office, only intermittently. I returned from lunch and saw I had a message from a number I didn't recognise: '*Understand that you are likely to get NFA. Would love to give you some money for an interview.*'

Who was NFA? I immediately thought my remortgage inquiries had come up trumps. Then it dawned on me. With trembling hands I called the number.

I knew that voice. It was my friend from *The Sun*. I asked what she was on about.

She told me she'd heard I'd be getting 'No Further Action' from the police. My heart started racing.

'Who told you?'

'The news desk heard from someone this afternoon.'

This was good news, of course. But how come *The Sun* had heard and we hadn't?

She told me she'd find out where the story came from and call me tomorrow. I called Henri and he said, '*Hmmmm...*' I called Laurie and he said, '*Hmmmm...*' as well, followed by the more profound, 'let's not start sucking yet.' I agreed.

I told Michelle. She threw her arms around me (*swoon…*). My brother Bill said, 'Someone at the police must have leaked a story to *The Sun*.' I looked at the text again: '*Understand that you are* likely…' That was the key word, 'likely'. This was based on hearsay.

I had to drive back to Stockbridge the next day for photos to promote the tour. On the way, my friend from *The Sun* called me. She said, 'The story didn't come from the police…'

Shit!

'…but from the man who started this entire Jimmy Savile thing off. The ex-detective that did the TV programme exposing Savile's behaviour.' (Or perhaps she should have said his 'alleged behaviour' – here I go again.)

He'd told the news desk that he believed the file on me was very thin and that the CPS would not bring charges. But how did he know? Was he in regular contact with Yewtree? The file on me wasn't thin at all; it was full of my statements for one thing!

I thanked my friend and reassured her that when all this was over, I'd be available for an interview. Still, I kept telling myself, '*It's only hearsay and should be ignored.*' But *The Sun* thought it'd all be over soon and wanted to put a marker down. Henri said that type of rumour was better than a negative one, and I agreed.

Meanwhile, Michelle had turned into a detective. I was sitting in my office, watching The Rolling Stones impersonate the walking dead at Glastonbury, when she came flying in and said, 'I've been watching *Big Brother* – the filming of the housemates was done six months ago.'

'What are you on about?'

Apparently, someone had thrown a tennis ball into the *BB* garden with a note pinned on it saying, 'Dan is an actor' – referring to Dan Neil, the policeman from Yewtree. Henri had written to the police to ask some questions about DC Neil but had received no answer. One of the things we'd like to know is when negotiations for Dan to enter the house began.

Michelle heard two housemates discussing the tennis-ball incident. One said something along the lines of, 'We'd have noticed something when we were filmed six months ago at our auditions!' This would indeed put Dan in the timeframe of applying to be a contestant at the same time as, or very near to, my arrest. Was he the policeman that told me, 'I've spoken to *Big Brother*'? Was he made privy to the fact that I was going in one day late?

The *Daily Star* today (1 July 2013) has the front-page story of the tennis ball with the note on it. They are reporting that a member of the public threw it in. Michelle tells me that the ball must have been placed there by *Big Brother* as the note was plain to see and landed in precisely the right place for maximum effect. The theme of the show was 'Secrets and Lies': they were trying to create an atmosphere of paranoia by suggesting Dan wasn't a policeman but an actor.

We know a Yewtree copper is in there because of the flap the police were in. But the police have not confirmed the officer's name and they certainly haven't issued a picture of him. Is this Dan an actor after all? If so, then one of the other housemates must be the Yewtree detective!

'Kin 'ell!

Chapter Thirty

Another puzzling part of the Yewtree enigma is my arrest and how it was planned. As I've said, Op Yewtree made their move on 2 January, the morning I was about to enter the *Big Brother* house. However, everyone else went into *Big Brother* on the first of the month; I got a twenty-four-hour pass. They must have known this.

I got a call at about nine o'clock from my PA, Sam, telling me a policeman wanted to speak to me. We still don't know who the first contact officer was. (Henri has asked the Met if it was the officer now in the *BB* house. As I write, on 3 July, he's received no answer.) It wouldn't have been someone from the arresting team, as I believe they turned up at my house at eight in the morning, 2 January, expecting me to be there and to nab me just before I set off for *BB*.

It was reported in virtually every paper that I was going into the *BB* house, but very few people knew it'd be on the second: only Michelle, Laurie, Sam, the celebrity liaison team (BBLT) and me. So the puzzle is...

Why did the arresting team arrive with Hollywood speed and style, not knowing I wasn't there? BBLT knew I was arriving from Scotland that morning; they'd sent a car to the airport. When I got arrested, I'm convinced BBLT didn't know about it. It was a shock to them. But everyone at *BB* knew there was something brewing in the papers back in October. Laurie had spoken to them but they seemed unconcerned; they didn't believe the rumours in the *Sunday Mirror* and persuaded us not to cancel, as it'd give out the wrong signal.

When I called and told them I was off to a police station, they said they'd hang on and I could come in later. Then, however, they went into a huge flap.

The next day, 3 January, the day of the start of *BB* and my release, Richard Desmond was desperate for me to go into the house. So was this his plan? What a scoop for his show and his papers that would have been. But Richard is a mate, he wouldn't do that...would he?

No. Apparently a big argument broke out between him and the bosses at Endemol, the Dutch company that owns the rights to *BB*. They didn't want me in, but Richard did.

So let's go back to the morning of 2 January, the day I was arrested and the other *BB* housemates were in isolation at the *BB* hotel. The mystery policeman who first made contact in the morning said, 'I've spoken to *Big Brother*.' In which case, why didn't he know that I was at Heathrow waiting for the *BB* car?

I wasn't at home; he knew that, otherwise he wouldn't

have asked me where I was. So he must have had had a phone call from the arresting team.

When I arrived at the airport I couldn't find the *BB* car. I called BBLT and they told me its whereabouts, so I went to look for the driver. He was supposed to have a board with 'Davidson' written on it; I even continued to look for him as telephone conversations were going on between the mystery copper, Henri and me.

The car was nowhere to be seen. Did someone know I wasn't going to need it? It seems doubtful. BBLT seemed concerned that I couldn't find it – at least they sounded convincing! Here's how it all went;

Plane lands. Go to baggage hall. Call from Sam. Bags arrive. Call from mystery policeman. Leave baggage hall. Call to Henri. Call from mystery policeman, tell him to call Henri. Call from mystery policeman, tells me a colleague will contact me. Call to Henri. Call to BBLT. Call from arresting copper Danny Root, who told me his name (thought he said 'Danny Boot', name of a friend and fellow comedian), told me to 'wait there', he'd be an hour. Checked my bag into left luggage. Called Michelle. Called Henri. Called BBLT. Went outside. DC Root called and I directed him to me.

So had Root come from my house? The trip from Stockbridge to Heathrow is about one hour, the time he told me it'd take to come and get me. He said later he was based at Earl's Court, only fifteen minutes away from Heathrow with the *ner-ner* siren on! He had my policewoman in the car with him and an older lady who disappeared when we got to Heathrow police station. Who was she?

Now then, guys and gals, here's the thing: if the arresting policeman (Root) didn't know I'd be at Heathrow, he couldn't have spoken to BBLT. The mystery copper did, he told me. The first-contact telephone officer had spoken (according to him) to *BB* yet didn't know where I was. So who did he speak to? Not BBLT; they were the only ones who knew I was arriving from Glasgow; if he did speak to anyone, they weren't privy to all the minor details. He must have spoken to people who knew when I was going in but not where I was coming from. Neither *BB* bosses nor the police contact knew I'd be at Heathrow at the precise moment that the arresting team was knocking at my door in Stockbridge.

It wouldn't be necessary for my itinerary to be passed up the chain of command at *Big Brother*. This would be left to the two girls who'd been handling me from the word 'go', the Big Brother Liaison Team. Someone from *BB* gave the contacting officer only half the facts. He must have been shocked when he got a phone call from Root; I've often thought about how that conversation went. Here's my slightly twisted version:

'Hello Dan? It's Danny here; Davidson's house is empty. Are you sure he was going in the BB house today? He never went in yesterday like the others, did he?'

'He should be there, he's due at the BB house at 10 o'clock today...I'll check with my contacts... stand by.'

Anyway, back to the facts. He then speaks to Peter Mansfield from Laurie's office who immediately calls Sam (his girlfriend). Sam calls me, then calls the mystery officer back and gives him my mobile number. He calls me and finds out I'm at Heathrow, telling me to wait for a call back from his colleague. My imagination kicked in once again:

'Hello Danny. He's at Heathrow, can you get up there? I'll call you back, how long d'you reckon it'll take you?'

These raids and arrests take a while to plan, and we should also take into account that The Stoker was lifted the same morning. Would you risk jeopardising an arrest operation for two suspects at different locations, unless you had prior knowledge from a reliable source that I wouldn't be entering a location (i.e. the *BB* house) until the morning of 2 January?

They don't just turn up. The timing was planned for maximum publicity. However, it went wrong slightly because the mystery policeman on the phone didn't get all the facts from his contact. He felt secure in the knowledge that I was going in twenty-four hours after everyone else. That gave them another day! Somewhere along the line the left hand didn't know what the right hand was doing. But it created a conspiracy theory in the windmills of my mind.

Can you imagine turning up for a dawn raid and there's no one in? It must have pissed the arresting team off no end. He then repaired the damage and told Root to go and clean up his mess. Here's my version, with a bit of imaginative licence:

'Dan, you fucking dickhead why didn't you tell us he was coming from Glasgow by plane? Were you too busy

243

feathering your own Big Brother *nest? Thank God we didn't inform the press we were going, like we normally do, we'd have looked right arseholes!'*

'Fuck you lot, I'm leaving anyway, I'm orf to be a TV star, bollocks to the lot of yer! Evenin' all.'

Chapter Thirty-One

3 JULY 2013

SIX MONTHS AFTER I WAS ARRESTED.

I was to return to answer my bail on 11 July – which also happens to be my father's birthday. At two o'clock this afternoon I received an email from Henri. He forwarded one from DC Root: '*Unable to do your client's bail date please be advised the next date will be in approx 10 weeks.*'

Fucking hell!

Henri is out as I write, so I can only speculate. My best positive guess is they've not got enough to charge me. The CPS has told them get some more evidence. My worst negative guess is that some more allegations have come to light and they're investigating them. Let's see. I wish my heart would slow down!

* * *

Henri called at three o'clock. It was good to hear his voice. We speak every day and have done for six months. I'm starting to sound like him! I've adopted his speech patterns; if people ask me a question, I start to answer like a lawyer.

They'll say, 'What do you think the weather's going to be like on Friday?'

'Well, allegedly, as I'm only led to believe this on account of listening to the BBC weather report, it could be cloudy in the morning and sunny by lunchtime. However, that is just my own opinion and not to be taken out of context.'

I've started driving people bonkers. But why have the police moved the bail date without explanation? Here is what Henri thinks, and I agree:

'Firstly, we must understand that if they had enough evidence to charge you, you would be charged, make no mistake about that!

'Secondly, if they had other allegations they would have informed us, as they did before, and we would be discussing them when we returned for our bail date.'

Phew!

Bill Roache has been charged. Stuart Hall has been convicted and sentenced. These were not part of Operation Yewtree but were carried out by the Lancashire police. But Yewtree will be aware of the sentence that Hall received. The public and press are moaning like hell and calling for another review. The Director of Public Prosecutions is being pressurised into increasing the sentence.

Yewtree have arrested thirteen. So far, only Max Clifford and another bloke have been charged. They must be working like beavers to get more convictions. But it's the CPS that gives the go-ahead to press charges, not the police and certainly not my arresting officer. Danny has told me himself that he has no say on whether I'll be charged or not. All he does is fill in the forms, writes out the transcripts and give them to his boss, who then passes them on to the CPS.

My case must be a pain for them as:

1/It does not relate to underage sex.

2/It has no pattern.

3/We've presented twenty-five statements to the police. They've already acted on one of the statements that resulted in the Palladium/Pavilion fiasco. They must be aware that, if things go further and I'm charged, those twenty-five statements will turn into at least sixty. The trial will last for months!

4/DC Root has said on record that he didn't encourage one of the complainants to change her allegation after we proved it was flawed. He was aware of this because we *told him*; we also told him that any future changes of testimony will not go unnoticed.

5/I am a five-times married man who has made no secret of liking the ladies.

6/One complaint is not of UK jurisdiction. It's not up to the CPS to decide as the decision lies with the Falkland Islands Public Prosecutor.

We believe the evidence they've received has sent their heads spinning. DC Root has not even acknowledged receipt. The CPS or Yewtree bosses must be telling him, 'Go and find some more evidence,' but how can he? He's in possession of the complainants' testimony and our counter evidence, and ours outweighs theirs! Our QC points out that the evidence the police now have in light of our representations does not meet the CPS's evidential code 4.4:

Prosecutors must be satisfied that there is sufficient evidence to provide a realistic prospect of conviction against each suspect on each charge. They must consider what the defence case may be, and how it is likely to affect the prospect of conviction. A case which does not pass the evidential stage must not proceed, no matter how serious or sensitive it may be.

They also have a problem with this *Big Brother* policeman. They must be cringing. Dan Neil, as nice a man as he is, is quite frankly becoming a laughing stock in the public's eyes. To them, he's the one doing Jim Davidson's job after arresting him and preventing him from entering the *BB* house.

The police have been silent on the issue. The inspector has not even answered Henri's request for details. DC Root is maintaining radio silence and I imagine he may be hoping someone else comes forward with an allegation or two to help them form a pattern.

So far the police have interviewed one person with regard to the allegations. That was my PA, Sam. They were under the impression she worked for me in 1988; when she told them she was seven at the time, their response was, 'Oh.'

If the police want to interview anyone who sent a statement in via us, as they requested, they have to do it with Henri in attendance. In short, they're in a quandary.

We believe they'll be taking advice right from the top.

In the meantime, our lives are on hold again as we avoid snakes and wait for the next ladder.

* * *

My detective work continues. The policeman who made the call to Laurie's office on the morning of 2 January was DC Paul Marrion. Dan Neil is off the hook... for now!

A bail date has been set for 2 October 2013. That's a long time. What are they up to? They just can't let it go, can they?

I got loads of texts and messages wishing me good luck for the 11th. I had to reply and tell them that it's been moved. People's reactions vary from 'Shit!' to 'What the bloody hell's going on?' to my favourite: 'They've got fuck-all.'

The 11th of July saw me whizzing down the Solent instead, in my mate's boat. Better to be a boat owner's mate than a boat owner. Darren Ridge made a packet from the mobile phone business and has a fabulous boat. He's generous and great fun to be with, and also aware that I might get fed up answering questions. We went for a blokes' piss-up and for four hours I was free!

Another pal, Steve Lamprell, has invited us to France for two weeks but we can't go... dogs! Who'd be a dog lover?

Steve knows me inside out. He knows that two weeks away, although it sounds idyllic, would be as stressful as being at home. As he said, 'If this was me I'd never go anywhere until it was over.'

He's right to a degree. The trouble is, he and Gillie are so great to be with and are such generous, caring friends that I'd be afraid to bring them down with my constant worrying. Anyway, the dogs have put the kibosh on the whole thing!

* * *

I've had another of those wake-you-up thoughts, concerning Sassoon:

I met her in Eastbourne on the afternoon of the show; she turned up later in her best frock; she must have gone all the way to Brighton to get changed; she wanted to look her best – why? Did she go to Brighton? Or was she living in Eastbourne at the time? It's only a small thing but she says she was heading home after work; if she rushed all the way home to Brighton and then back for seven o'clock, she was on a serious mission; if she was staying in Eastbourne, it had to be somewhere where she had her best frock hanging up!

The father of her third child lives in Eastbourne. Surely she wasn't cheating on him? But no – I 'forced her', remember?

* * *

Bobby and Suzy, our friends from Dubai, came to dinner. I explained a few legal details to Bobby, who looked concerned. 'You should have told them nothing, what proof could they have?'

I don't agree with what he says. I believe that helping with statements, being open and truthful can only help convince the CPS that my case does not match their code with regards to the decision to prosecute.

I hope I'm right and we've made the correct decision. Only time will tell.

Michelle is pissed off with it all and piles on the negativity. She turns a shower into a storm but I can't blame her. It's different for me; I'm always on the computer researching and probing. She just has to wait. She knows nothing of the CPS code and bail conditions; she just thinks the whole system is cruel and uncaring. She's right, of course. The police must surely be aware that their actions cause great stress for the families of the accused. Nine months is a long time to be on bail. After a while your body adjusts to a life of stress; it becomes normal. This morning (Monday, 15 July), for instance, I've been up since 5.30; I went to bed at 11.30 after falling asleep in the armchair.

I've read these notes so many times I can virtually recite them. Sometimes I sit and stare at the computer screen for ages. I should be writing my book of short stories but I can't concentrate. It's as if my ability to imagine or create has been erased by some unseen force. The person I used to be is now gone, and all that's left is a man whose life depends on a group of unknown people who'll decide my fate.

Fancy a joke? Okay, here's one:

Judge: What do you have to say for yourself?
Accused: Fuck all.
Judge: Clerk of the court, what did he say?
Clerk: He said, 'Fuck all,' your honour.
Judge: Don't be a twat, I saw his lips move!

Chapter Thirty-Two

I feel like people must have felt when the 'phoney war' was declared in 1939. It was a Sunday. The air raid sirens sounded straight away. People were terrified and then... nothing happened. Nothing has happened here either – well, nothing much.

Henri has responded to another letter from Penguin's lawyers. He's told them he'll ask DC Root if we can actually correspond without breaching the bail condition of 'no indirect contact to be made'.

Otherwise, it's all gone a bit quiet. It's nerve wracking. Stuart Hall has had his sentence doubled by the DPP and some appeal court judges. But this hasn't affected me – I am *not* Stuart Hall.

I've now watched series seven of *Dexter*. Consequently, I now speak like a serial killer rather than my lawyer Henri. People should watch out!

Dan the copper has been evicted from *Big Brother*. Detective Michelle Davidson immediately said, 'What has he done that they've had to evict him?' I said that the public voted him out but the ever-watchful Michelle thinks otherwise. We'll see...

All this 'nothing happening' is giving me Henri-withdrawal. I don't know whether it's his reassuring tones that I miss in my periods of worry or the fact that, however bleak things look, he always makes me laugh my head off. But I've just put the phone down after a half-hour conversation with him and it's as if I've had an intake of happy pills. I can't begin to tell you how good he is, both as a lawyer and a friend.

The main problem, as I see it, is now twofold:
1/To be able to concentrate on work and be happy; to ignore these allegations and plan for the future; to keep going as if all will be well.
2/For Brian Shaw to convince the theatres that all will be okay.

It's a problem because I don't know what the police are up to. All the coppers and ex-coppers I've spoken have warned, 'Be careful what you say or do as they'll be looking to stitch you up.' Even my old mate from SOCA said, 'Don't trust the bastards.' He went on to tell me he thought the Yewtree brigade had acted disproportionately:

'Why the dawn raids and searches? Why the high profile arrest? Why the instant press coverage on accusations that go back twenty-five years? Don't get friendly with the arresting officers or they'll have you over in seconds if they can.'

He believes that if there's no further action to be taken, I should sue the police for wrongful arrest. He has a point. I believe the Yewtree mob didn't check anything in the first two allegations, otherwise they wouldn't have arrested me.

The first complainant – or 'victim', as they're now called – went to the police twice according to her story in the *Mirror*. She went on to say they did nothing because of lack of evidence. Well, has new evidence come to light? I don't think so, so why did the Yewtree officers believe they could get a conviction when the Lancashire police threw it out twice?

It's plain and simple: they arrested me because of some political agenda. Op Yewtree must be seen to arrest high-profile historical sex offenders. My arresting policewoman said as much herself: '*We must take these accusations seriously no matter how flaky they are.*'

It must be on the police's mind. They arrested me as a kneejerk reaction to Savile without checking or validating the 'victim's' statement. That to me is wrongful arrest, and it's the same with 'victim' number two. We told them that this girl was mistaken and we proved it. They then allowed her to change her allegation.

It could be argued that it was these first two allegations and my subsequent arrest that caused the problems. They got the most press; they did all the damage and cost me my livelihood. But let's put this to the back of our minds right now and wait for the police to come to their senses.

* * *

31 July 2013. Normal routine: up at seven and scan the newspapers online. Nothing.

I have to take Bertie to the vet's, as he's having his nuts off. And I thought I had problems. (Maybe they'll... but no, don't say it!)

Richard Digance and I have taken adverts in *The Express* for this Friday and Sunday. I hope it sells some tickets. Times are hard out there and people are fussy about what they spend their money on. I can only hope it's us!

Chapter Thirty-Three

1 AUGUST 2013

I've had very little sleep, this time for a different reason. Bertie misses his nuts. He hasn't been able to get comfortable at all and has taken to licking my face at every opportunity. I just about manage to drop off, dreaming of DC Root tongue-tied and crying in the witness box, when the little bugger barks, jumps on the bed and turns into the canine equivalent of a car wash.

I'm also starting to worry about going back onstage. It's always the same after a period of 'resting': I forget how to do the act. It's a good thing in a way, as it forces me to improvise and create some new material. It's still terrifying though. Thank God for Proprananol.

I start on the fourth in Bridlington – the heart of British show business! It's bloody miles away. By the time I get there I'll be a nervous wreck. I've been walking onstage in a suit, saying, 'Do you think this will look good in court?' but the trouble is that everyone's forgotten all about the arrest. I bring it up in conversation and people say, 'Eh?'

Lloyd Hollett is the support act. I'll watch him and hope to get into character before I take the step at 8.30. I wonder what I should wear. Michelle thinks my new suit looks smart, but in Bridlington? I'll look like a debt collector. I might take everything along and see how I feel on the night.

There's no news in the papers, apart from Simon Cowell expecting a baby. Andy D texted me tonight, an old mate from the Regiment who's now a barrister. He imagined that, because he hadn't heard from me, I was awaiting a trial. I called him and explained what had happened. I'm used to people saying the right things – 'They have nothing,' etc. – but Andy's tone was more measured. He's convinced there are other elements in motion, and that the police will look for a conviction as opposed to seeking the truth. He feels the CPS will be working their arses off or will be praying for something to come up: 'They hate letting people off.'

He's concerned and offered himself as a character witness, should things go the wrong way: 'You are not a sex offender.' Thanks, Andy.

Dexter's sister has gone mad and I'm going to bed. I hope Bertie sleeps and dreams of big bollocks.

* * *

2 August 2013. Bertie slept like a log. I didn't. Andy's hesitation was on my mind. Barristers are always cautious but they're clever buggers, which is why they're barristers.

I'm now worrying. It's funny, isn't it? I read these notes and realise that the allegations are silly. But Andy D is aware of the dark side of the coppers and the CPS. As he said, 'People go to court and lie like fuck!'

The feeling I have is indescribable... but I'll have a go: it's like being on a life raft floating down a river. You have no control of the steering. You know there might be a waterfall around the corner, or it might be a marina with a bar! Sometimes you think all will be okay and then... splash!

I'm only going to write now if anything significant happens. Fingers crossed, eh?

* * *

5 August 2013. Something significant has happened. Rolf Harris has been arrested again. He returned to the police station to answer bail and was arrested for other offences. It hardly made the news and there are no stories on the front pages. Why is this? Is it because people are fed up with it all and don't believe it? Or is it the fact that Syria might have chemical weapons?

I've just done three gigs. Once again, people were really supportive. They ask me if I'm worried that Rolf has had further allegations laid before him. They obviously want to say, 'Are *you* worried that more allegations will come?' Of course I am. Anyone can say anything now and the coppers *have to* listen. What have they got to lose?

And Charlton have lost their first game of the season. @*^&%$%£@! (This is a bad swear word.)

Chapter Thirty-Four

15 AUGUST 2013

I t's our anniversary today. We've been married for four years. Actually, it was yesterday – but Scotland were playing England at Wembley for the first time in fourteen years, so Michelle let me go. It was a great match, with Scotland narrowly losing 3–2.

The usual early morning flick through the online papers brought nothing to attention. However, this afternoon it was reported that Dave Lee Travis has been charged with eleven counts of indecent assault and one of sexual assault. They date back to 1977 and one alleged victim was fifteen.

Michelle started to worry. My heart rate went up a bit. Then I thought things through: I read with interest what the woman from the CPS had to say regarding the 'hairy cornflake'. She said that seven allegations would receive no further action because of lack of evidence. *Hmmm...*

Penguin's civil case lawyers have sent an odd letter to

Henri by mistake. Its heading is 'Penguin v Kings Agency'. It then rambles on about doctors and gives us Penguin's address... how strange!

I'm cooking paella tonight while Michelle is trying not to worry. I'm sure it'll be fine... the trick is to use hot stock.

* * *

'We must have a plan.

Secondly, we must have a man.

When we have a plan and a man we shall succeed: not otherwise.'

—Field Marshal Bernard Montgomery

The little summer shows are fun. There is something about a show in a little theatre during the great British summer; the weather has a lot to do with the size of your audience. First of all, it has to be sunny to get the people to the seaside resort in the first place; then the problem is if it's too nice they won't want to go to the theatre. The ideal thing is for it to be sunny all day and then to pour down at about 4.30, so that they leave the beach, and then for the rain to stop at six so they won't get wet on the way to the theatre. The trouble is that the cost of going abroad is now so cheap that people who used to flock to the seaside for their holiday bugger off to Benidorm!

I like driving when touring. It gives me time to think because it's the only time I'm on my own. I usually have some cunning plan for the future but all that has been taken away. I've realised that not only can I not plan for the future, but I must plan for the worst.

I left Skegness, a haven for mobility scooters carrying oversize creatures, at 10.30pm and set off for Great Yarmouth. Five miles on I decided it was likely I'd be charged and I'd better prepare for trial. I'd worry about where the money's coming from later. Right now, I needed to be found not guilty.

We'd done most of the groundwork but what we needed now was a job lot of character witnesses. By the time I got to Yarmouth (sounds like a Glen Campbell song), I had a list in my head of people who could explain what I'm about.

The first on my list was Lord George Robertson. I first met George when he was the Defence Secretary. I was asked to fly to Gibraltar and join HMS *Invincible*. They'd been away in the Caribbean for five months and, on their way home for Christmas leave, were diverted to the Middle East. The crew were pissed off slightly and I think I was a sweetener provided by the MOD.

I was accompanied by my old friend and the head of CSE, Richard Astbury, who'd later make a statement for me about the Falklands. We arrived in Gibraltar and had a lovely meal on the quayside, sleeping alongside and sailing in the morning. The ship was quite empty. The Sea Harriers had departed with the carrier air group and only the sailors remained on board.

The captain was James Burnel Nugent, a no-nonsense, get-up-and-go sort of chap. He was full of energy and seemed to be enthusiastic about everything. He looked like a young Eamonn Andrews and was great fun, though also very naval officer-ish. I did a show on the flight deck as we sped around the corners of Spain and Portugal at 26 knots. The show went well and afterward I visited every mess I could, having a ball. I even joined the captain for aerobics on the poop deck. I know why they call it that now – I was pooped!

As we entered the English Channel, the ship went into party mood. I learned how to 'duck race' in the CPO's mess and Richard learned to pole dance in the wren's mess. I found a poster of me and stuck it on the wall in the CPO's mess, scrawling on it: 'Vote Conservative and be home for Christmas.'

Midway down the channel, after a heavy lunch, the captain asked me if I'd make an announcement on the ship's tannoy system. I was taken to the radio room and handed a mike. I was at a bit of a loss as to what to say, having already met everyone, so I decided I'd make a speech as George. I depressed the TX button. I do a good George impression and it went like this:

'Do you hear there? This is Secretary of State George *RRRR*Robertson speaking... For those who don't know me, I've got the smallest fucking mouth in history, no teeth, a lisp and a Scottish accent thrown in fe' good measure.'

I heard the laughter echoing around the ship. The captain feigned horror and hid his head in his hands. I continued for a bit and got huge laughs. We'd just returned to the captain's cabin when a helicopter landed and the real George Robertson got out...

Shit!

I watched in horror as the first place he visited was the chief's mess, the one with my poster. After a while I could hear his distinct voice coming down the corridor.

It's no secret that I'm a Conservative, and George would have been aware of that – don't you worry! He entered the cabin and we all stood. I looked at Asters, who was struggling to stifle a laugh with a grimace. He was also a bit unsteady on the old pins... okay, he was royally pissed!

'Who stuck that bloody poster on the wall?' asked George.

'I did, Secretary of State.'

'Well Jim,' said a smiling George, 'I wasn't going to talk politics, but I said to them if you vote conservative you'll all be home for Christmas, 'cos there'll be no bloody carriers.'

He laughed his head off. We joined him. I liked him instantly. Asters let out the laughter he'd been trying to hide. The more George said, the more he sounded like my impression of him. Asters was turning purple, but I really liked this charismatic politician. He is without doubt one of the nicest, cleverest men I've ever met. But things were about to go wrong.

Asters, feeling no pain, slurred, 'Now then, Secretary of State, this strategic defence review... is it going to be a cutting, slashing budget?'

The captain's eyes rolled back and senior naval officers found something interesting to look at through a porthole. George was not put out one bit. He described to us in plain English what he had in mind, telling us about the plans for new aircraft carriers. He was very impressive.

'I'm going to speak to the ship's company on the microphone, Jim... you must come with me.'

Oh shit!

Asters collapsed. George was taken to the radio room. I made my excuses and stayed put.

Asters said, 'Sorry Captain, did I overstep the mark?'

'By miles,' said James without a smile.

Meanwhile, in a room at the bottom of the ship, George hit the switch and said, 'Do you hear there? This is George Robertson *sssss*speaking.'

The ship roared. Back in the captain's cabin I laughed, the captain went red and Asters wet himself.

When George came back to the cabin, he said, 'I don't know what you've done, Jim, but they're in *sssssuper spriritsssss*!'

I thought Asters was going to have a heart attack.

George became a trustee of my BFF charity a few years ago. He's regularly at meetings and is a valuable asset. He speaks a great deal of common sense and is a fun guy to be around.

The second character witness on my list was old pal Simon Weston. He was so upset that I wasn't invited to Maggie's funeral and he's been around me for years. What's more, he knows that rape is not my game.

Then there was Andy D, the ex-Regiment barrister, and Lea Kristensen – the co-host on the last series of *The Generation Game*. She is a lovely person as well as being drop-dead gorgeous. I really fell for her, but then a gay monk would have. She'd have none of it, so she knows I definitely knew the meaning of the word 'no'.

I'd put the complete list together when I got to Great Yarmouth. Yarmouth never changes. I have a love-hate relationship with the place. I spent a fortune on one of their piers once, renovating the theatre and transforming a glass beer garden into a fabulous nightclub. The theatre has now been pulled down and changed into a bowling alley. The glass nightclub is closed for health and safety reasons.

I arrived at the hotel at 12.15 and had a Scotch or two. I slept well and by 10.30 the next morning I'd emailed my list to Henri.

Later in the day we had a chat on the telephone. I told him Michelle went down a snake when she saw DLT had been charged.

'I knew it wouldn't put a spring in her step,' said Henri. He was in full flow: 'We must concentrate on our case and not look for possible similarities in anyone else's. It is pointless seeing as we don't know any of the details.'

I asked if he'd got my list.

'Yes and it is a very good list if, Gawd forbid, we go to trial.'

Henri now spoke about the trial. I'd always thought he was unhappy talking about a negative outcome, but seeing as I'd instigated the 'prep for trial' conversation he told me his plan.

'We will give them the pattern we think they are looking for, only it will be *our* pattern. We will, by way of direct evidence and witnesses, point out and make clear that *our* pattern suggests we have a person who likes the ladies and can charm them into his arms. More importantly, we have a person that respect women's wishes. He understands the word "NO!"'

Whenever I spoke to Henri I felt there was some hope. He looked at things the way that a judge would. Other people would say, 'You'll be okay,' and I'd take no notice even though I was happy they felt that way. With Henri it was different. He may have hoped we'd be okay, but we still planned for the worst.

The Great Yarmouth show was a bit iffy, simply because I had had a bit too much to drink. I had the witness thing on my mind and the niggles had started. John Cannal had taken me for a tour of Norfolk during the day. He is an expert on the county and to hear him talk about the place was a break from the black dog that was chasing me. We chatted to fishermen and gave them a few tips, ending up in a pub in Thurne. The landlord, an ex-Met Police detective, gave me hope and took it away at the same time. Like Henri he made no prediction, but he couldn't believe how incompetent and lazy the Operation Yewtree procedure was.

After a good day I returned to the hotel and waited. Then I started to pace and panic. Ten milligrams of Inderal sorted me out. I lay on the bed and closed my eyes. Sleep came for twenty minutes. I felt better and joined the lifeboat boys at the bar for a laugh.

The show was different this time, as I'd had a few and was messing about. They loved it. 'A lotta new stuff there, Jim,' said John, raising a knowing eyebrow. I'd been pissed and waffling about bullshit, and he was trying to be diplomatic!

I have one more show next week in Torquay. I think I'll take the boat. That should focus the mind.

Chapter Thirty-Five

AUGUST 2013

The weather looked good as I arrived at Ocean Village in Southampton for my trip to Torquay. Gone were the days of huge cabin cruisers; in their place was a 36-foot sports fishing boat named after my old vessel, *Afghan Plains*.

She is narrow, fast and low in the water, so it was crucial to get the weather right. The sea off Portland Bill can be dangerous in a frigate! The sea was like glass as I slipped and proceeded; it was 7.15am.

Half an hour later I passed Calshot Spit, at the corner of where Southampton Water joins the Solent. The Solent was like a skating rink and I had to force myself not to open the throttles. I'd need to conserve fuel; open her up and she'd drink more than my daughter Sarah.

The last time I tried this trip I had Brother Bill and Goose with me. It went sort of wrong when we got pissed in Weymouth. We'd set off at 4am to round Portland Bill. The sea picked up and was so lumpy during our 40-mile leg across Lime Bay that beer cans were exploding and spinning around like gas canisters. Bill grabbed them and sucked the beer out of the cracked cans, bless him.

We had to slow down dramatically and poodle into Torquay because we'd too little fuel to continue at warp speed. That was my fault for not filling her up, relying too much on my calculations and believing my fuel gauges.

This trip would be different. This time I had 900 litres on board.

The Needles approached and it became clear that the flat calm had gone away. I kept the revs at 4,000 and trimmed the nose down.

According to the weather forecast, the wind would be force one at most. Well, I don't know who predicts these things but he's an idiot. I sung a little ditty from my friend Richard Digance's act:

'*Michael Fish, he missed a hurricane of a hundred miles an hour. / So how can he detect an isolated scattered shower?*'

It'd been an hour since I set off. The plan was to head into Weymouth and wait for the early evening calm. The sea was a bit lumpy as I crossed the outskirts of Christchurch Bay. She was pushing 26 knots through the water and I was feeling good. This was what I needed. I'd had eight months of stress and worry; now all I had to worry about was staying alive and getting her into Weymouth.

I looked out at the sea and thought, '*If it stays like this I'll be laughing.*' Of course, it didn't! I got my first taste of what was to come was at a point called St Alban's Ledge, a piece of water that doesn't quite know what to do with itself. The water boils and the waves stand upright and growl at you.

I slowed to 20 knots and trimmed the nose up. I'd be doing some surfing and didn't want a breach, the moment the sea pushes the back of the boat up and she surfs into troughs nose down. My heart started to race and I reached for the hip flask in the back pocket. One quick swig followed by another got the old 'Para head' on; I faced the confused and scary sea with renewed vigour.

Within ten minutes I was free of the nasty water. Spurred on by the fifteen-year-old Glendronach, I decided to skip Weymouth and head straight to Torquay, 45 miles to the west. The sea looked calmer as I altered course and set a waypoint midway along the eastern side of Portland Bill. I'd tuck in behind some other boats and take the inside track around the Bill, avoiding Portland Race, which can literally sink you or cause you to commit suicide to get out of it! It's that scary, ask any sailor...

The sea was big but not breaking as I approached. The swell was about six feet, which was good. I put the nose down and slowed to 10 knots. The tide can flow through there at an amazing speed so I needed my wits about me and another huge swig. I rounded the Bill and set a course west for the 45-mile trip to Torquay.

I increased the speed to 28 knots and checked the fuel gauge. At this speed she'd be using 120 litres an hour. I wanted to get as far away from the Bill as possible then I'd slow down a bit, should conditions allow.

At 11.10 I was 12 miles from Torquay and started to relax.

By 11.45 I'd arrived in the bay, where I slowed down for a celebratory tin of beer and a sausage roll. I'd done it, and for a few hours I was free of my demons. I felt positive again... I was going to win!

I first performed at Torquay about a thousand years ago. It was a summer season with Peters & Lee. The first thing I did was buy a speedboat, a Fletcher. Halfway through the season I sunk it and broke my collarbone, just for good measure! But I had some great memories of the place and some old pals I was looking forward to seeing again.

Having checked into the Grand, I made my way down town and grabbed some pasta. As I sat outside, I noticed a smart old chap strolling along in the sunshine. It was my old friend Tony Rider, one of the Normandy veterans, a sprightly eighty-four years young. We had a good old natter; he was disgusted at what was going on and found it hard to understand. We ate dessert together and I arranged for the veterans to collect money after the show on Thursday.

By 7.30 I was battling tiredness. I'd been up since 5.30 and was feeling knackered. I'd arranged to meet Kevin the roadie's ex-wife, Elaine, and her second husband, Terry, for a drink in the Hole in the Wall pub. My old guitarist, Colin Reece, was also coming and we'd watch Drew Millen, another friend, strum his guitar and knock out some good old drinking songs.

What a night! The vodka took away the tiredness and Colin took away the blues. What a laugh we had, and I needed one. After Terry and Elaine left, I joined Colin and Drew for a drunken sing-song. How embarrassing...

Colin had been with me for years. He's a brilliant singer and guitarist, with a placid nature and a wicked sense of humour. He felt awful for me as I tried to explain the limbo I was in, giving up to sing 'Help Me Make It Through the Night' ('Take the ribbon from your hair') instead!

Breakfast made me feel sick. I hate the morning after, but I've learned not to beat myself up about it. It does, however, bring on the 'beer fear'. I started to worry about money. Things were getting tight. I wasn't going to get rich from these summer season gigs.

I flicked through the witness list and added some more, and scanned the online papers. I'd skip lunch and take the boat to Babbacombe, drop the anchor and chill out.

I called Mitch; she sensed I was worried. She's wonderful at sniffing out a problem, even from 200 miles away.

My phone rang. It was Elaine. She'd been to town with a friend; I said I'd pick her up from the harbour and we'd have a spin. We went to Brixham and had a good catch-up, talking about her husband Terry and how different Kevin had been. *C'est la vie*, eh?

Elaine dropped me off at the hotel; it was four o'clock. I lay on the bed and felt sorry for myself. Torquay was lovely but my mind was in a darker place. Where was I going? How would this end up? How would Michelle cope? Maybe she's better off without me. Maybe....

I dropped off to sleep and dreamt of Benji, my poor dog. He was lying next to me, looking sad. Suddenly he started barking.

The buzzing of the mobile brought me back to my senses. It was Henri. I knew something had changed. I had an immediate feeling of '*Here we go, phase two, I'm being charged.*'

'Hello Henri...'

'Jim, I will say this quickly... I have been a lawyer for thirty years and this is one of my happiest days: "No further action."'

I think I did a little dance. I congratulated Henri. We'd taken a risk, done a lot of hard work that could have been used against us and made the right decisions. I asked him to thank Trevor for me. Henri explained that the Falklands Police were still to consider that particular allegation, but all the UK ones had gone away.

'Go do your phone calls and then call me when you are ready.'

I called Michelle. No answer. I cursed and called again. This is her account of that moment:

I was sitting in the middle bedroom sorting out our clothes. I wasn't expecting a call from Jim, so when the phone rang I thought, 'Oh God, who's this now?' It had rung before and I ignored it as I was busy. But it was Jim. He said, 'Are you sitting down?' I didn't have time to panic. 'Henri has just called.' My heart sank. 'No further action.' I said, 'What? Are you sure?' I lost my breath and felt sick at the same time, thinking, 'Has this just really happened?' Jim sounded choked; I had tears in my eyes and felt strangely numb. He hung up to make some more calls. When I put the phone down, I put my head in my hands and wept. It'd been a long nine months and I hoped it'd now be over. I went and had a cup of tea.

Chapter Thirty-Six

22 AUGUST 2013

We'd done it. Our plan had worked. So what now?

That evening I walked to the theatre and had a drink in the bar with wonderful Wendy, the manager. She was thrilled. My phone was ringing off the hook. Richard Desmond called, offered his congratulations and asked me – no, *told* me – I was going in the *Big Brother* house tomorrow. I told him I'd speak to Laurie, switching the phone off just as I heard him say, 'Fuck Laurie.' I had a Scotch or three, went back to the hotel for supper, called Michelle and went to bed. I slept for eight hours.

The next morning was the perfect Torquay day. I wished I could have sailed off home to Michelle. I wanted to be with her. We'd been through the most awful nine months and now we had our first bit of good news. A load had been lifted but we were not together to share our relief. First there was the small matter of a show, and the dreaded press.

I walked to the marina, cranked *Afghan Plains* up and set off on a trip of 500 metres to just outside the harbour, dropping the hook in a small bay overlooked by the Imperial Hotel.

The phone was still ringing. I tried to duck Richard Desmond's calls as I was convinced an appearance on *Celebrity Big Brother* would be like sticking two fingers up at the police, and would look as if I was treating this whole episode as an escapade to further my career. Nothing could be further from the truth. I was determined not to look victorious, or to try to cash in, or to use the Operation Yewtree accusations as a gimmick. And I certainly didn't want to fuel accusations that said, 'How dare he be on the television now after all he's been accused of?' I love Richard, but if he doesn't get his own way he can be really scary.

My friend from *The Sun* kept calling; I ducked her as well. She then texted me: '*Call me you bastard!*' She loves me really.

Laurie was worried to death that I might say the wrong things. He called and told me not to speak to anyone, but I don't like that approach. It always looks rude, as if you have something to hide, which I haven't.

The sea gently lapped away at my tension as I took it all in. Laurie called again, really panicking. He told me what I should say onstage or, to be more precise, what I shouldn't say. We were expecting a lot of press. It was vital that I didn't put my foot in it or give the impression of 'I told you so'. I still had the Falkland Islands issue hanging over me and didn't want to tempt fate in any way, in the unlikely event that the accusation became an on-going process.

Lloyd Hollett called. I upped anchor to pick him up at the marina. He was excited, but then he's always excited. He's a good lad, is Lloyd; he's been my opening act for a while now and is coming on in leaps and bounds. He lives for comedy and showbiz, working hard at his act. But he's amazed by my lack of preparation and can't quite understand how I seem to breeze through it. I sometimes see him in the wings, open-mouthed in astonishment at what I'm saying. He's been very supportive of me and is now firmly in the 'sue everyone' camp.

We were soon whizzing to Brixham at 30 knots. Lloyd loved it; I loved it. It was the first day of the rest of my life. Still, the Falklands thing was unresolved and prevented a feeling of total relief. What I'd thought was a silly allegation, with not one iota of truth, was now the thing that stopped me from rejoicing.

Lloyd and I returned to the marina to face the media. There were three TV cameras outside the theatre. As we arrived at the stage door they sprang into action. I was careful not to slag off the police – what good would it do? I was also aware that dodgy questions would be put to me, in this case from ITN.

Their reporter asked what I thought of the women who made the allegations and the fact that they were still out there. Why did I think they made the allegations?

I swerved around it. How was I to really know why these women made the claims? I didn't say they were after money; I didn't even call them liars.

The rest of the questions were fine, but when I called Laurie he was furious.

'What are you doing at the theatre at that time anyway? You just can't help yourself, can you?' I was slightly pissed off by this. 'You should have just brushed past them,' he went on. I said nothing. I was now very pissed off and starting to realise this was not going to be easy.

Laurie was convinced we should say or do nothing until the Falklands accusation was over. He was right to an extent, but we still had to sell tickets. Laurie is also ducking Richard Desmond. Richard calls Laurie 'The Pensioner' – which is not very nice, even if it is from a friend! But then Richard doesn't like anyone to stand in the way of what he wants, and that includes an artist's agent – he can't see the point of having one.

I walked on to a tremendous reception, but the stage show was an anticlimax really. I had to be careful not to look as if I'd 'got away with it' as the press was in, plus a camera from Sky News.

Afterwards, I was drinking with the Krankies. Ian and Janette live in Torquay, so we had a good blather about the old days. They were pleased for me but angry that it'd gone so far. Val from 1976 was also there – as was Jo Urch, who I'd dated as a sixteen-year-old back in 1986. She looked well, as well as being £20,000 richer thanks to the *Daily Mail*. I thanked her for being nice in the article. 'I only told the truth,' she replied – for which thanks again, Jo.

Kevin's ex-missus, Elaine, was also there. It was a great turnout, but Elaine and I left them to it and went to the hotel bar with stage manager Martin Jenkins, and had a dram or two.

I was taking the boat back to Southampton in the morning.

All thoughts escaped me apart from Portland and its fearsome waters.

* * *

I woke at eight and had a bacon sandwich. As I looked out to sea from the hotel lounge, I glanced across at a chap reading a paper. I was on the front page. The weird thing was that I was 'the news', and a man two feet away was unaware that the news he was reading was appearing live at his elbow.

The sea looked lumpy. The wind was easterly, not good. It was a spring tide; in fact, the highest tide of the year. I studied the laptop and tried to work out a suitable time for my 100-mile trip back. In the end I took the boat out to Thatcher Rock and had a look. Five minutes later I was tied up alongside and looking at train times. The last thing I wanted was to be freed of all this and then to drown!

The train took me to Southampton, where I picked up my car and set off for home. I was looking forward to seeing Michelle. She looked wonderful and we hugged in the way we'd been looking forward to for months.

Then, within ten minutes, we'd had a row and I stormed off to the pub! Laurie had called, moaning about my 'posing' for pictures. Michelle joined in, blaming me for 'posing' on the boat, but the papers had taken long-range pictures of Lloyd and I in the marina. I told them both I didn't like their attitude.

Brian Shaw called and asked if I was doing *Big Brother*. I explained why I wasn't. He thought I was mad, as I was entitled to get something out of all this.

The next morning, my mobile rang. I answered it without thinking. It was Richard Desmond.

Shit!

'I've got someone to speak to you.' He handed the phone over.

'Hello Jim... it's Roger Daltrey.'

'Hello mate.'

Roger had been well briefed by Richard. 'Jim, why don't you do *Big Brother*? You can get your own back... tell your side of the story.'

'Roger, I can't. I don't want it to look as if I'm cashing in.'

'I see your point. Mind you, they cashed in on you!'

He had a point. Roger is a good man, like all the other people who think the police had dealt me a bad hand.

We chatted for a bit. I told him, 'Tell Richard it's against the law to put guns against rock star's heads.'

Richard took the phone. 'You're fucking mad... what's pissed me off is you never answered my calls!'

'I was scared.'

'Don't be an arsehole! What can I do to you on the phone?'

'Richard, you could rule the world on the phone... I'm sure I'll be there for you when you need the ratings lifted!'

I said it with a smile. His answer really made me laugh.

'You go fuck yourself... go do your gigs in Potters fucking Bar!'

It was Richard at his best! I told him that wasn't very nice and hung up. What a coincidence though – arrested on the day before *Big Brother* and 'no further action' confirmed on the day before *Big Brother*.

I couldn't do the show; I still had Penguin lurking in the

shadows. Richard doesn't know about the civil proceedings that are still bubbling under the surface. This really is frustrating. I've just turned down the best part of £200,000 because of this fucking woman. I look at her face on Facebook and my thoughts are unprintable, which for me is saying something!

I made the four-hour drive to Yarmouth, for the last of the summer shows, while running through her stories. There are three different ones: one for the papers, one for the police and one from her lawyers. She can't seem to make up her mind if she was raped or not.

Richard Digance called; DC Danny Root had phoned him with regard to his statement. I listened with interest. It seemed the police were now subverting due process by interviewing our defence witnesses without the presence of Henri.

But when Richard said, 'He's all for you, this copper,' it started my antennae twitching. Danny had said he was after a 'neutral statement'.

What the fuck does that mean?

He asked Richard if he knew the whereabouts of our driver, Corporal Smith. Richard had mentioned this chap in his statement, but I don't recall him at all. They spoke for a long time. Richard explained that we hadn't really seen one another for fifteen years. Danny was taken aback.

'I thought you were great mates and worked together?'

Root said he'd spoken to the other two girls in the troupe and had 'now got a picture', telling Richard he wanted to 'close the book'.

I put a call in to Henri, but he was out. I spent half an hour pacing. What was this policeman up to? He'd never bothered speaking to any witnesses to the other allegations. Something was afoot!

Henri called. I told him the story. 'It sounds like he is doing the work he should have done with the last lot.'

We agreed. 'Is he allowed to speak to our witnesses?'

Henri said he'd call him. DC Root later sent a reply to Henri, apologising for the break in procedure and promising it wouldn't happen again. How odd! But we're agreed that, because DC Root is preparing this file for another police force, he's actually being forced to do some legwork.

I wonder what he thinks about the allegations being 'NFA'd'? If I were a betting man, I'd have money on him being in agreement with the CPS. He's a good copper and the reports on Google say he's a winner with regards to rape cases. But you don't have to convict to be a good copper; one need only find the truth.

According to the newspapers, Freddie Starr is suing the woman who accused him of groping her in Savile's dressing room. Good for him. I sometimes daydream about suing the police, but in a strange way I don't wish to drag Danny and Paula through it. They're just coppers doing their job. I might be wrong but I always suspected he wasn't happy arresting me. Having said that, he was now probably scouring the country for Falklands witnesses. Good luck to him though; he won't find any. It never happened.

* * *

It was time to return to Torquay and pick up the boat. The longer I left it, the worse the weather would become. I studied the forecast and found a window. I'd go to Torquay by train and leave either Thursday afternoon or Friday morning.

I slept, dreaming of smooth seas and sunny skies. In reality it was lumpy ogging and cloudy!

The train ride down allowed me to look at the sea in Lime Bay. It seemed do-able. I arrived at Torquay, had a quick bite to eat and set off at 2.30pm. The sea was hitting my boat starboard side. The swell was about four feet and just breaking. I had a swig and told myself the boat would do okay... would I though?

I maintained 22 knots and arrived at Ocean Village, bruised, battered and shaking, at 6.45. It'd been hellish but exhilarating. I'd needed to beat something so I had to do this trip on my own. I'd needed to test myself.

I think I'll get a yacht.

* * *

Laurie and I have decided I won't be speaking to the press with regards to any Scottish dates. Six gigs in Scotland were booked when I still had the office in Glasgow. Now that I don't have the office they seem daft. Most are little gigs that were fun to do when they were around the corner; now they're 400 miles away and I can't do anything to promote them!

We've started to put together statements from people connected to the Falklands. I spoke to Anna King on the phone, who I've known since 1983. Her mum and dad, Des and Ning, owned the famous Upland Goose Hotel in Port Stanley. She was appalled that someone would make such an accusation and offered to state how long she'd known me, etc.

I also emailed David Crwys-Williams, who was the big boss of CSE, and contacted Dave South, who was the sound engineer at the time of the allegation. Both want to help, and that's all I can do at the moment.

Henri and QC Trevor have decided to send *all* the allegations and statements to the Falklands. Now it will be up to the Attorney General of the Falkland Islands to review the facts and make a decision.

People keep slapping me on the back and congratulating me, but I have to keep telling them it's not over. Richard Littlejohn has done another piece; note his astute comment on Yewtree:

This week, it was reported that the BBC had agreed to pay £33,000 each to 120 of Savile's alleged victims, at a cost to licence-payers of £4 million.

How many of the women who claimed to have been assaulted by Jim Davidson thought they might be in line for a nice little drink if they said it happened while he was presenting The Generation Game *or* Big Break?

We shall never know, but the implications for justice are disturbing. In the fevered atmosphere stirred up by Yewtree in the wake of the Savile affair, anyone in the public eye is fair game...

Davidson... has suffered serious career damage. He was due to make his TV comeback in Celebrity Big Brother, *but was dropped like a spinning plate on* The Generation Game *following his arrest.*

He is entitled to sue the blue serge pants off Scotland Yard...
Meanwhile, Jimmy Savile remains dead.

Chapter Thirty-Seven

SEPTEMBER 2013

It's the anniversary of the Twin Towers attack and America has changed her mind about bombing Syria. I'm pleased. I don't think you can solve things by bombing people. The French are sabre-rattling, saying they might attack on their own; well, I hope their air force is up to speed with Russian SAMs.

Nothing much seems to be happening in Yewtree World. *The Sun* have offered a king's ransom for a story. They say I can have editorial approval as well; it's tempting, but there's still the Falklands thing to sort out. Anna King from Port Stanley has sent a statement; so has Sir Rex Hunt's driver, Don Bonner. Henri has asked DC Root three times for a contact in the FI police, so that we can send more representations. These include statements from two former commanders of British forces in the islands.

The longer this goes on the more difficult it is. The main

problem is I can't do interviews with the press to advertise the tour; they'll want to know the ins and outs of the Yewtree stuff. As much as I try to say nothing on the subject, something will be blurted out.

My QC has prepared the package to present to the relevant authorities as soon as Danny Root pulls his finger out. As Danny is in charge of the investigation on behalf of the Falkland Islands, I'm assuming he'll be interviewing people as well. We need to get a move on.

Michael Le Vell from *Coronation Street* has been acquitted of sexual offences. I thought he would be. I listened to the news and read reports of the case, and it seemed to me that the 'victim's' story was confused. The CPS always says that by advertising the fact of the arrest, more 'victims' will come forward, but they didn't, not even bandwagon jumpers – or none that we know of, anyway.

Today's papers are full of scorn for the CPS. I'm not surprised. Michael has had two years of hell, and the jury took only five hours to find him innocent. I doubt if the evidence came anywhere near the CPS code regarding the possibility of conviction, yet they still went ahead. In yet another high-profile case, the very self-satisfied CPS representative has faced the cameras and announced it was in the public interest. Oh yes, but of course it was...

The Le Vell jury must have been thinking, '*Why was he arrested in the first place?*' To find the answer to that, I'll take you back to the police station at Heathrow:

'*We must take these accusations seriously no matter how flaky they are.*'

Arrest now, investigate later. Thank God we decided to

gather our evidence and present it before charges could be brought. That's what we're doing now with the Penguin allegation.

The Deputy Speaker of the Commons, Nigel Evans, has been charged with sexual assault and rape. I met him once; he was charming and young men surrounded him with stars in their eyes. I think that a lot of people in the public eye must be as nervous as hell right now. There is nothing to prevent people with a grudge dragging your name through the mud. I said this a year ago: just pick someone famous and say they groped you when you were young. The CPS and the police will leap with glee; the poor bastard will be inundated with bad headlines; his life will be ruined, but all you have to do is invent a credible story and stick to it. If he gets off because of lack of evidence, you can walk away with anonymity and his life will be in the sewer!

The Sunday papers are awash with stories on Michael Le Vell. The columnists and comments pages speculate on why the CPS brought the case. Some are furious and rightly so.

It has to be asked: why did the QC advisor to the Director of Public Prosecutions overrule the CPS's camera-friendly top man in the North and bring the pointless case to trial?

There are also reports of Le Vell suing the CPS in an attempt to claim back the £200,000 costs as, since 2011, you can't claim costs if you win. This seems like lefty bullshit to me: 'If you can afford to pay for your own defence and not claim legal aid, then tough shit.'

But then I would say that, coming from the right – or so they say...

Henri has sent his third email to DC Root, asking for

contact with the Falkland Islands authorities. He's had no reply so he's now sent forty-six statements. It's the responsibility of the Yewtree detective to forward those to the attorney general in the FI. Laurie, Brian and I are unanimous that we'll wait until the FI authorities make their minds up before we broach any publicity. But it's a pain in the arse – a very costly pain in the arse.

* * *

18 September 2013

Henri has now had a response from Root. The stuff will soon be winging its way to the Falkland Islands. Danny has also furnished Henri with the contact details in Port Stanley. It's strange, but never in all my wildest dreams did I ever think I'd be part of a police investigation in the islands that I love.

Danny Root is going to bring my stuff back – although I'm not sure what was taken. There was certainly nothing missing from the house that I thought would be of any use to an investigation – unless they were looking for bad-taste crockery. He'll come personally on Monday. Weird, eh? How will he be? I quite like the guy so should I be friendly? Should I talk about the case? And why is he bringing the stuff personally? What's his game? I'll report further in a paragraph or two...

It's quite late now. I cooked dinner and we watched a show about the kids of famous people. The kids were obviously coached. Why do TV execs treat us, the viewers, as morons?

I've just watched the latest *Dexter* on the laptop. When the end music played it took me right back to Glasgow, where I'd watch the episodes one after the other in an attempt to block out the nightmare. For a moment I thought I was right back there, at a time when the future had ceased to exist. It's a weird feeling.

God, I hope this ends soon. This year has definitely changed me. Will things ever be the same? Will *I* ever be the same again? Let's get the Falklands sorted and we'll see. Goodnight Ovalteenies...

* * *

Monday, 23 September 2013

Well, I think I know what Danny's game is. He's due here in a mo to give me my kit back. We were wondering why he was doing the job and not some lowly copper, but I think I have the answer.

Michelle and I went to Glasgow last Friday. We were invited to the opening of an exhibition by Jack Vettriano, whose wonderful paintings make you nostalgic for an era you didn't even experience. While we were having a spot of lunch, Henri emailed a strange request from DC Root: he asked for my help with an accusation against Freddie Starr. The email said I wasn't implicated in any way, but would I speak to a colleague on Op Yewtree? Our first reaction was, 'Cheeky bastards!' I believe they wanted to ask me a question that related to part of Freddie's defence, but in any case I felt I couldn't help. I still had my own problems; to be under investigation by one part of Operation Yewtree and to help them in their inquiry into someone else was too much to ask.

Henri agreed, emailing him to say that Jim was concentrating on his own outstanding allegation.

Now we know why he's coming to my house. He wants to hear what I have to say. I was wrong about DC Root... I think. I'll continue writing after he's gone. See you then.

* * *

They've just left. It was strange to see Root in jeans. Paula, the WDC, was with him and it was a bit like a school reunion. They brought with them the items they took away: two laptops from the office and a hard drive; a picture of me leaning against Brother Bill's police car; a picture of me at San Carlos Cemetery in 1983; some CDs and discs, most of my stage act or our wedding, which Danny said 'looked like a nice day'.

He was jolly and chatty, saying he understood my declining to help the police with the Freddie Starr case at this time. He didn't fish for anything, though he told me his file was sent to the Falklands on Friday. Laughing, he said perhaps he should buy some snow shoes...

We had a cup of tea and he asked me about Charlton's recent record. I reminded him Henri was West Ham's lawyer; Danny said that Henri was very good, an extremely clever man – but then he would say that, he's a West Ham fan!

They were very professional and I thanked them for that, and for being kind to me. 'Jim, all we were doing was looking for the truth and I think the right decision was made,' said Danny. With that, they were gone.

It's weird, but I hope we can be friends one day. I think I

now understand the Stockholm syndrome: I've grown fond of my captors and I don't blame them. I'd been through a lot and they were there throughout – even if they were the enemy. But they did their job and I do believe they were looking for the truth, after all.

I'll find Danny Root on Facebook and send a friendship request. You never know...

Chapter Thirty-Eight

10 OCTOBER 2013

Walter White is dead; Dexter is hiding in a forest; DLT has had more charges brought and Max Clifford has been in court again; no news on Freddie; Rolf has been to court and, ironically, a sketch of him in the dock was shown on the news. Imagine being the sketch artist in that court: 'Your honour, can you guess who it is yet?'

I'm still waiting for the Falkland Islands police to read through our stuff and get it to the attorney general. Until then I can do nothing. The tour is suffering and if I'm not careful, the momentum could be lost.

Ros from *Big Brother* has called Laurie; let's see if Richard Desmond still thinks I'm an arsehole. I hope not.

Richard Digance and I did our show in Dartford and it went well. This and the last show, in Glasgow, had sensational receptions with huge standing ovations at the end. It was really moving.

I wish the FI police would hurry up and come to a decision. I can't imagine they'd want a trial in the Falklands as it'd cost a fortune. And how would I pay for that? But I will somehow, if that's what it takes.

* * *

23 October 2013

It's now one year since the rats were lurking about. A whole year! My new habits are now set in stone. I still scan the newspapers every morning, a habit I'll probably have for life.

DLT has been to crown court; Stuart Hall is about to have his OBE taken away; Alex Ferguson has released an autobiography; a pretty woman has won *Bake Off* and a Kardashian woman has had a picture published showing her huge bum!

Richard Digance and I are having a ball. We're five gigs in and the shows are going well. However...

Business is bad. We're playing to 300 people per night, sometimes less. The theatres are ones that took no notice of the arrest situation and believed that 'innocent until proven guilty' still means something. Good on 'em. Promoter Brian Shaw says he's done 'all I can', but the trouble is that they're still faffing about in the Falklands and I'm in limbo.

The Sun is waiting to pay me money for a story, but I can't do it until the Falkland Islands authorities decide what to do. Consequently, I have a problem promoting the tour. I can't do any press interviews. No one could do an interview with me without asking about the Falklands, which I can't talk about, which would then piss them off and grant me an unfavourable article. It's the same with television programmes: no one wants to speak to me when there's an on-going situation in case they bring themselves into disrepute in any way. So the best thing for them was to say, 'No, let's wait and see what happens and then we'll speak to Jim,' but of course by then it'd be too late. The shows wouldn't get promoted. But Laurie says no one will touch me while this is still hanging over me.

My old roadie, Terry Draper, has found some pictures of Penguin in her stage underwear costume and sent them through to me. I agree with Henri that we should sit on them for a rainy day, so to speak. But then I remember that it's always raining in the Falklands...

I read the Penguin thing again and it doesn't make sense. That doesn't stop me from worrying that the demons are still around, circling about like lazy vultures.

What if the Falklands police fancy some headlines? It doesn't bear thinking about. But if, Gawd forbid, they feel there's a case to answer, at least we'll know what's going on and be able to plan our defence.

I'm in danger of disappearing if I'm not careful. The longer this goes on, the more remote that the moment of opportunity to move on becomes.

I'm appearing in Swansea tonight and there are 300 in. Two years ago it was 600, five years ago it was 1,100! Recession is kicking in big-time, either that or I've stopped being funny. But I firmly believe that tickets are too dear for people. Who can afford fifty quid for two tickets without parking and drinks? No wonder the theatres are struggling.

Of course, this has financial consequences and this year is turning into the perfect storm: recession, arrest, and Charlton lying fourth from bottom.

Roll on 2014...

Chapter Thirty-Nine

24 OCTOBER 2013

Stuart Hall has been taken out of prison and rearrested; Jimmy Savile's driver has also been rearrested on further allegations; someone has said that the Yanks are bugging the German chancellor's phone; Steve Davis is going into the jungle for *I'm a Celebrity... Get Me Out of Here!*; and the Irish police have returned the small child they snatched from its Roma parents: 'Sorry!' (What is a Roma person anyway? Someone from Rome, or a politically correct term for someone who lives in a caravan?)

I've had a sleepless night trying to plan the next move:

Plan A/NFA from the Falklands.

Plan B/More shit to deal with!

Plan C/Go to the pub and bollocks to everyone!

* * *

30 October 2013

One of the first Yewtree arrests has killed himself. David Smith, a former driver to Savile, committed suicide on the eve of his trial. Two more people have been arrested in south London; the Yewtree police used the term 'others' to describe these two.

As for me, I've heard nothing, which is causing me trouble. I still have my hands tied with regards to work. Brian Shaw, my friend and promoter, is feeling the strain; we've started to disagree on how we should be promoting the tours. It'd be much easier for us if there were no further allegations still pending.

The Falklands authorities have had all the stuff for best part of a month now; I have a week's break from the tour; the boat is out of the water; Ebbsfleet FC are out of the cup; Yann Kermorgant is injured and I've replaced *Dexter* with *Boardwalk Empire*.

Chapter Forty

1 NOVEMBER 2013

No news, apart from two more people have been arrested by the Yewtree police; I've caught my biggest pike (22 lb 2 oz); Charlton play Birmingham tomorrow.

I've spoken to Laurie. We're both getting frustrated by the Falklands thing. We have a good mind to ignore them and plod on. We'll give them two more weeks and decide then.

* * *

3 November 2013

It's Sunday morning. I've been up since six and have been checking the papers. Strangely, there is no news on Paul Gambaccini, who's admitted he was one of the two men arrested last week. I've met him; he is a gentle and kind man. He is also gay, so I wonder what Yewtree think they have on him. I'd thought the operation was winding up but it obviously isn't.

Charlton beat a poor Birmingham City team. I went to Brum and had a wonderful day with the locals, who are a great lot. Lots of laughs all day. People were patting me on the back and expressing their pleasure that I'd got off! I took the time to remind them I hadn't 'got off' – I just hadn't been charged with anything.

Still no news from the South Atlantic!

* * *

6 November 2013

Stuart Hall has appeared in court. I ask myself why he was handcuffed. He's an eighty-three-year-old man, for Christ's sake! I have no feelings about him either way, but it just seemed cruel and medieval.

Henri and Trevor felt it was time to ask the Falklands police what was happening. Henri got a prompt reply from Chief Inspector Len McGill, who told him the evidence had been passed to the attorney general who wasn't on the islands at present, and that he should contact his assistant. He did, and got a reply saying there would be an answer soon. I've stated to feel the weight of this now. No matter how daft I think the allegation is, there's a chance the FI authorities might want to take it further.

The tour hasn't done well. Brian Shaw and I have had words about how things should have gone. It's hard, we both know that, but the strain on our relationship has proven too great. This tour will be our last, I fear.

Steve Farr is also becoming a worry. He's always been indecisive but, since the operation on his head, he's become worse. He's forgetting to do things and getting humpy because of it. His wife, Sue, is also worried about him. He should be resting, retired even, but of course he thinks he's fine. He isn't, and I must make a decision soon.

What a year.

* * *

17 November 2013

It's a beautiful, frosty Sunday morning. My daughter and granddaughter have come down to stay. I've a leg of lamb to cook for lunch. All in all it's a perfect Sunday – except I'm sitting in the shed as I write this, worrying!

The last three gigs were a disaster. Because of the fallout from the arrest, the theatres were not ones we'd normally choose. They were in Stoke, Grimsby and Bradford, all economically depressed areas. The tickets were too expensive for people; the theatres also added a ridiculous booking fee and other surcharges that put the prices up to £3 over what we were charging. Twenty-three quid for a ticket is a lot of money these days.

I've decided that Brian Shaw and I will no longer do business. He agrees it's for the best. He could be said to be another victim of Operation Yewtree. I've asked my old friend Chris Davis to take over. He'll also be my agent and handle everything I do under the ever-watchful eye of Laurie, who'll still be my manager.

There's still no news from the Falklands. *The Sun* are waiting for a story and there are other things in the pipeline as soon as the Falklands make their minds up. I have three more gigs to do before Christmas. I can't imagine they'll be busy, but I also can't help feeling that if the Falkland Islands thing was settled sooner, I could have promoted them.

What a nightmare... but no, that'd only apply if the Falklands wanted to take this further! Once again, I can see the shore but I can't swim to it yet.

* * *

18 November 2013

I'm angry today. Steve Farr called this morning and told me his van was broken into in Great Yarmouth. They've taken my entire monitor speaker setup, my radio mikes, and all mine and Richard Digance's merchandise. I shouted at Steve, who hadn't even called the insurance company. He called me back later and told me his insurance would only pay £500 – which later turned out to be £250! That won't even cover Richard's losses.

I was incensed that we weren't insured properly, which was probably my fault. I was also unhappy that Steve had left the gear in the van in a dodgy road. I did my nut and told him to forget the rest of the tour. We had no PA and no merchandise, so there was nothing for him and Sue to do. I told Steve I'd pay for the lost stuff and he could keep whatever insurance he gets. Nice, eh? I know Steve fucks up. I'm used to it, but it drives Richard mad. He could never understand why I employed him – because I love him, that's why. He is a friend and a great bloke.

But goodbye Steve.

* * *

21 November 2013

There is a piece in the wonderful *Mirror* saying I still face sex charges in the Falkland Islands. Why they've done it I've no idea.

But it does at least keep the story alive. I'm aware that, as time goes on, *The Sun* might go off the idea of a story about the allegations against me in Britain. I'll lose the fee I so desperately need after this year from hell.

* * *

25 November 2013

The tour is over. Brian and I have gone our separate ways. I've not been paid as Brian is 'waiting for figures and money to come in'. Richard has been a star and has played the last couple of gigs for expenses only. Brian has paid him up to date, so I don't have to worry about my old friend.

There's still no bloody news from you-know-where.

Steve Farr called and confessed that the van is only insured for £250. He did offer to pay the £500 himself but, seeing as the gear and merch were worth three grand, it's no help, even though he feels bad about it. He'll be okay though. He lives in France, up a bloody great mountain. He's happy there; he should retire, enjoy life and stop worrying about everything – even John Cannal's toilet, which now flushes hot water since Steve fixed it.

* * *

27 November 2013

I know we're getting closer to the end of the year because the demons are cramming more shit in! I've always used Marc Voulters' company as my accountants, but last year I decided to save a few quid and go with Brian Shaw's bookkeeper. I don't have that much accounting: there's the VAT and wages to do every month, and the yearly accounts to present to my mate the taxman.

But then earlier this year my nice new accountant was taken ill. This has put the poor chap behind somewhat; as much as I wished him well, I had to make a change. With much relief I've now gone back to Marc. However, there are now big holes in the accounts due to my former accountant becoming sick. You'd think the taxman would say, 'Look Jim, you've had a shit year, don't pay anything!' But Marc will sort it.

Chris Davis is now firmly in control of my diary and I dare say next year will be better. I've taken on a job that will take me full circle. I can't speak about it now, but I'll tell you more when it's confirmed.

No news from the Falklands still. I'm wilting!

* * *

29 November 2013. 3.22pm

I've just this second been doorstepped by two reporters from the *Sunday Mirror*. Michelle spotted them as she went to the Co-op. Within a second of the dreaded knock, my heart rate went through the roof. I started to shake. It took me back to last year. I called Henri but he'd seen nothing on the net.

I decided to open the door to the two lads.

'Yes?'

'We're from the *Sunday Mirror* and we want to know if you've heard anything from the Falklands?'

I told them that I hadn't, my dealings with the Metropolitan Police were over and the Falkland Islands authorities had all the relevant stuff. I also reminded them I hadn't been arrested. I shut the door after declining a photo and came in to call Henri.

We feel it was a fishing expedition on behalf of the *Mirror*, but it made me feel horrid. It took Michelle and I back to the days of doom and gloom. We can only wait to see what prompted them.

* * *

1 December 2013

It's Sunday. There's nothing in the papers, so I don't know what the *Sunday Mirror* boys wanted.

* * *

18 December 2013

It's three in the morning. Nelson Mandela has died; a Royal Marine sergeant has been jailed for killing a Taliban fighter; Spurs have sacked their manager; I'm now in my sixties and I have a hangover!

Let me explain that last part: Michelle and I flew to Dubai on 8 December. Steve and Gillie Lamprell had invited us to their magnificent house in Emirates Hills. The rest promised to do us both good, although, knowing Steve and Gillie, there'd be a busy itinerary and rest would be scarce!

My last gig of the year had been at the Lakeside Country club; Bob Potter, the owner, who is now eighty-five and works just as hard as he ever did, was there to greet me. Was it really a year ago that I sat backstage with everyone, moaning about the Jimmy Savile witch-hunt?

The gig, as always, was tough. Dave Franks was there; he's a car dealer and has always sorted my cars out. He'd come because my tyres were suffering from Kojak syndrome. Dave's been a mate for forty-five years and he doesn't mince words: 'Christ, that was hard work wasn't it?' Yes, it was.

I arrived home at 1.30am and grabbed some sleep before we set off for Gatwick the next morning.

Dubai had changed a lot since we were last there two years ago. Michelle was apprehensive that being back would upset her. We'd loved it there and, of course, it was in the good old days before my life was hijacked.

But the sun was shining and I took some money from Steve as he tried out his new knees on the golf course. The 13th was my birthday, so Steve and Gillie had invited some friends round for a dinner in my honour. It was a fun night – but it would have been more so if the Falklands nightmare had ended.

Henri had written again to the authorities and I had a feeling their answer would come soon. That put us both on edge a bit. I told the guests about some of the stories, and they were open-mouthed. They all wished me luck as they departed.

The week itself was sensational. Michelle went brown and

I went pink! On the Monday, Steve and Gillie flew off on a business trip, and Michelle and I went to our Indian friends' house for dinner. Bobby and Susie are Glaswegian, so there'd be some drinking involved. They'd also invited my old pal from SOCA (the '*sue the bastards, don't let them walk all over you*' man from a few chapters ago). He asked how it was going and was disgusted to hear it hadn't ended. Criticism of the Yewtree approach was good to hear from someone considered one of the brightest minds in law enforcement.

I was expecting a call from Laurie. We'd been talking about various plans for the New Year but the Falklands thing would determine how we'd proceed. Then the food and wine appeared and all good intentions flew out of the window. We pushed our worries aside for a while until my phone rang. It was Henri.

'Jim, I have some very good news.'

I held my breath.

'DC Root has called. There will be no further action by the Falkland authorities.'

It was over! I shouted to Michelle; she leapt into my arms; our friends cheered. I felt so happy for my dear wife, who'd been wonderful throughout.

Henri told me to call who I had to and he'd phone me back. I called my kids; Michelle called her family; I called Steve and Gillie.

Bobby produced a bottle of something horrible and told me, with typical Indian hospitality, 'I am so pleased that you heard the wonderful news in my house.'

So that was that! And it *was* wonderful.

* * *

We were so uplifted that we arrived back in the UK about twenty minutes before the plane. Billie and Bill, who were house sitting, were so happy for us. And there were, of course, no reporters outside the house. What does that tell you?

We opened the champagne Mitch had been saving. She took the Falkland Islands coin out of the bowl of stones with holes in that our neighbour Liz had collected for us; we lit the candles we'd saved for a year, had a takeaway Indian and got boss-eyed!

So here we are. As I'm typing this, Michelle is asleep. My brother is snoring and I'm wondering what the next year will bring. I feel strangely hollow. It hasn't sunken in yet and I've gotten into a routine of worrying. I guess I'll have to change that. But I'll always be a lot warier of people – and also, I hope, a lot closer to the friends who have stood by me during this awful year.

Steve and Gillie were as pleased as punch; I reminded them that, without them, life would have been impossible. Goose called and was not surprised at all. My old friend had been right all along, as was the inscription carved inside Rosslyn Chapel: '*truth conquers all.*'

Chapter Forty-One

DECEMBER 2013

By the time the Falkland Islands authorities had made their minds up, I was considerably out of pocket. Henri had done a best mate's deal, but he and our QC, Trevor, had put in a lot of hours... thank God! So it was time to make some money.

Most people said, 'sue the police for wrongful arrest'; some said, 'sue the papers'; some said, 'sue the women'. All these things would be futile. It was time to go back to work, to do what I did best and get back on stage. The trouble was, would ticket sales improve now that I was free of police interest? The time between the NFAs from the Met police and the Falklands police was so long that people had forgotten I'd ever been arrested.

But I was commended on my handling of the situation. People praised me for not running off to the papers with my tale of woe. Some believed I was mad not to cash in, but the truth was that I couldn't do anything until the Falklands thing had gone away.

It had seemed to take forever. I'd turned down money from *The Sun* and the *Mail*; Richard Desmond had fallen out with me for not going into *Big Brother* in August; the theatres weren't interested. Remember also that it needs a six-month run-in to play a theatre; you just can't play one next week, there's the advertising, the printing and it all takes forever.

Laurie called *The Sun*. They were still interested in the story – thank God. Then he called the *Mail* – they offered even more. We had a day to think about it, and we decided to go for *The Sun*. Laurie called but they replied with: 'Ahh, the editor is not so sure now… it *is* an old story.'

So Laurie called the *Mail*: 'Ahh, we can only offer a small amount.' Laurie asked what had happened to the fortune we were offered: 'Ahh…'

He knew we were being fucked about, so we devised a cunning plan. We'd speak to the *Express*!

Bad idea – they were disinterested. But their owner, Richard Desmond, had something else up his sleeve. I'd be going into the *Celebrity Big Brother* house.

I told Michelle, who went white. She then remembered the bedroom extension and said it was a good idea.

Laurie did the deal with Richard and we were in. It'd start on 1 January. They wanted me on the very first day, taking no chances of a repeat of last year's fiasco. The show would commence live on the third, and I'd have to be in isolation in a hotel for two days prior to that. I was also told that if anyone found out I'd be cancelled.

The next day, the *Daily Star* announced who they thought

would be in the *Big Brother* house: I was named, along with Katie Price – which made Michelle raise an eyebrow, I can tell you. Other people I'd never heard of were also named; I made a mental note to Google them and start a file.

Both Michelle and I had a *déjà vu* moment. It was a year ago we were planning an entrance to the house; now we were reliving it and all the stuff that came with it. Both of us had a deeply gloomy feeling. What was to come? Would the end come with me sensationally walking out of the *Big Brother* house after calling them all arseholes, and making an even bigger one of myself? If that happened it definitely would be 'goodnight nurse' – the last thing you say before you pass out. Or die. Or your career ends.

We pushed the negatives to one side and planned for the Christmas invasion. The plan was for Michelle's nice family to visit one day and my loonies on another. I really couldn't see Michelle's mum getting any Christmas cheer from Sarah vomiting red wine all over her!

It worked a treat. We all had a good time. The kids were thrilled I was going in, though Mitch's mum and dad weren't so sure. Neither was I.

Michelle bought me a signet ring engraved with the Davidson crest; I bought her lots of silly things. We had a great time even with the dreaded *Big Brother* on our minds. We were both aware that it was quite a mountain to climb; one slip and I'd be dead!

On the 28th of December we set off to Steve and Gillie Lamprell's house to celebrate Gillie's birthday. The journey took three hours. By the time we got there we'd had a blazing row that carried on through dinner, ending with her in tears,

Steve's friends pissed off and me pissed. This really was *déjà vu*, complete with another talking-to by Gillie!

The drive home was a bit quiet; both of us needed our own thoughts. New Year's Eve was to be a quiet night, too, spent with my brother Bill and Billie. I drove to Dartford to pick them up, but we were all asleep as the last firework fizzled out over the London Eye.

The car was picking me up at 3.45, which gave me plenty of time to pack. Anything with a logo on was a no-no. *Big Brother* must have tied up some serious sponsorship deals and the housemates were not to be seen to advertise. So Michelle and I spent most of the morning gaffer taping up my personal admin stuff – which included Kiehls facial products and Amouage aftershave.

Michelle plonked me in a chair and started cutting the barnet. Halfway through, the car turned up. I'd got the timing wrong. Michelle speeded up like an old film of someone cutting a hedge.

I knew I'd be out of contact for a couple of weeks and wasn't looking forward to it. I tried to seem matter-of-fact and so did Mitch, but deep down we were feeling sad. The longest we'd gone without speaking was five days. The show was scheduled for three weeks but I was confident I wouldn't get past the first eviction.

Laurie was on holiday with Nigel Lithgoe. This really was *déjà vu*! He called and wished me luck: 'You can do this, Jim.' I hoped he was right.

I took my same green bag and put on my same fishing coat as last year. Was I tempting fate? Or was I saying, 'Come on, fate, come and fucking get me if you dare!' Michelle and I shared a look and I stepped out of the door. Bill and Billie were very quiet as I loaded the kit into the car.

Michelle ran out to me. She said something I'll never forget, grabbing my face with both hands: 'Listen, I'm your wife... don't get pissed!'

The car journey took forever. I was dropped at the back of the Village Hotel in Borehamwood. I was then met by a group of young *Big Brother* women who acted as if we were at Checkpoint Charlie during the Cold War!

I was shown to a bedroom and introduced to my chaperone, a nice lad called Phillip. He was pleased to meet me and promptly told me the rules: 'No phone, no TV, no contact with anyone.'

Shit, this is real!

My cases were brought in and an ex-bootneck security bloke took my mobile phone. I noticed that there was no phone in the room and no TV remote control. The television mounted into the wall looked dead. I was stuck there with nothing to watch and no one to talk to.

Phillip was really helpful although he gave nothing away. He told me the schedule for the rest of the day: it was to be pictures, filmed pieces and more pictures.

Charlton were playing Ipswich, so I made a mental note to somehow find out the score. That was my mission for the day.

A nice girl from the wardrobe department came in and selected what I should wear for the photo. That done, I went to a room downstairs to have my mugshot taken. *CBB* had taken over huge chunks of the hotel. There were young production girls everywhere; beefy security guards stood at all doorways. Security was tight. Not *that* tight though. On my way to the photo room, I stole a mobile phone from a young person who'd left it unguarded on a table next to her.

After the photos of me doing silly things and pulling funny faces, I was taken back to my room. On the way I noticed one of our young TV escorts acting as if I was to be assassinated at any minute. It was very cloak and dagger. She was paranoid about any of the housemates being seen or, more importantly, seeing each other. I asked if her job was op sec.

'Yer what?'

'Operation security.'

'Yes,' she said proudly.

'Right, you better have this then.' I handed her the mobile phone. Her jaw dropped open. I'd had my fun; her face was a picture.

Back in the room Phillip and I ordered our dinner. I had my usual hotel fare, a hamburger. While we waited I changed my clothes and we went to be interviewed by last year's winner, Rylan. He was in the show I was supposed to do and now, by some strange irony, was dating Dan Neil – the Yewtree policeman!

Rylan was lovely: very tall, overly made-up, but lovely. When he smiled, his new railings dominated the room. I couldn't stop looking at them when he spoke. He wished me luck and I was whisked away by the secret squirrels.

I stole another phone on the way back. I had dinner with Phillip in my room and, when he left, I gave him the phone. He roared with laughter. I was keeping myself amused.

While he was out of the room, I took two panels off the wall and reconnected the TV. I then figured how to operate it without a remote. The next problem was a little red light that appeared on the TV; some tape and a black marker pen Philip left in my room quickly hid this.

Charlton drew one-all after being one-nil down. Things were looking good.

Philip returned and then it was off for more interviews. People guarded their phones with vigour this time. The rest of the evening was spent filling in endless forms. Phillip left at ten o'clock; I watched TV until 12.30 and fell asleep.

The next morning, a producer came and checked my clothes. He searched every nook and cranny. He was quite thorough – or at least he thought he was. I wasn't sure about being allowed to take prescription sleeping tablets into the house, so I hid some. It was simple: I just put them into the things he'd already searched when his back was turned. Then a doctor came to visit and cleared the use of sleeping tabs, so the smuggling was redundant.

There was a lot of downtime so I persuaded Philip I'd catch up on some sleep. He left me to sleep so I watched a film. Then, while he was in his room next door, I took the screwdriver I'd 'borrowed' earlier and took off the window restraints. I climbed out onto a ledge and shinned down a drainpipe for four floors, to get to the pub across the road. Just kidding! (Or am I?)

My clothes, minus my shreddies (they had 'Calvin Klein' on them) were packed into two *CBB* cases and an overnight bag. There were a few interviews still to do and then lots of downtime. Philip and I had dinner together in the room, and I had my first glass of wine. He was very helpful. I was now fully prepped to enter the house.

The following morning, we transferred to a hotel next to the studio and a long, boring wait of ten hours began. I started to worry. Was I doing the right thing? I thought of Goose and the cover story we'd planned: 'Keep it simple, just tell the truth and prove to the viewers you are *not* the man the papers make you out to be.' I hoped I could remember the wise man's words. 'Jim, you are on a mission and you are armed with the greatest weapon of all... truth.

'Be yourself – if you want to drink, have a drink. If someone upsets you, stand your ground. Get into a routine. Routine kills boredom: get up first, do your personal admin and then find time for yourself to reload the game plan. Clean yourself of negativity and be yourself.

'Jim bro,' he continued, 'you've had a terrible time but you've been saved by truth. It will be the same with this show... you will win, brother, because you're not finished. Your journey is just starting. You will now have a purpose in life, the rebirth of Jim Davidson – a truthful man.'

These were strong words indeed. I reminded myself of the terrible depression of the previous year, of how Goose's words had helped and eventually come true.

Ah well... he who dares wins, eh?

Chapter Forty-Two

Make up done, suit on, a last-minute bit of chilling out or meditation and we were off. Phillip came with me.

The car entered the studios. I'd been instructed to wear headphones and a blindfold but I took no notice. My heart was racing and my biggest concern was whether the crowd would boo. I started cracking gags and being hyper. The driver was hysterical.

Then Ros, the nice producer, opened the car door. Philip wished me luck and I thanked him. Backstage was similar to any film shoot: people standing around in warm coats and techies with earphones and miles of cable. It was a shabby threshold to the magic behind the doors.

The atmosphere was electric. I walked past blurry faces and stood behind a sliding door. On the other side was the future; success or failure was up to me. I was on the tailgate. I had to check myself, calm down and take the step. The door opened to reveal smoke and bright lights.

Come on, legs, get going!

I walked towards the figure with the mike, Emma the presenter. It was a surreal moment, one I'd never previously imagined. I thought briefly of the police cell. As I walked in the crowd cheered.

'Kin 'ell!

It made me feel a little better. I told Emma that I was sorry to be a year late. She muttered something I can't remember and I was ushered down some stairs to await the next housemate. I watched the big screen.

It was Linda Nolan. I'd met her a few times twenty years ago in Blackpool – she was always in Blackpool. The oldest of The Nolans, she was a bit of a lush and, as I recall, had left them in 1983. I watched the big screen as her pre-recorded babble was played. To my horror, she said, 'I hope that male chauvinist Jim Davidson isn't in the house.' This was going to be fun!

Suddenly she was there. She looked as if she'd been eating well and her blonde hair blew in the breeze. I stared at her face and remembered those scary eyes. Linda was known for a quick temper she used to the best of her ability.

I was led up the stairs and stood next to her. We hugged. She then blurted out, 'Oh, he's okay when he's sober. It's when he's pissed... sorry for the language.'

Dear Pot... Yours sincerely, Kettle.

She also blurted out that she'd had me thrown out of a nightclub once, but I can't remember that unlikely event. Then, before we knew it, we were handcuffed together and shown to the door. It slid open and we were in.

It looked really nice inside the house. Smaller than I

expected but beautifully fitted out. We trotted about, talking bollocks, and wondered who would be joining us. I also wondered how long I'd be handcuffed to Linda.

The rest of the housemates were soon marching down the stairs with their best painted-on smiles. First in was Dappy. I'd looked him up on the net: he was a Greek bloke pretending to be black, one of those gangster rappers.

Shit!

He was wearing what looked like Chinese restaurant wallpaper with the arse of his trousers halfway down his legs, and was handcuffed to a tall, dark-haired woman. Dappy dragged her over and said hello. His smile was disarming. I liked him immediately and felt a pang of regret for my initial thoughts. Perhaps this was my first *CBB* lesson.

The tall woman was Liz Jones. She was a journalist. *Hmmm...* what was she doing there? Was she stuck in to write about us all, to do an exposé?

More people arrived. I was relaxing, thinking how I could win Linda over, though I didn't like her much and never had. Too scary for me.

In came Lee Ryan from boy band Blue. I knew Lee from my time in *Hell's Kitchen* – he isn't shy and he's also a Charlton fan! He was handcuffed to a pretty girl with enormous knockers, the first of the *CBB* eye candy. She introduced herself as Casey and she was delightful. Maybe this wasn't going to be so bad after all.

Next came two pretty girls. One I recognised as Sam, the girl from *The Only Way Is Essex*, a programme featuring real people in false situations. The people who are in it refer to it as a 'docu-drama'. That's always a problem when I do a programme like this – I've got years of being onstage and having 'a job' in show business, and then you get these other people who are there because they're there. That's what was worrying my wife: that I'd get on there and call 'em all arseholes!

The other girl, Jasmine something-or-other, turned out to be an American. She was very attractive and had a look of danger about her. Her tattoos looked as if she'd done them herself and she'd had a drink or two, I think! Then came Lionel Blair and the posh bloke from the other 'docu-drama', about toffs in Chelsea. He was very handsome; Lionel looked pleased to be there.

I'd known Lionel for years and he was a treat to be around. He was one of my judges on *New Faces* in 1976, and I wondered how long it'd take him to remind me of it. Lionel is gushing and showbizzy. *'Thank God he's here,'* I thought, not having seen him for years, *'he's great fun.'* I wondered why I hadn't kept in touch. Within a week I'd have my answer.

Next came four-time world heavyweight champion boxer Evander Holyfield, famous for having his ear bitten by Tyson, and a sexy looking girl with great legs – I think she was the bird from *The Apprentice*.

That was the twelve of us. All seemed very pleasant. Then Linda and I were called to the diary room

What, already?

We were told to pick one couple to release from the handcuffs, and chose Dappy and Liz. Linda and I thought they looked so mismatched; even Ollie, the posh kid, and

Lionel looked quite happy in comparison with Dappy and Liz.

We returned from the diary room and joined the others in the living area. We thought they'd be pleased at our unselfish action, as we could have released ourselves, but there was a twist.

'This is Big Brother! Jim and Linda have chosen to release Dappy and Linda from the handcuffs, but they must pay for the privilege. They will now be the first couple to be nominated for eviction on Monday.'

We weren't to know, but the housemates were cool about it. We were given lots to drink and our American lady took advantage of the kind gesture. She fell over twice, broke the furniture, nearly broke Sam's wrist and then, after exposing her breasts, started a conversation with great charm about sticking fingers up arses. Lionel's face said it all. We were in for a laugh!

It was 3am when we were shown to our bedroom. I was supposed to sleep in a double bed with Linda, but sod that! I kissed her on the cheek and slept on the floor.

I woke sometime later. It was dark; Linda was snoring. I was aching and had no idea what the time was. It was a weird feeling to sit in the dark knowing the infrared cameras could see my every move.

I saw the girl from *The Apprentice*, whose name, as it turns out, is Luisa. She'd been handcuffed to Evander but now, like all of us, was separated for sleeping. Evander was a big bloke so Luisa did the same as me, kipping on the floor. I waved and she crawled over. We whispered about this and that, though, to be honest, I couldn't hear a word she said. Too much rock and roll did my lugholes in years ago. But we seemed to get on well – two strangers sharing a similar burden: one handcuffed to a scary giant who took up half the bed and snored like a diesel express; and one chained to Evander.

The blinding light soon came on without warning.

'This is Big Brother: can housemates ensure that they are handcuffed at all times?'

I connected to a sleepy Linda. Luckily, the handcuffs had a chain that extended five feet so you could go to the toilet while the other one waited outside the door. You could take the handcuffs off when you got into bed, but you had to put them on when you woke up. Mine made my hand swell up quite badly; I kept asking them if I could take them off but they never answered.

Linda and I went into the kitchen to see what was on offer. There were chickpeas, lentils and tins of tomatoes. We weren't going to get fat on these rations. Linda, an expert on the show, explained that we had to perform tasks to get food.

I had some toast and a cup of tea. The first conversation of the day was about how Sam had put up with the American whirlwind. The second was about the complete lack of food. The fridge was full of onions, cabbage and celery; we had tea, sugar and milk but no decaffeinated tea, which was making Ollie freak out a bit. We had gluten-free bread because Jasmine wanted it – she wasn't really wheat intolerant, just American!

And then, in the afternoon, we had our first task. We were led into the living area, now stripped of furniture and with lots of building blocks. These had slogans on them:

'MONEY PROBLEMS', 'I'D DO ANYTHING FOR FAME', etc. The idea was that each person would select a building block and tell a story related to it. It had to be a true story. Whoever won would be released from the handcuffs and immune from the first eviction.

The game was fun but it lasted three hours. I don't think the producers realised how much dysfunctional people enjoy talking about themselves. I told them about my alcohol addiction and the steps I took to get off the Colombian marching powder. They showed that on the programme; what they didn't show was my story of 'PUBLIC HUMILIATION':

In 1976 I'd appeared at the Alexandra Theatre in Birmingham, playing the part of Idle Jim in *Dick Whittington*, starring Frank Ifield. I got very friendly with Brum rock star Roy Wood, who was very partial to curry. Birmingham is famed for the best Indian restaurants in the world, so I went off with Roy most nights after the show; we'd get a bottle of wine served to us in a teapot, as they weren't licensed, accompanied by the strongest curry I've ever had.

But all this had a terrible effect on me. While I was onstage, bouncing around dressed as a Bay City Roller, I felt a blow-off go into the departure lounge. I took it into the wings, where all the crew was playing cards. I thought, '*Right, I'll leave this there with them,*' so I attempted to blow off and made the most terrible fucking mistake, following through spectacularly!

They burst into laughter. It was soon packed with dancers who'd heard over the tannoy system: 'Everyone to the wings – Jim's shit himself!' I then went back onstage, facing the audience without turning my back on them – it was the most humiliated I've ever been, but the show must go on. After ten minutes of being onstage in the lights, my fucking suit started to set! I staggered off to the wings, like Douglas Bader in *Reach for the Sky*, scraped my costume off and threw it away.

It was this story that convinced the group Linda and I were the best. We were released from the handcuffs and made immune from the first eviction, and I think that's when the trouble between she and I began. Though to be truthful, the trouble had started twenty years ago and was soon to erupt in HD.

We were all still being nice to one another at this point. Linda and Sam said they would share a bed, leaving me a double to myself, which was much appreciated. Jasmine moved in with Dappy for the night; he's believed to have an enormous 'Cory' as she was to find out! That'll learn 'er...

The task the next day was a strange one in the garden: the handcuffed couples had to undo huge knots in a thick rope. Lionel and Ollie won; they were released and spared eviction. Ollie was later to be seen weeping about it in the diary room. I don't blame him; being handcuffed to Lionel Blair would be too much for anyone.

Lee and Casey seemed in no hurry to be separated, and Evander seemed oblivious to everything. I was starting to like him. He never swore and started every sentence with, 'My mama told me...' I was getting to know them all now.

I'm writing this after the event. In fact I've had to watch it to remember what happened, but it showed me what a terrible bunch of two-faced bastards they were. (Well, all except Dappy, Evander, Ollie and Sam. I'll never speak to the American girl again – Lee, you're welcome to her!)

A few niggles had started to creep in. One of the tasks was to kit out half the team in bondage gear, real cheapie black-leather sexual-deviant fashion, and get them at it. The other half that included me was tasked with doing a children's version of the show. I enjoyed this. Casey was very funny but when I joined in Linda got shitty!

We were taken into a little room where we had to role-play a kids' version of *Big Brother*, dressing up as children's entertainers and putting makeup on. Casey was brilliant at this, because a man dressed as a monkey came in with a custard pie about four times and kept smacking her in the face with it. Because Casey is rather beautiful, with enormous knockers, it leant itself to innuendo; she was saying in a childlike voice: 'That naughty monkey has creamed all over my face!' I said, 'Yes, he *is* a naughty monkey, isn't he?' Liz just sat there not knowing what was going on, and Linda tried to join in, which confirmed that she didn't have a clue about comedy. But we did well and won some food.

We were eventually let out and joined in the living area by the others, still in their porn gear. I didn't think it was possible for Luisa and Jasmine to get any cruder and louder than they were, but they did. Ollie and Sam seemed a bit shocked and hadn't enjoyed it at all; Lionel said he didn't either.

Luisa told us all about the sex parties she'd arranged, so this was just a walk in the park for her. Jasmine was in her element; I found out that night that she has a sex film on the net, though I made a note *never* to see it...

The niggles had really started now. Linda was stirring the shit about me. I really didn't know what I'd done to upset her but she could turn like a London taxi. I was determined not to be dragged down by her hatred. Linda had said, right from the off, that I was rude to her husband and because of it she'd got me thrown out of a nightclub in Blackpool. I thought that highly unlikely, as the people I was with in Blackpool could have demolished the whole club.

I usually went to bed early after a few drinks, but this proved impossible as the kids wanted to play. Jasmine and Luisa thought it was fun to piss me off and tell the camera I was a miserable bastard, or the more subtle American version: 'Fucking miserable prick!' What a charming girl she is!

I found a quiet corner. I was missing home and wishing I was there. I'd smuggled in a small picture of Michelle which kept me sane and reminded me why I was doing this, and why I was trying not to tell people what I really thought of them. I thought of Goose: '*Just be yourself.*' That's what I'd do. Bite my lip and let the public decide.

During the night we heard this noise and thought, 'What's that?' In the morning a 'spaceship' had landed and these ridiculous aliens came out: a great big bloke and a small actor, one of the people formerly known as 'midgets'. I was invited into a room and ate the most awful food – rather like *I'm a Celebrity...* in the jungle. It wasn't bugs and grubs but a sheep's head; I had to eat an eyeball, and I thought I was very clever by sneaking in a raw green chilli. I thought, '*If I eat this chilli first I won't taste anything else*'; it sort of worked, but my stomach felt like it'd had an epidural. During the night I was desperate to be rid of the awful grub, but the toilet was occupied. Lee and the nice American had bonded. They didn't show me shouting in desperation, 'Hurry up mate, I need a shite!'

Jasmine was working her way through the cast list. She'd already had lesbian romps with Luisa at the bottom of my bed, prompting me to say I thought I heard someone whisking an omelette! The girl was certainly earning her money.

Me? I wanted to go home. They were bound to nominate me, so I was happy.

Casey had started pining for Lee by this point. He'd promised her the world when they were groping and then changed his mind and given Jasmine half-a-yard in the khazi! A huge row erupted between Casey and Jasmine. ('A storm in a G-cup,' a lesser comedian might have said.)

Little things were beginning to annoy us. Ollie had lost his electric toothbrush, and it turned out that Luisa had used it as a sex toy on Jasmine. I would have fucking burnt it afterwards…

On the Monday, Lee and Casey were evicted in a fake vote. We thought we'd seen the last of them, but they were spirited off to a little room to watch our antics for a few days. It was a clever twist which none of us foresaw.

While they were away, Dappy had a huge stand-up row

with Luisa. It was a cracker, with Luisa showing us mortals how many swear words she could spout. I consoled her later. She was receptive to my sympathy but soon changed when Linda started stirring the shit again. I walked in on the girls listening to Linda slagging me off at that point, with Jasmine joining in. I said sorry for whatever I'd done and walked away... fuck 'em!

I was now aware I had a problem with Linda, Luisa and Jasmine. They'd be playing their game against me but I was past caring. I got the feeling I was being picked on. The public apparently were getting that too, although I wasn't aware at the time. We were in total isolation; we didn't even know what time it was until I worked out a way of gauging it.

I wished Luisa was a little less 'her'. She was worse when Linda was about and it was causing a small rift in the team.

I still missed home and it was round about this time that I was at my lowest. I cheered up when Lionel had a row with Luisa, and she stormed off crying. So much for not giving a shit what people thought of her. There may have been a human being lurking in there somewhere after all, and I made a note to try and find it... if I could.

The factions within the group were now becoming apparent; there was Linda with her coven of Jasmine, Luisa and a reluctant Sam; there was Lee with his two women – all he wanted to do was fuck anything that moved and still look good in the public's eyes; Evander was trying to work out what it was all about; Lionel was being Lionel; Liz was in her own world; Ollie was bouncing from one group to another, being nice – he'd lie on the bed talking to the girls for hours. (What did they talk about, apart from fake tan?) I was with Dappy.

Dappy was great fun but needed taking care of. Two glasses of wine would send him into alcohol heaven. He was a funny cartoon drunk, reminding me of a meerkat on Duracell batteries. He was also nearly in the Ollie and Lionel mirror-checking team; I've never seen so many men checking themselves out so much. (I stopped doing that years ago!) People have since commented on why I looked so red faced, but I can only put this down to my routine in the bathroom. I was unaware that you should only exfoliate your face every now and then; I was doing it every day and I'd taken several layers of skin off!

Luisa and I kept our distance. Lee was suffering from TMT (too many targets) and the pressure was getting to him. The coven and Lionel also got onto Evander about the time he admitted punching a horse. This was becoming fun!

By now my sleeping was getting worse. I tried everything but the kids took no notice of my suffering (the bastards!). And *Big Brother* was about to play its first real trick.

It was the second live show. Someone was to be evicted. I, of course, was nominated by everybody and sat awaiting my fate. At least I wouldn't be the first out: Lee and Casey had that honour.

All the nominees had to pack their stuff into suitcases, put the cases in the storeroom and wait in the living area during the live show. We couldn't hear what was going on as they played a loop of cheering on the house PA system. It was like aural torture. Then, without warning, we heard Emma's voice:

'Housemates, for the last forty-eight hours the British public has been voting.' What she said next took us all by surprise. 'The most votes for staying in the house are for...' There was a huge pause. We all stared at one another. '...Jim.' There was a huge cheer from outside. Linda's face said it all. The rest were open-mouthed.

The next to be saved was Liz. That left Luisa and Evander. Now came the twist: BB revealed that Lee and Casey were not removed but had been secreted in a little room, watching our every move. They appeared on the screen in front of us. BB asked them to choose between Evander and Luisa. I crossed my fingers.

Lee picked Evander to be evicted, and Casey agreed with him on the basis that Luisa was a friend. So out went the great man, having apparently not known what he was doing there in the first place.

Lee and Casey returned. Lee was so pleased to be back, full of life and ready to face Jasmine. The fun had started. We had a soap opera featuring a three-way love triangle, a series of rows and people who were feeling malnourished, sleepless and liable to explode at any minute. Add to that a grumpy old bastard who was hated by the coven, and no wonder the ratings were going through the roof.

With Evander gone, it was time to nominate. This time we had to do it in the diary room: I nominated Linda and Liz. I knew Liz wanted to go home so I made up a bullshit reason. I said, 'She's not mixing with people and she's making everybody miserable.' In fact it was quite the opposite: she was like a breath of fresh air in there. But I had to have a proper reason, otherwise my nomination wouldn't have been accepted. Of course, I got the most nominations.

But the next live show would see Jasmine leaving, then Lionel. Most of us were shocked by that, though I wasn't. Lionel could come across as very two-faced; he had a bit of a go at me that surprised a few viewers, though I'd enjoyed being with him and we'd shared lots of show business anecdotes – in fact I got told off by Big Brother for Lionel and I doing impressions of Danny La Rue. We were saying in speech marks, in Danny's voice, 'Twenty-five years in the business, feathers up me arse!', which is what Danny used to say. But I got taken upstairs: 'Jim, you were told about homophobic behaviour!' I said, 'What do you mean – Danny La Rue was *gay*?'

Anyway, Lionel spent most of his time reminiscing about show business or talking about the people he'd met. He'd sing lots of songs and he'd dance, and he was great fun – though the *Big Brother* people couldn't show it because of the copyright problems. But I think at the end of the day we all came over exactly how we really were – or how we wanted to be seen. No one really wants to be seen as two-faced, so one must surmise that Lionel was being himself. (I'm starting to sound like Henri Brandman again – fucking hell, it's rubbing off on me!)

Jasmine was no shock. I think she was too much for us Brits. This now left Lee alone. I wondered how long it'd take for Casey and him to hook up again. We didn't have to wait long.

Linda was still sniping and stirring. Now the rest of the housemates wanted to know what the problem was. Luisa asked if we'd had sex, but fuck that!

It was time to get the reason out in the open. I was sick of her saying I was awful to her late husband, Brian. I thought she was playing the 'dead person card': how dare he be horrible to someone who can't defend himself because he's dead, that nasty Jim Davidson? In fact, she never told the real reason why I was nasty to her husband – because he was stealing from us. The reason I was horrible to him was because he was arrested and charged with stealing from my friend the comic Frank Carson's dressing room. He was caught red-handed after a police surveillance team rigged up cameras. Money had been disappearing on a regular basis. The CCTV revealed all, and Brian pleaded guilty.

I just rolled that little hand grenade under Linda's bed and she pulled the pin. And I regret that I had to, but I was sick of this woman having a go at me and not telling the reason why – which just fuelled everyone's imagination. How was any of this my fault?

I didn't expect her venomous reaction and regretted that I'd brought it up. She fell to bits and blamed me. She came storming out of her bedroom, walked over to me, calling me every name under the sun, and asked, 'How dare you?' Well, how dare I what? Tell the truth? I apologised. I was truly sorry, but...

Look at it another way. I knew why she hated me, though I didn't tell anyone. She tried to say all sorts of things: 'He's sexist, he's dismissive; he's terrible when he's drunk.' She even confided to Luisa that I'd been 'inappropriate' with her sister. I don't know what 'inappropriate' meant, but I got the connotations. Obviously, being bad to her ex-husband wasn't enough for the public to hate me. She had to find another reason. But she hated me – that was plain for all to see.

* * *

The next nominations were imminent. I nominated Luisa and Sam; they were all upset that I nominated Sam, but the reason I did it was that I was desperate to leave and wanted to be up with someone who'd get more votes than me. She was upset but I told her not to worry; she'd have no problem. The same couldn't be said for Linda.

The public had spoken and Linda climbed the stairs. I kissed her on the cheek and wished her good luck. I knew she'd start blaming me for everything, including global warming, and I was right. The *Mirror* loved her and gave her a soapbox: 'I've self-harmed in the past and I did it in the house... that's what Jim's behaviour made me do. He made me feel the need to do it again.'

One must question the producers' reasons for booking her. In my opinion, I didn't think Linda was very well. She was steeped in anger and misery, and by her own admission was taking antidepressants. If you look at the show or bump into any of the housemates, they'll all say I tried my best with her but her hatred runs deep.

On one of the *Big Brother* 'Bit on the Side' programmes, the pundits were furious with me. They seemed to revel in knocking me, but Emma interviewed my son Fred, who said, to the amazement of everyone: 'I feel sorry for Linda...' A gasp went up in the Davidson camp, but he then added:

'Anyone who carries around that much hatred is not right.' The viewers agreed with my son, it seems.

While I was in the house, Breamteam was handling the Twitter stuff. Dan Bream is my friend from Charlton; his company design and manage all your media needs and they're brilliant. The Linda controversy was pushing Twitter followers up to the 100,000 mark. All were supportive but, looking back, they really should have gone easier on her. Linda is just Linda. She should dump the hatred and move on... nuff said!

Liz was next out. Then, one night without warning, Emma entered the house and told Lee he'd been voted out. He left immediately, the poor sod. He'd worked his arse off in the house and earned every penny they paid him.

Before he left we all had visits by our loved ones. I was the last, though we weren't allowed to speak to them as they entered through a clock! The first was my darling daughter Elsie, and behind her was my beautiful wife Michelle. She looked well, if a little nervous. They hugged me and kissed me, telling me all was okay. I was choked, but so pleased that all was well.

We'd been asked if we'd allow them to extend the show for another five days; we all said it was okay. Mitch told me she was pleased and that Bobby Davro would cover the gig I had to miss. She also brought two ironed shirts, making a point after hearing Luisa say she would never iron a man's shirt. Well done, love!

With that Elsie said, 'You're gonna win, Dad.' For a moment, I thought she might be right. They thanked a tearful Dappy on the way out, giving him a kiss: 'Thanks for being

Dad's friend.' He couldn't say anything; we weren't allowed to say anything. But he just sat there with tears dripping down his face, he was so happy for me.

They were suddenly gone and my life was a little empty once more. I went to the bedroom and got myself together. My Special Forces friend Goose's words were constantly on my mind: '*Be yourself and get the job done.*'

After Linda left, things calmed down. There were no more arguments. Luisa started to like me and Dappy had adopted me. He said at our last supper that I was like a dad to him; his father had died suddenly and I was filling the gap. I was overwhelmed and the tears flowed.

We were now the last six. We'd made it to the final. It'd been tough, with more than a few ups and downs. Lee had admitted to me he probably had an attention deficit disorder, which explained a lot about his behaviour. He's a talented lad who gets frustrated at not having an outlet for his talent. His band Blue are great blokes, and when they came through the clock as a surprise for Lee, one of them came up to me and said, 'Bet you're glad Linda's gone!'

When Lee left I was called to the diary room: 'Hello Jim, you were warned about offensive language. But at 9.22pm, when Lee was leaving, you shouted, "Yid Army, Yid Army!"'

I tried to keep calm; this was my third incorrect bollocking and I'd had enough. I asked for the accusation in writing.

'Big Brother does not put things in writing.'

'Well you better fucking start, because this is going to my lawyer!'

'Big Brother is just warning you, Jim.'

'And I'm warning Big Brother... you have my lawyer's

number. I need him to hear that you've just accused me of racist comments and, worse still, anti-Semitism.'

Big Brother went quiet.

'I'm a Charlton fan, why would I give a Tottenham chant? If you look at your recording you'll see and hear that I said, "Red Army."'

Big Brother asked me to wait: 'Jim, Big Brother is sorry that this accusation was made. It will not be included in the show.'

I stormed out. I was pissed off and went for a sulk in the garden. In fairness to the producers, they're worried about offending people. But then they don't mind showing vulgar females talking about anal sex, they just can't have any non-PC stuff. The show was under Ofcom's microscope and I can't blame them really, but I was tired and they were sloppy.

* * *

The live finale was now upon us. We'd been together for twenty-eight days and we were like a family. After Linda left, the house was quite pleasant. We all got on well and have since stayed in touch. We were the last six and we were proud.

Emma's voice came booming into the house. The first out was Casey. She was happy enough to be in the house, let alone be in the final. I kissed her and said I'd see her at the nearest bar.

Next was Sam; she'd not been well while she was in the house but she's a classy lady. And then there were four.

It seemed to take forever before Emma announced Luisa

was leaving. She'd made it to be the top female... against all odds. She was such a different person during the last week, chatting to me and confiding in me. She had this wall of protection around her, saying, '*I don't give a fuck what people think of me.*' But the first thing you learn in psychology is that the opposite is often true for people like that. She became more vulnerable and more human, and actually really nice to be around. She also became aware, while she was in one of the little rooms watching what the rest of us were doing, of the game Linda was playing. She swapped sides, so to speak.

Now a cynic would say she knew I was going forward and Linda was going backwards; there's the old saying: 'Stick with the winners'. Was she that calculating? I don't know. All I know is that she became a nicer person and I began to like her.

I was in the last three. Would I win? I thought I might. But the trouble was that everyone loved Dappy and he had millions of young fans. I was a sixty-year-old comedian that most young people had never seen.

Emma came on again. Ollie, Dappy and I shared a look; by this time, Dappy was about to spontaneously combust. I put my arm around him and told him he'd win. But he couldn't believe it.

We said goodbye to Ollie and walked him to the stairs. Dappy and I were alone. He was manic. I was calm and really not fussed. I knew that, whatever happened, I'd made it to the last two.

Emma came on again: 'The winner of *Big Brother 2014* is...'

Dappy crossed his fingers and muttered, 'Please, please...'
I held him tight for the agonising pause so popular on this
kind of show.

'... JIM.'

Dappy leapt up and said, 'Told you, man!' We said our
brief goodbyes and he left like the star that he is.

Big Brother spoke to me as I waited alone in the house. It
was a strange feeling to think we'd never be here again. All
the fun and the tears came flooding back: cooking
hamburgers for the world champion boxer; soup for Dappy;
stir-fry for Linda.

It was all over. I'd won, but I couldn't take it in. I felt like
someone else should have won. I was just being myself;
surely they'd made a mistake? But the public had voted
and they'd voted for *me*. I think they'd wanted to say,
'*Never mind the accusations, you're a nice bloke.*' It was a
great feeling.

I now had to leave the house as series champion. I was
numb as I stepped into the lights. I was out and I was the
winner!

I looked to my left and saw Michelle cheering. She was
with Elsie and her boyfriend, Liam, but Michelle's face said
it all. She looked the happiest and the most beautiful I'd
ever seen.

It was unreal. Michelle had worked non-stop to get people
to vote and she was a winner too, as were all my family and
friends. I soaked up the glory and rejoiced by punching the
air in sheer joy. What a year I'd had. Was it really over?

I fell into her arms. 'I love you, Michelle... I won it!'

The tears fell as we shared our joy and relief. Elsie hugged me. Laurie, my manager and friend for forty years, said, 'You did it!'

'Yes I bloody did!'

A year ago I'd been arrested going into the *Big Brother* house. Now I was coming out of it a champion. The British public had spoken and I'd come full circle, against all odds.

Michelle was smiling and, up in heaven, a little dog wagged his tail.